PRAGMATICS OF
COMMUNITY ORGANIZATION

4th EDITION

Bill Lee M.S.W., ED.D.
McMaster University
School of Social Work

CommonAct Press
Toronto, Canada

CommonAct Press
telephone (416) 410-3770
fax (416) 410-1664
email: commonact@commonact.com
website: www.commonact.com

Canadian Cataloguing in Publication Data

LEE, BILL, 1942-
Pragmatics of Community Organization
4th Edition, 3rd Printing

Includes bibliographical references.

Library and Archives Canada Cataloguing in Publication

Lee, Bill, 1942-
    Pragmatics of community organization / Bill Lee. -- 4th ed.

Includes bibliographical references and index.
ISBN 978-0-921159-11-7

    1. Community organization. 2. Social action. 3. Social work
education. I. Title.

HM766.L43 2011   307   C2011-905191-5

Printed with Union Labour

CommonAct Press is a participating publisher with both Markets Initiative (Canada) and the Green Press Initiative (USA) and is committed to the goals of the Book Industry Treatise on Responsible Paper.

Pragmatics of Community Organization has been printed using paper that is 100% post consumer paper and is Ancient Forest Friendly.

The production of this title on Rolland Enviro 100 Print paper instead of virgin fibres paper reduces our ecological footprint by :

Tree(s) : 14
Solid waste : 1,426 lbs.
Water : 13,939 US gal
Air emissions : 4,678 lbs. CO2 and 6 lbs. NOX
Electricity : 12 MMBTU

This is the equivalent of :

Tree(s) : 1 tennis court
Waste : 13 waste containers
Water : 151 days of water consumption
CO2 emissions : 8,871 miles driven
NOX emissions : emissions of one truck during 8 days
Electricity : 58,640 60W light bulbs for one hour

100%

PCF

BIO GAS
ENERGY

PERMANENT

Printed on Rolland Enviro.
This paper contains 100% post-consumer fiber, is manufactured using renewable energy - Biogas and processed chlorine free.

Dedicated to all the community workers, community work students, and activists, so many of whom have all contributed to my understanding of the importance and dilemmas in our practice and struggle. At this time I also wish to acknowledge Wendy Weeks the late Australian-Canadian Feminist-Activist and academic who was so instrumental in my thinking about social justice and so important to community practitioners in Canada and Australia, and I also wish to acknowledge the inspiration of the late Paul Eisenbarth, doctor, farmer, peace activist, environmentalist and friend.

Almost every significant social progress in our respective countries starts out with one or two or three people saying, "Something is wrong and we are going to make it right."
— *Ralph Nader*

Good travels at a snail's pace. Those who want to do good are not selfish, they are not in a hurry, they know that to impregnate people with good requires a long time.
— *Mohandas K. Gandhi*

Our struggle as women, men, blacks, workers, Brazilians, North American, French, or Bolivians, is influenced by our gender, race, class, culture, and history – conditionings that mark us. Our struggle, nevertheless, departs from these conditionings and converges in the direction of being more in the direction of universal objectives. Or else, for me at least, the fight would make no sense.
— *Paolo Freire*

Foreword

Community and community practice should be understood as crucial elements in all social work practice. They are particularly important for those who must make the journey of healing and struggle that Aboriginal people must travel as a result of ravages of colonialism. It is important to understand and remember, as Native people do, that community life has been targeted by the colonizers, historically and in contemporary life, and that therefore the health of communities is central to the regeneration of the Aboriginal nations. We therefore need to think about the community as a major focus of intervention and to reflect consistently and critically on what we need to achieve and how we can go about doing it.

This text book is very familiar to me. I have used it as the required text for my community practice courses for over twenty years now – indeed since the very first edition which came out in paperback form, with a binding that broke apart when you opened it. Most recently in my own work in Indigenous healing and holistic practice within First Nations communities, I realized that texts like *The Pragmatics of Community Organization* are rare. Hoping to achieve healing among people and to find ways of informing their struggle requires books that "speak to them" and not simply to academics. This book does that.

In other ways, community practitioners need to carry a spirit, exhibit a nature, and demonstrate a character that is tangible to people in their communities. I have over the years challenged Bill in what I call an "Indian Way," where each of the four elements of the person – their spirit, their nature, their character, and their intellect – is real. This means they are discernable and tangible, and for hurt and marginalized people these aspects of the person are very evident. "Do you believe what you write?" For an Aboriginal person, like myself, I was: a) actually testing his character; b) determining whether the source of his knowledge was rooted in common people (who are residents of the communities); and c) whether his character was consistent with the sentiment of his words. This was important for me because, like many other people particularly those in Aboriginal and other marginalized communities, I have come across too many academics who publish for the sake of publishing; who have usurped the knowledge of the people for their own aggrandizement and promotion; or whose work was not really understandable by average people and thus not so useful for practice. One of the reasons for asking these questions was the following: I was going to ask him to work with me in a very delicate situation involving a First Nation community which was asking for some help with its work of evolving into a fuller functioning reality. We would be given the opportunity to put ideas into practice and, as Freire would say: "...to make intellectuals meaningful to the common people."

So Bill passed the test – the Indian test. And so has the content of his book.

The outstanding feature of this text is its rootedness in the *real* situation, and the dynamics of the people. It gives solid advice to the practitioner on how to be human in a human context; how to be respectful of people in their intimate context, which is their community; how to read situations in which people find themselves while interfacing with institutions (and the people who work in them). All of this is done so that a positive outcome can occur, in spite of the power difference that exists in these scenarios: to show how to struggle without unnecessarily making enemies but, importantly, without accepting and maintaining a powerless position; how people can learn to assess their own situation and its political, social, and economic dimensions; and how they can create strategies from this information, and then mobilize into action in an informed way.

As an Aboriginal person, I am pleased that in this and the previous editions of the text, Bill acknowledges the spiritual realm, and the need to recapture hope; it is an important part of the make-up of the community. To develop a community is to change it and this change must be a conscious choice which shows itself in the way people experience the spirit of the community, and of themselves. Empowerment, by people, for themselves results more in the tangible sense of spirituality that they possess and not in the material change that occurs. I get this from this book, and I get it from practice which I gather from this book.

One of the biggest challenges faced by Aboriginal communities, which are very diverse in nature and culture, is to re-capture the Indigenous notion of community. This, as Bill notes, requires work to heal the effects of oppression and to resist on-going oppressive policies. The community for the citizens who live there is a vital identity development instrument. This challenge of community building is central to our struggle and to the struggle for all marginalized and colonized peoples. The development of a genuine "civil society," which for most societies is evidence of a competent community, is framed by a strong organizing effort that serves to strengthen its people.

Mac Saulis
Waterloo, Ontario
January, 2011

Introduction To The Fourth Edition

Initially when we published the first edition of *Pragmatics of Community Organization (1986)* it was to fill what we thought was a significant need within a fairly small population: a coherent, practical guide to thinking about the practice of working with communities, for community work teachers and students. It has turned out that the book is being used by students, teachers, beginning workers and activists in a whole variety of community settings in Canada and the U.S., as well as in countries outside North America as far away as Japan. It was also nice to discover that activists and "old hands" were finding it useful.

The focus of the first edition was on the so-called phases and political nature of community organizing. In the second edition, I added a framework to assist us in thinking about what we were trying to achieve, the objectives of our work. The third addition brought the context of practice into the nineties and added a chapter on roles and skill required by the practitioner. This fourth edition, I hope, will provide another update on context and a clearer conception of the place and character of community – particularly its political character. There has also been a range of material injected throughout the book that tries to address our ability to think about strategy and tactics. We have attempted to make the book more user-friendly, introducing more summary charts and diagrams. Readers will also note that the bibliography has been expanded and updated to reflect the interesting material that has appeared in the last eleven years. There are recommendations regarding useful additional readings accompanying most chapters, for those who wish to explore more deeply the ideas and notions discussed in the work. Finally, I have been able to do what I love to do most: work and talk with community workers, teachers and activists. With their assistance we have been able to add to the number of examples and bring in new ones which reflect and highlight the contemporary context and struggle. As well, these conversations have helped me maintain my sense of hope in these troubled times. Indeed, many of the quotes found throughout the text are reflections of the importance and the reality of what community work can engender.

Acknowledgements

As with the first three editions of *Pragmatics*, this book owes its existence to a number of people and when I start to thank them I know and fear I will forget some. Nevertheless, I believe it would be churlish to try and fob the responsibility off by thanking a mysterious "all of the people who meant so much to this effort." So I embark on this attempt to acknowledge everyone and not to screw things up too badly.

First, I very much appreciate the Foreword written by Mac Saulis, who has been a friend as well as a challenging colleague. My wife, Cecelia, read and re-read chunks of the manuscript, and gave me valuable editorial comments as well as a lot of encouragement. Mike Balkwill encouraged and badgered me to "get the damned thing done." Marnie Cuff's encouragement and suggestions for re-organization are evident in the final shape and look of the book. Sarah Pennisi was likewise encouraging and pushed me to add depth to various sections. Abigail Moriah was essential to putting together the new sections on the use of the world wide web for organizing. CommonAct's Beth Gray did everything a person can do to be helpful and keep my nose to the grindstone. Saada Branker slogged through all the confusion in the final editing process. Finally, Anthony Rapoport added polish and coherence to the book's layout.

There are some people within the Aboriginal struggle who have indirectly provided this book with a valuable grassroots perspective: Barb Nahwegahbow, Rene Masching, Dorothy Peters, Harry and Eva Sock and Sheri Pictou.

A number of my colleagues at McMaster University, particularly Gary Dumbrill and Sheila Sammon, have encouraged the community development approach to social work. I also wish to thank Sue Watt for helping me get to Uganda and Nigeria. My four excellent colleagues – Susan McGrath (York University), Ken Moffatt and Usha George (Ryerson) and Mirna Carranza (McMaster University) – have provided me with important insights, particularly around the importance of diversity and citizenship.

There have been many community organizers and activists who have shared their experiences with me, and who let me share mine with them, particularly Mike Balkwill, a friend and colleague for over thirty years; Louise Martin in New Orleans; Pat McNaughton in Nicaragua; Nelly Rivera in El Salvador, Janet Fishlock, who I have worked with in

Toronto and Nigeria and in various international development projects. I especially wish to thank Marion Porter in Cork, Ireland, and Shannon Beard in Toronto who opened my eyes to the great strength and energy of those fighting against disability discrimination. Nobuko Takeda and her colleagues from the Community Work Practice Study Group, and the Foundation for Children's Future in Japan were incredibly generous in helping me understand the Japanese community practice terrain. I also wish to thank Mary Jo Leddy and the folks at Romero House in Toronto for stimulating my recent interest and helping me to know some wonderful activists in El Salvador.

Finally, and most importantly, the members of various communities, particularly the women of Banamwandu Tumelin'dde Co-operative Group in Uganda; the community research team at Jos University in Nigeria; the CEICOM team in El Salvador; members of the Affordable Housing Action Association in Mississauga; the workers and staff at the Chetwynd Project in Toronto; the workers and community health worker trainees at Anishnawbe Health Toronto; the workers of the Children's Aid Society of Toronto's Community Work Program; and the First Nations people of Big Cove (New Brunswick), the Moose Cree Nation (Northern Ontario), and the local groups in Toronto and Hamilton, who have allowed me into their lives to learn along with them. In many ways, to me this seems like a collective project.

Bill Lee
Toronto, Ontario
August 2010

Design and layout by: Anthony Rapoport
Cover photos by: Gary C. Dumbrill, Mary Jo Leddy and Paul Prescott
Illustrations by: M.J. Lee, A. Martin and Anthony Rapoport

A Note on the Use of This Book

In this book, the process of assisting communities with change is divided into three sections. The first deals with the broad strokes of community organizing, in its historical and present forms. The second describes context, objectives, and roles and skills. The third section covers the more detailed "how" we go about our work. It is broken down into phases that appear in sequence, and are more or less discrete (see Figure 7-I, pg 123). This is a bit ideal, however; I do not wish to suggest that each phase represents a bunch of tasks that, once done, will set up the next phase perfectly. The phases are meant to represent clusters of issues that need to be dealt with in the work of community organization. Though there is a general and logical sequence to when these issues need to be addressed, the phases will often overlap in your own experience in working with a community of people. Things, of course, will not be so ordered and logical. Thus, when you are using this book in practice, feel free to skip around according to the needs of your situation. It would be a good idea to give the book a quick initial read, to get a sense of what is in it and where things are, then use as your requirements dictate.

TABLE OF CONTENTS

TABLE OF FIGURES

SECTION I

An Introduction
to Community Organizing[1]

---

[1]   While we agree with Wharf (in Wharf and Clague 1997), that *community orga-nization* is probably the most appropriate term, at this point other terms *community development; social development; adult education; and community work* are used. The variety actually reflects the state of the practice.

Chapter 1

HISTORICAL PERSPECTIVE

Power concedes nothing without a demand. It never did, and it never will.

- Frederick O. Douglass

Community organization – the purposeful bringing together of people and structuring their effort to achieve some alteration or development in the life of a group – is usually thought of as a modern intervention, a creation of the "activist" and "idealistic" 1960's (Biklen, 1983). Certainly Barack Obama's successful run for the presidency of the U.S.A. highlighted the existence of community organizing in that country. More recently, the New Democratic Party of Ontario elected a former community organizer (from Hamilton) Andrea Horvath to be its leader. While small-minded folks like the failed vice-presidential nominee Sarah Palin have attempted (unsuccessfully) to question the importance of community organization, it has perhaps taken on a certain cachet as a "modern" approach to social problems. In reality, however, it has probably existed for as long as recorded history. There is ample evidence of its antiquity, of people taking responsibility for solving local problems or challenging unjust social conditions. It is easy to identify examples of its practice throughout the history of most societies.

The Old Testament tells how Moses and his brother, Aaron, organized one of the first recorded non-violent revolutions in history. Enslaved for generations by the Egyptians, the Israelites banded together and began their great exodus out of oppression. Centuries later, Saul of Tarsus (St. Paul) organized the first Christian groups into small strong communities founded on principles of equality and sharing.

In medieval Italy, Francis of Assisi, after experiencing a deep spiritual conversion, came alive to the poverty and corruption around him. Rejecting all class distinctions, he took to the road to organize religious communities dedicated to the relief of poverty, contemplation, and work for the poor. His efforts provided the impetus for a movement of religious orders that swept through all of Europe (Boff, 1982).

In the 1700s, the brilliant Shawnee organizer and leader Tecumseh emerged. In response to the long series of encroachments and violations of the advancing Euro-Americans (who were threatening the way of life of Indigenous North Americans), he formed a powerful Confederacy of North American First Nations against the land grabbing of the border states (Berton, 1980: 52-69). Recognized by friend and enemy alike as a gifted orator and organizer, he is considered the forefather of the twentieth-century First Nations movements (Edmunds, 1984).

In the 1790s, Church of England pastor Thomas Clarkson began the long and arduous organizing journey with the campaign to end the slave trade in the British Empire. It took his movement, which included politician William Wilberforce and a former slave Olaudah Equiano until 1807, when the British parliament finally passed the act that outlawed this odious and immoral commerce (Goff, 2007).

Harriet (Ross) Tubman (1822-1913), was born a slave but after her escape in 1841 she became a key organizer and leader in the Abolitionist movement. Her ability for planning and managing escapes during her involvement in the Underground Railroad gained her the nickname the "Moses of her people" (http://www.incwell.com/Biographies/Tubman.html). In this pre-Civil War period she assisted at least 300 people in escaping their slave condition, first to safe havens in the northern U.S.A. and after 1951, (the year of the Fugitive Slave Act) into Canada. Subsequently, in 1869, she also became community activist and an important figure in the suffrage struggle for women's rights in the United States. (http://www.harriettubmanbiography.com/).

Mary "Mother Jones"[1] Harris (1837-1930), Irish born and Canadian-raised, was one of the most committed organizers for the rights of workers during the period of the Robber Barons of the U.S.A. Elizabeth Gurley Flynn, herself an important figure in the American Labor move-

---

[1] She married and had four children with George Jones, a member of the Iron Molders' Union. Years later in 1867, her husband and their children died during the yellow fever epidemic.

ment, called her "the greatest woman agitator of our times" (http://www.kentlaw.edu/ilhs/majones.htm). While she was important particularly to the struggle of mine workers, she was noted also for organizing the wives of workers and thus imparting a community base to labour organizing. She also was among the founders of the most radical democratic union, Industrial Workers of the World (IWW, the "Wobblies"). In 1898 she helped found the Social Democratic Party. Jones was and is an inspiration for anyone interested in social justice for labour, women and children.

Before and during World War I, Sylvia Pankhurst was one of the most effective organizers of the Women's Suffrage Movement in England (Tremain, 1973). Inspired by a belief in socialism and a well-developed social conscience, she fought for women's rights, particularly among the poor in London's East End. She also helped to build strong and effective organizations for the poor and for peace. She believed that no society was just if any of its citizens were political or economic slaves (Romero, 1987).

The late 1800s to mid 1900s witnessed, perhaps, the world's most remarkable leader and organizer: Mohandas K. Gandhi. Through his work as an advocate for the rights of oppressed Indians, he gained a reputation as the father of Indian independence. Of greater importance, however, were his creative innovations in the philosophy and practice of nonviolent resistance (Brown, 1989; Gandhi, 1951). Gandhi believed not only that every individual should pursue truth and individual spiritual realization; but also that this could only be accomplished through interdependence and mutual responsibility. He maintained that the way to address injustice is to reconstruct socio-economic life, basing it on principles of truth and non-violence, which stress the interconnectedness and mutuality among all living things (Brown, 1989).

A. J. Muste was perhaps one of the most influential persons in the peace movement in the United States during the first half of the 20th century. He was a major player in the Fellowship of Reconciliation which led pacifist resistance to both WWI and WWII. It was during the Vietnam War however that he perhaps played his most important part, influencing key activists such as David Dellinger and Bayard Rustin (Tracy, 1997).

From the late 1930s to the early 1970s, North America saw the abrasive organizing style of Saul D. Alinsky. Working in ghettos throughout the U.S. and in his training program in Chicago, Alinsky - with his emphasis on mass-based organizing and confrontation - influenced organizing activity all over the continent (Horwitt, 1989; Finks, 1984). His message was that freedom and equality do not come as gifts; they are acquired through struggle. If people join together, he felt, they can generate the power to make the necessary changes to live with dignity.

During roughly the same period, Dorothy Day worked with colleagues to establish the Catholic Worker Movement, a potent force of social change for poor people in the United States. A writer and activist, Day was influenced by A.J. Muste (above) and found in the Gospels an understanding of human liberation, and a sense of community and solidarity, much larger than traditional politics could provide. Her writings were frequently confrontational and contentious, and her actions always challenged the institutional forces which lead to poverty.

In the 1930s, Moses Coady emerged on the east coast of Canada as the Co-operative Movement took root and flourished. Believing that the capitalist system had failed the people, Coady struggled to convince people that through co-operative principles, community action, and planning, they could obtain economic stability and become masters of their own destiny (Laidlaw, 1961). Before he died in 1959, he helped to set up many working peoples' co-operative economic enterprises. The institute at St. Francis Xavier University in Antigonish, Nova Scotia (which bears his name) was set up to assist people from all over the world in learning the principles and techniques of co-operative development.

From the 1950s until his death in 1993, the founder of the United Farm Workers of America, Cesar Chavez, waged a non-violent battle against the environmental, political and economic exploitation caused by agricultural producers, local and state governments, the Teamsters Union, and multi-national corporations. Chavez, like Gandhi, attributed his perseverance and commitment to his beliefs in non-violence, God and truth. He believed these were the ultimate ways to work for social change.

African-American civil rights and socialist activist Bayard Rustin played an important, largely behind- the-scenes role in the civil rights movement of the 1960s. He was the principal organizer of the 1963 March on Washington for Jobs and Freedom. He played a pivotal role as a key adviser to Martin Luther King, Jr. on the techniques of non-violent resistance. Rustin eventually came out as gay and advocated on behalf of gay and lesbian causes in the latter part of his career (Anderson, 1997).

In the 1960s, George Manuel was one of the leading organizers in First Nations communities (McFarlane, 1993). Drawing on his experience growing up in residential schools – where he contracted and recovered from TB which left him with a serious disability – and living in Native settlements in British Columbia, he worked to develop local, provincial and finally national organizations that would fight for the rights of Aboriginal people. He was the first president of the National Indian Brotherhood, now called the Assembly of First Nations.

The convergence of the environmental crisis and the struggle of Indigenous Peoples in Latin America have produced the extraordinary organizer and leader, Paiakon.[2] Born in the mid-1950s in the Brazilian rain forest, he realized that the European civilization posed a serious threat to his people, the Kaiapo. At the age of fourteen he left his village to spend two years with a Portuguese missionary to learn the language and customs of the people invading the Kaiapo lands. He returned to lead a successful fight against a mining company that had devastated their territory. Subsequently, they established a new village deep in the rain forest. Paiakon has dedicated himself to bringing together the many nations of the Para and Mato Grosso states in Brazil. This Pan-Indian coalition works on resisting the logging, mining and hydro-electric interests that are devastating the physical environment and killing the First Nations people of the rain forest.

In the 1960s during the Quebec's Quiet Revolution, Michel Blondin encouraged, *animation sociale*, a novel approach to community practice. Focused on rural areas he promoted a combination of Alinsky's confrontational approaches (see above) with the more mainstream orientations of locality development as articulated by people like Murray Ross. Its hallmarks were broad-based participation and group self-advocacy. This approach influenced practitioners beyond the borders of the province.

---

[2]   I am indebted to environmentalist/broadcaster Dr. David Suzuki, who is both a friend and co-worker of Paiakon, for providing me with the story of this remarkable individual.

In the 1970s, George Hislop emerged as a key figure in the early development of Toronto's gay community, and became an extremely effective organizer and leader of Gay and Lesbian issues in Canada. In 1971 he co-founded the Community Homophile Association of Toronto, one of Canada's first organizations for gays and lesbians. Also in 1971, he organized the first Canadian gay rights demonstration on Parliament Hill in Ottawa; and in 1981 was a leader in galvanizing the community to respond to the infamous Bath House Raids that took place in Toronto[3]. He also organized the Gay/Lesbian community around supporting gay affirmative politicians, and was one of those responsible for keeping their issues on the Toronto and Ontario agendas.

In the 1980s, Brazil's Francisco Alves – better known as Chico – Mendez, an environmentalist, and union organizer, worked fearlessly to bring about the twin issues of forest protection and a union of rubber workers deep in the world's most extensive rainforest. Though confronted by ruthless business interests, he succeeded in influencing global environmental policy. His death made headlines around the world when he was gunned down by thugs hired by the companies he was fighting (Revkin, 2005).

From the 1970s to the present, Mike Gecan has worked to organize marginalized groups in the U.S.A. Affiliated with New York's Industrial Areas Foundation (founded by Saul Alinsky) he has been lead organizer for East Brooklyn Congregations and other New York-based community organizations. He is the executive director of United Power for Action and Justice, a Chicago-based affiliate of the Industrial Area Foundation. He has also written about organizing, in his book *Going Public: An Organizer's Guide to Citizen Action*.

John Clarke is the founding director of the Ontario Coalition Against Poverty (OCAP) a direct-action, anti-poverty organization based in Toronto. He is a strong believer in the dictum that struggle is an absolute necessity for the attainment of social justice. From the 1980s to the present, Clarke and OCAP have been mounting campaigns protesting against regressive government policies as they affect marginalized/poor

---

[3] The raids were staged by the police to gain maximum media coverage and thus humiliate the men, many of whom might not have been "out." In recent research by myself and my colleagues (Moffatt, McGrath, George and Carranza) queer respondents often mention the raids, and the community organizing that responded to it, as key in the development of the movement to fight discrimination.

working people. OCAP provides direct-action advocacy for individuals against welfare, public housing and others who deny poor people that to which they are entitled.

Internet and Community Organizing

While not historical in the long-term sense, the internet has had an important impact on organizing over the last 10 to 15 years. Communities have moved from only connecting face-to-face, by newsletters and phone calls to email, websites and other sophisticated online methods. Political candidates have also used online methods to campaign, and social action groups have used them to pressure the government on international issues.

The internet is now playing a critical role in communications of community organizations, individual citizens, and advocacy groups. Clearly, the internet has impacted the way organizing has occurred over the last decade, and has altered perceptions of how future organizing might take place[4]. Given the continued potential of internet technologies in organizing, it is worth taking a closer look at specific ways the internet might influence organizing in order to discuss the negative or positive impact that may result.

One of the first widely known instances of internet-based organizing was in Mexico during the mid-nineties. In 1994, the Zapatista National Liberation Army (EZLN), a Mayan group in Mexico which was organizing against injustices perpetrated by the Mexican government, used the internet to bolster local and international support for their political cause. They were able to apply the technology to increase local support and put their agenda into an international forum.[5] They communicated with and reached out to individuals and organizations around the world sympathetic to their cause and this was used to gain a lot of support. The internet-based Zapatistas rebellion was a catalyst for

---

[4]   Lopez et al. "The Organic Internet: Organizing History's Largest Social Movement," 2007. http://www.lulu.com/items/volume_57/862000/862780/7/print/ organicinternet.1.5.pdf, Retrieved June 12, 2008

[5]   M. Martinez. "Civil Society, the Internet and the Zapatistas", Peace Review, 13:3, 2001. http://www.desal.org.mx/IMG/pdf/MEMartinezPeaceRev.pdf, Retrieved July 31, 2008.

activists and organizers to use online strategies for mobilization and action.[6] Wireless technology played a similar role in the 2011 demonstrations in the Middle East.

In 1996, Zapatista supporters met in Chiapas in support of Mexican peasants; and as a follow-up in 1998, anti-globalization supporters from different continents met in Geneva during the Second Ministerial World Trade Organization Conference. They formed the anti-globalization group, People's Global Action (PGA) against Free Trade and the World Trade Organization.[7] The PGA was created as a forum to communicate and coordinate anti-globalization efforts. Shortly after, in 1999, the PGA played a key role in using the internet to communicate with and organize people from all over the world and finally stage protests against the G-7/WTO meetings going on in Seattle.[8] The actual on-the-ground protest became famous as "The Battle of Seattle." Participants were confronted by well armed police, however, it was the role played by the internet that sparked much of the comment.[9]

Around the same time, internet technicians or 'techies' were exploring ways to make the web more accessible to the general public. They were investigating how the internet could become truly "public," a tool that anyone could use for communicating, information sharing and even organizing.[10] A key emphasis was developing 'open source'

---

[6] Harry M. Cleaver Jr. "The Zapatista Effect: The Internet and Rise of an Alternative Political Fabric", Journal of International Affairs, Vol. 51, 1998.

[7] People's Global Action http://www.nadir.org/nadir/initiativ/agp/en/ Retrieved July 30, 2008. PGA Conference http://europe.pgaconference.org/, Retrieved July 31, 2008.

[8] IndyMedia.org played a key role in facilitating collaboration and dialogue. IndyMedia was set up by activists in 1999 to collect and share information and to strategize in preparation for the WTO summit.

[9] Naomi Klein, *New York Times:* Toronto, December 10 1999 "Rebels in Search of Rules" (http://www.globalpolicy.org/globaliz/cvlsocty/stlcomnt.htm); Canadian Security Intelligence Service: Ottawa, August 22, 2000 "Report No. 2000/08: Anti-Globalization - A Spreading Phenomenon" (http://www.csis.gc.ca/pblctns/prspc-tvs/200008-eng.asp).

[10] A. Lopez. (Lopez et al., 2007) argues part of the role of progressive technologists is to keep the internet out of the control of the government.

material – software that could be freely used and shared by anyone – to promote a culture of collaboration and openness. Some of the innovations that arose as a result of this early work include:

- Internet access for people within a particular range through Wi-Fi.[11]
- OpenOffice word processing suite as an alternative to Microsoft Word.

One of these groups, IndyMedia (IndyMedia.org) led to the expansion of similarly focused innovations in Canada, where groups of technicians began to explore ways they could make the internet more accessible to the public – as a tool to be used and manipulated – and to use their technology skills to affect local issues. Ile Sans Fils (Wireless Island), a nonprofit community group established to use technology to impact local, not global, issues, grew out of the community wireless networking movement which emerged in Seattle in 1999.[12] Today Ile Sans Fils provides free wireless internet access to the public in Montreal. This community group believes that free access to internet promotes interaction between the public/users and also provides locally relevant info.

Concluding Comments

As these few examples suggest, community organization has been a basic and constantly evolving function in society. Its work transcends divisions of history, gender, race, religion and national boundaries. First Nations, Labour, Black, and Women's movements, for example, have had many good organizers who developed communities that have made significant achievements.[13] Most community development workers have not attained the same high profile as the people above. Indeed, organizers who become well-known leaders are the exception.

---

[11] Kahn and Kellner (2004) note the potential for Wi-Fi to provide internet access free of charge for others within Wi-Fi range if networks aren't secure.

[12] Interview with Michael Lenczner, co-Founder, Ile Sans Fils, June 17, 2008.

[13] See Indian Country by Peter Matthiessen (1992); Chief by Roy MacGregor (1990); and Feminist Organizing For Change by Nancy Adamson, et. al. (1988), for discussions of some of the issues and personalities in these movements in North America.

The role of the organizer in this kind of work is to develop leadership, as well as active people's organizations, that can exercise their ability to affect the social contexts in which they live. This is what community organization is most about – people realizing their citizenship, their right and ability to influence their environment, and taking responsibility for their lives. The organizer has and will act in ways that assist people to utilize whatever skills and technology they have at hand in order to bring themselves together and struggle for social justice.

Chapter 2

THE CURRENT CONTEXT OF PRACTICE

This new era in social policy reflects the increased power of the corporate sector and the influence of globalization. Governments no longer seem willing to insure conditions of citizenship implied in the social contract. They are no longer committed to full employment, unwilling to redistribute resources in ways that alter the structure of wealth, and are not prepared to create programs that protect citizens against the forces of the global economy.

- Jim Rice and Michael J. Prince (2000)

You don't have to create class conflict. There has always been class conflict.

- Howard Zinn (attributed)

Growing Inequality

The questions and issues that this book attempts to examine are framed at a specific time and within a particular set of social, political and economic conditions. The people mentioned in Chapter 1 confronted the issues of conflict and used the strategies and resources of their own times. We live in a period in which principles of materialism, efficiency and the "bottom line" appear to rule. Inequality is growing (Wilkinson and Pickett, 2010) and the rich are getting richer (Mackenzie, 2007; McQuaig, 2007), paying less of their fair share of taxes (Dobbins, 2007-2008; Whittington, 2007) and making obscene profits within an increasingly less regulated marketplace (McQuaig, 2008). Middle-class folks are increasingly squeezed, and less secure in the lean and mean

global economy (Barack, 2008; Francis, 2004). Through the manipula-
tions of the centrist and right-wing media, the labour movement, one
of the greatest forces for the well-being of working class people is increasingly under threat (Contenta, 2009; Carr, 2002). And the poor are
getting poorer and poorer (Whittington, 2007). This is not accidental;
nor, as we can see from the last number of years is it a short-term trend
that the "market will straighten out." There is a continuing deliberate
attack on notions of equity, citizenship and social responsibility. Linda
McQuaig (2008: AA8) puts it forcefully,

> ...during this era [1960s, 70s, 80s] the share of income received by the
> richest 1 percent actually declined – from about 20 percent in the early
> part of the century to about 7 or 8 percent by 1980. The rich didn't like
> this, and have been waging a kind of class war ever since, convincing
> governments to impose "neo-conservative" policies like lower minimum
> wages, tighter monetary policy, less social insurance protection, open
> markets and shifting the tax burden from capital to labour.

When we raise questions of fairness, equality and social justice (and
we will get into this in more depth in Chapter 4) we do so within a society
dominated by neo-conservative ideology and propaganda (Albert, 2009)
– an ideology that seeks to have us accept a world safe for companies
but dangerous for people (Klein, 2007). The response then is typically:
"Yes, those are very laudable goals but we must be practical, and be
thankful for what we have. There are global forces at work here." Hart (in
Choudry and Shragge, 2007, p. 8) puts it well:

> What is called for ... is a psychological, mental and behavioural prepa-
> ration for living with instability, and for being able to think of oneself in
> terms of a renewable, exchangeable, and updateable resource rather
> than in terms of a human being with unique experiences, hopes, wishes
> and dreams ...a self-sufficient nomad [and] generic worker [able to] ad-
> just to indeterminate change and ...characterized by low expectations
> regarding pay, work conditions, and above all job security.

The attack has of course worsened since the 9/11 assault on the
World Trade Centre (Klein, 2007). This makes for a problematic context
for all branches of human service work with community practice being

no exception. Ours is a collectivist, egalitarian and process orientation; facing trends that are individualistic, elitist, material and inhumane (McQuaig, 2008). At the same time, it is these very individualistic
and competitive notions that make community organization particularly relevant and important. As we can see from the wreckage of the
2008 meltdown, the apparent triumphant economic philosophy of the
"neo-cons" has had profoundly negative implications for the vulnerable sectors of our populations, whether in the Global North, Canada,
the U.S.A., Europe or the Global South. The movie, "Roger and Me"
documented the complete callousness with which General Motors (in
the 1980s) dumped 30,000 workers at its Flint, Michigan plants and
brought a thriving urban centre to its knees. As we know, things have
gotten only worse. The banking system, the backbone of the supposedly triumphant Capitalist system underwent a staggering crash,
thanks to deregulation and corporate and elite greed; it occurred
first in the U.S.A. but then around the world in the summer and fall
of 2008 (Chossudovsky, 2008) At the same time, the auto sector has
been brought to its knees in the U.S.A. and Canada stemming from
the inability of the capitalist brain trust to devise vehicles that meet
the needs of consumers – people who are beginning to wake up to
the issues of global warming and that an economy cannot expand for-
ever. As would have been predicted by Marx or Polanyi, governments
came to the aid of the system rather than questioning its assumptions.
Companies and governments continue to downsize and export good
paying jobs off-shore to jurisdictions with lower labour costs, with the
same lack of concern for workers. An expat in Nicaragua said of the
elections in the early 1990s, "Since the Americans bought the election
the bottom has dropped out of everything. You can see the Mercedes
all over the place as the rich return from Miami. But you also can't
avoid seeing the begging, prostitution and crime that have returned
with them." Perlas (2003) puts the situation very starkly but powerfully:
"The current economic system, divides us, and perpetually drives us
against each other, like animals under the whip, fighting for the master's favour. This is insulting."

Since the last incarnation of this book appeared in 1999, three important issues have clearly (or more clearly) emerged for the work of
community organization practice: the threat of human environmental
degradation, the world financial upheaval, and the internet.

Environmental Degradation and Crisis

In 1944 the great economic historian Karl Polonyi wrote *The Great Transformation*. One of his smaller but very important points was that it was in the nature of the free-market Capitalist system to wreak havoc with the natural world (2008: 139). Now, due to years of the unthinking exploitation of the earth's resources, we face an unprecedented environmental crisis (Kempf, 2008; Speth, 2009; Friedman, 2008). While acceptance has been slowly making its way through society, the situation has been made more grave with the denial of the issue by western neo-conservative governments such as the U.S.A. during the Bush Jr. presidency, Australia from 1995 to 2008 in the long Howard government tenure, and Canada since 2006 when the Harper Conservative government came to power. Community workers will increasingly find themselves working directly on the issue, as well as with groups, who are involved in complex situations that connect to the environmental crisis.

World Financial Upheaval

If nothing else, our current economic crisis has exposed the financial system's rotten core. The various claims of efficiency, dynamism, and innovation spouted by its most ardent boosters were, it turns out, simply a façade hiding unbridled greed, unethical lending and unfathomable financial assets.

- Robert DeFina (2009)

As Diane Stone notes "... economic globalization and regional integration are proceeding at a much faster pace than processes of global government" (Stone, 2008: 23). This has seriously negative effects on the ability of the nation state to exercise regulation on the activities of financial elites. In the terms of American social critic Chris Hedges, "The free market and globalization, promised as the route to world wide prosperity, has been exposed as a con game" (2009: 30). But as he also says, "... this does not mean that our corporate masters will disappear. Force and fraud are all they have left, but they will use both" (Hedges: 2009: 30). (More will be said about this in Section II.) This is not to suggest as far as the right-wing onslaught is concerned that we should simply "lower our sights." Nor does it mean that being aware of the context leads us to understand why we "can't win." Focusing on the real material conditions in which we live can (and must) also lead us to ask questions which will point to analysis and action that are likely to be more successful, in terms of empowerment and the search for social justice.

The Internet

As well, as noted in the previous section, the exploitation of the internet has come to be seen as a key resource for organizing. The very successful efforts to bring people to Seattle in 1999 to protest the WTO (World Trade Organization) Ministerial Conference (Shah, 2001) gave organizing through the internet a high profile. Of course community organizing has used internet technologies to various extents since the emergence of the World Wide Web. It would be difficult to find a community organizer who is not at least somewhat familiar with the internet and its diverse tools (Dobson, 2006). Regardless of the extent to which staff, volunteers, and community members have access or ability to use internet technologies, the internet has created space to engage in community organizing in new ways, and to redefine traditional organizing techniques. This offers exciting potentials and creates challenges for us, for although the internet could strengthen organizing efforts and enable desired change, it risks undermining or further marginalizing efforts of communities that are not using this tool. Importantly, the internet cannot replace face-to-face organizing efforts which allow for relationship and trust-building, as well as a way for online activity to be translated into action. Finally, the internet provides a lot of tools that community organizing can adapt to traditional organizing efforts to achieve their goals. The culture of the web provides organizational techniques that are aligned with more grassroots community organizing efforts. At the same time, not all internet tools are appropriate for community organizing. If community organizing practices could inform the development of internet technologies, the technical tools developed would create powerful spaces for action and social change.

Chapter 3

THE LANGUAGE OF COMMUNITY ORGANIZATION

One of the aims of this book is to keep things as simple and straightforward as possible. Sometimes, however, a form of academic or technical language (or jargon) is unavoidable, maybe even preferable, in cases and in some others, downright useful. Either the issues or the topics are themselves complex or no simple language that is available is adequate to express the precise meaning of what we need to talk about. What is offered here is a more or less quick guide to some of the specific terms that may not be in current use outside of community work. The idea of placing it at the beginning of our discussion is so that it is apparent and easy to find. It may be useful to scan it before getting into the book, so that you may have a sense of some of the terms that will be used.

Advocacy: The act or practice of taking action by and for ourselves (or on behalf of some group or individual) upon a more powerful public or private institution, individual, or group; to gain or maintain resources or rights that will allow for the meeting of some legitimate need which has been denied or threatened.

Action Targets: Those people and/or issues which are identified as a focus of planning and action for the alleviation of community problems.

Ally: A group or person who can be seen to have similar or complementary needs or goals as another group or person and they decide to work together on the issue. For example, feminist groups and unions might find themselves allies in the concern for good daycare.

Agency: People are said to have agency when they are able to act in order to affect the environment for their own interests. In this sense, folks have agency when they have power, understand they have power, and know how to use it.

Burnout: A condition whereby a person ceases to do the quality of work of which she is capable. It can be caused by simple overwork, by under-support, or by over-expectation of oneself or those around us.

Caucus: A private meeting of the people involved in a change event, a demonstration, or negotiation; for example to discuss immediate strategy and/or clarifying roles within the group.

Charisma: A natural ability to inspire people. It is related to a person's personality rather than, for example, her status or knowledge

Cinch Victory: The achieving of a particular objective that is easily attained or won for the purpose of building credibility of the community organization and the confidence of your people. A cinch victory is usually sought at the beginning of an organization's life.

Citizenship: Typically refers to being a member of a nation, and the concomitant rights and obligations. In different eras, however, different classes and groups have gained enough power to change and expand citizenship rights as new classes and other groups have come onto the political stage. As well, there continues to be a struggle for universal or social citizenship – the extension of rights to all adult members of society who have previously been excluded on the basis of gender, sexual orientation, race and/or ability. Some include the rights of humanity, meaning the right to peace, security, and a clean environment under universal citizenship (Lee, Sammon & Dumbrill, 2007).

Civil Disobedience: Actions that are outside the law, aimed at drawing to attention unequal or unjust treatment of a particular group or person. Indeed, the action may be aimed directly at a specific regulation or law (for example, lunch counter sit-ins during the civil-rights protests; or the occupation of disputed lands by Aboriginal people; or the blocking of logging roads by environmental activists.) Note that the action suggested here is non-violent. There are certainly all sorts of examples of violent civil disobedience, deliberately fomented riots and the like. But as will be discussed throughout the book, one of the key values underpinning this reading is that of respect for life in the broadest sense.

Coalition: The situation in which organizations agree to act in concert on particular issues of common interest, but maintain a clear identity. They give up the right to act independently on this particular issue.

Community: A complex notion of the way people live and connect with each other. When we live in community we occupy a space between personal and institutional spheres of life. (See Chapter 4)

Community at large: The majority of people in the society in which the target community (see below) occupies a part.

Conflict Situation: (See contest situation)

Conflict Strategy: (See contest strategy)

Consensus: A style of decision making in which all actors in a situation have the opportunity to express their ideas and feelings and to be heard seriously. It is not the same as unanimous consent. Rather it is a process which facilitates general support of whatever decision is made within a group while at the same time maintaining mutual respect among members. It depends on a process where people involved have an authentic sense that their voices are being seriously heard and considered.

Contest Situation: When an issue cannot be settled without confrontation between the parties; the two are too far apart on how they see their own interests. Similar to Conflict Situation.

Contest Strategy: Something that aims to neutralize or defeat the intentions of a person, group, or institution. Used when co-operative strategies are impossible. It should not be confused with violence. Similar to Conflict Strategy.

Co-optation: The use of a person's (or group's) energy and participation by government or industry to maintain the status quo and thus preserve political and social control by elites. It suggests the pitfalls of co-operating too easily or too early with elite power holders and losing the leverage of people power.

Culture: The sum of values, beliefs, and sets of norms that guide our ways of relating, and of acting in the world. It provides both a glue which binds us together and a boundary that identifies our differences from others.

Elites: Any privileged minority group who have more power than the majority and who use it, sometimes obviously, sometimes covertly, to maintain their advantaged position while disadvantaging others.

Emotional Tenor: The dominant feeling or feelings within a community. In effect, how a group of people feel about themselves as a group, their problems and their prospects.

Facilitation: Assisting a group or individual with a process. It is not the same as doing something for someone, but means helping them with resources (personal or instrumental) in a way that allows them to do what needs to be done.

Force Field Analysis: A popular education technique which allows us to identify and evaluate the forces, personal, organizational, historical, etc., that are at play in a particular situation. This technique assists in developing strategy and tactics in complex situations. (See Lee and Balkwill, 1996)

Generic: A general approach that would integrate or include activities that can be seen as separate and discrete.

Global North: The group of post-industrial nations, The U.S.A., Canada and Europe for example, that possess the great majority of the world's wealth. They tend to impose their systems of belief and means of wealth creation on nations of much less power, to their own advantage and to the detriment of the Global South. (See below)

Global South: The group of nations that did not go through industrialization or are now undertaking it, and whose development has been dominated by the nations of the Global North (see above). Their resources have been generally siphoned off to the advantage of the post-industrial nations. They have often been the object of development initiatives established by organizations like the World Trade Organization and The World Bank.

Goal: A desired state or result about which we are taking action expressed in general terms. For example we might wish to organize to reduce violence in our community. It is a clear idea but it is broad and needs to be specified before practical action can be taken. (See objective)

Government: The set of institutions, elected or appointed, which provides leadership and administration for the relationships and processes that we have identified as important for our well-being.

Guerilla Theatre: A sometimes formal, sometimes informal, theatrical event put on in conjunction with a demonstration to dramatize some aspect of concern to the community organization. It can range from something as stylized as a "burning in effigy" or a play to something as direct as a sit-in or the blocking of a street. Sometimes called popular theatre (See Popular)

Hegemony: The belief system of our culture fostered by the various major institutions of society, like the media and education. For example, part of the western hegemony would be the unchallenged assumptions that capitalism and democracy are inseparable concepts, as are socialism and dictatorship.   .

Ideology: Any system of ideas that describes and explains the experiences of certain individuals and either justifies their situation or proposes alternatives to it. Ideologies provide frameworks for making sense of the social world; they provide us with a worldview. They may be the product of, for example, a set of values, experiences, and political beliefs. Often, our ideology is implicit and unstated (and usually culturally framed), though it is impossible to be without one. An ideology will determine the nature and causal explanations given to social problems, as well as the solutions to these problems, including the types of interventions and social work activities to be used (Lee, Sammon & Dumbrill, 2007).

Internalized Oppression: The situation whereby an oppressed or marginalized group, or individuals, has come to accept the characterization about them put forward by the dominant group: that they are inferior in some or a number of ways. This is evidenced by group or individual self-doubt or even hatred. Thus individuals within groups may say things like, "We X people are unable to be good in business" or "We Y people are not ready to govern ourselves," (Lee, Sammon & Dumbrill, 2007: Memi, 1965).

Institution: In this book the term expresses two ideas. First it can refer to an organization, usually large, that wields power in a specific field; for example, the church or an oil company. Second, and somewhat related to this, is the notion of institution as being an established set of social practices that frame our social relationships; for example, the institution of marriage.

Left Wing: This has come to be associated with socialist and communist movements. More generally, it stands for an emphasis on human equality and takes the view that rights to survival and physical well-being supersede property rights. The left wing is more inclined (than the right) to make systemic changes to strive for economic equality, to push for strengthened state power in the economic sphere, to push to reduce state power in the sphere of personal liberties, to view the world in structural terms, and to value collective over individual activity (Lee, Sammon & Dumbrill, 2007).

Marginalization: A form of oppression that excludes whole groups of people from useful and meaningful participation in society, leading to material deprivation. It is a basic feature of injustice and oppression. Though often present, even without material deprivation people may be marginalized, for example people of colour, old and young people, many single mothers and their children, people with disabilities, unskilled workers and Aboriginal people. These groups constitute a growing underclass permanently confined to the margins of society because the labour market cannot or will not accommodate them (Lee, Sammon & Dumbrill, 2007).

Marshals: People chosen by the people's organization for supervising the actions of participants at public demonstrations like parades or rallies.

Mass-based Organization: A number of organizations form a single organization and surrender most of their individual group identity in order to mount a powerful united front to address a range of common concerns. (Saul Alinsky was one of the most well-known practitioners of this form of community organization.)

Militant: Strongly determined or committed to a cause. Again, not to be confused with violence, as this term is sometimes used in the corporate media. Some examples of people and organizations that have been militant are Gandhi, the father of the Indian independence struggle; Cesar Chavez the leader of the United Farm Workers in the latter half of the 20th century; and, feminist icon Gloria Steinem.

Networking: The development of a communication system among a group of individuals that enables everyone to become familiar with each other, share information and perhaps develop common issues to work on.

Neo-conservative: a belief that concentrating authority within the state is dangerous. Neo-conservatives defend capitalism as an imperfect, but manageable system. They value the defence of liberty over the pursuit of equality and tend to distrust the welfare state. They object to government action taken on behalf of minority groups because this is viewed as violating commitments to individualism. They also tend to see the need for a collective national identity that tolerates variety and emphasizes religion and family as sources of social stability. It is an ideology that tries to explain the world in terms of individual desire and initiative, which denies the importance of social relationships and suggests that the world will be best built by individuals pursuing their own interests (Lee, Sammon & Dumbrill, 2006, 2007). Some clear examples of neo-conservative approaches to governing can be seen in the administrations of George W. Bush in the U.S.A., Margaret Thatcher in Great Britain, and Stephen Harper in Canada.

Objective: A specific, concrete and measurable desired state or result on which we are taking action. For example, if we had a general goal of reducing community violence, we might then have an objective to reduce the number of guns in the community (see Goal).

Oppression: Refers to inhumane and/or degrading treatment of individuals or groups brought about by the dominance of one group over another. It is a process through which individuals or groups unjustly use their power to limit the lives, experiences and opportunities of others with less power. It is a dynamic process that is integrated into a society's institutional order, culture, and the consciousness of its people through socialization by key societal institutions (for example, education and media). Oppression never occurs in isolation; it involves multiple levels that intersect on the basis of age, race, sexual orientation, ability, class and ethnicity. Oppression involves disregarding the rights of an individual or group and is thus a denial of their citizenship. Furthermore, its intensity is not constant; it often changes in response to significant events and social action/movements (Lee, Sammon, & Dumbrill, 2007).

Polarization: The clarifying of a situation so that the most basic positions of those involved become manifest. This process then allows those involved to evaluate each other's actions in the most realistic light.

Politics: In this case, the term does not refer to the formal act of governing a country or region or city. Rather, it refers to the process of allocation or redistribution of resources within a society or group. This suggests the necessity for, and use of, power. Thus, in community practice we understand that every group will engage in politics internally as it sorts out leadership and resource issues, and externally as it seeks power to assist its members within the larger society.

Popular: This term is used as a qualifier throughout the book such as "popular education" and "popular action." It suggests that the people are at the centre of what is going on. It may be posed against "elite" or "expert" education or action.

Pragmatic: A concern that emphasizes practical values and concerns of cause and effect – a kind of nuts and bolts approach to issues and problems.

Problem Definition: The way in which the difficulties facing a community are perceived and explained. For example, a high incidence of delinquency in a geographic area can be defined in terms of psychopathology of the individuals, or structural problems (like underemployment), or something in between. Problem definition is crucial because we usually develop our strategy based on how we see the problem.

Protocol: A fairly detailed description of the way something can be completed. It is a kind of guide that might include the steps of a particular process (e.g. a survey or a demonstration).

Radical: A person or process that aims to understand and act on the roots of problems; the process of looking past the symptoms by analyzing them in terms of their basic causes. For example, we might look superficially at youth violence in a community as simply an expression of "youth out of control." Or we could attempt a more radical position where we look at underlying structural factors, like poverty and racism.

Right Wing: Associated with being conservative and less inclined to challenge existing institutions; more sympathetic toward property rights and more convinced that hierarchy and continuity of traditions, rather than equality, are essential in human society The Right is generally opposed to having the state do things like regulate business or redistribute tax revenues to equalize economic standing; but some parts of the Right are not opposed to having the state regulate personal behaviour, so it cannot really be said that all of the Right is consistently for less government. For example, restricting access to welfare tends to be a Right-wing policy – this is an area where The Right would like greater state intervention (Lee, Sammon & Dumbrill, 2007). (See Neo-conservative)

Root Cause Analysis: Generally speaking, the notion of thinking through issues to get at their basic or ultimate causes. Also, a popular education technique that facilitates the development of thinking about the problems a community is facing, and how these issues fit together (See Lee and Balkwill, 1996)

(The) State: A system of institutions (see Institution) that has the power to govern through the use of laws, regulations, and force applied to groups of people within particular geographic boundaries. It is the one entity to which people (citizens) cede the right to the use of force in regulating their behaviour. Some would argue that the state is able to articulate the common values and interests of its population. Others believe that the state expresses only those interests and values that reinforce the interests of the governing and economic elites (Lee, Sammon & Dumbrill, 2007).

Sociogram: A diagram representing the connections among members of a particular group. It might include such concerns as strongly positive and/or negative relationships among members. (See Lee and Balkwill,1996)

Solidarity: A profound understanding of a community of interest based on values as well as specific needs. It produces action in support of the needs and programs of another group. For example, in the 1970s and 80s, there sprung up a number of solidarity groups in North America that focused on assisting liberation struggles in parts of Latin America – like Nicaragua where the Sandinistas had taken power and thrown out the oppressive and American-backed Somoza government. Various groups raised money for that cause and some groups organized "brigades" that went there to lend labour to their liberation movement.

Strategy: The overall approach to solving a problem, which takes into consideration our goals, resources and the strength of any opposition. For example, if a community group is attempting to combat discriminatory behaviour by police or other officials they might develop an anti-racism public education strategy. That is, they would attempt to educate the larger public to the issue and the injustice in the expectation that the more people understand the more likely public policy can be affected. On the other hand, they may believe that a more confrontational approach may be required in the expectation that the police and officials will react in a positive way to direct demands for accountability. In this case, we need to consider how we will develop sufficient power to make the confrontation effective. Or they may choose a political lobbying campaign in the hopes that they will get politicians to reign in the officials and the police. In each case different resources and tactics (see below) would be required.

Status Quo: A situation which remains unchanged. We usually use it when referring to those conditions which maintain marginalized people in a state of material and/or social oppression.

Tactics: The specific set of actions that we use to accomplish specific objectives within the overall context of a strategy (see above). Thus, in a public-education approach, we might develop pamphlets with our position to distribute in various places, or we might call a series of public meetings where our issues would be articulated. If we were to choose a strategy of confrontation we might look to the range of allies that will support our position and actions; one action might be to call for our group and our allies to undertake demonstrations at public offices. If we choose political lobbying, we will look to find people with the best access to politicians and engage them in putting pressure on these representatives.

SECTION II

Conceptualizing and Situating
Community Organizing Practice

Chapter 4

SOCIAL STRUCTURAL CONTEXT OF COMMUNITY ORGANIZING PRACTICE

The exercise of power is never neutral.
- Jeremy Rifkin (1998)

While many of the strategies and tactics described in this book and others can be organized in support of a wide range of causes, not all of them would be considered progressive. For example, in the 1930s fascist groups in Germany utilized outreach organization of rallies and pressure campaigns to further their immoral ends (Kershaw, 1999 and 2000). More recently there has been a backlash against the strides that the Women's Movement has made (Cochrane, 2008). Most experienced community organizers are familiar with the basic organizing technologies used in these two examples. Thus, although organizing "technology" can be quite morally neutral, as it is articulated in the cases outlined above, community organization is not a neutral practice. We need to be clear about the values that underlie the initiatives in which we involve ourselves. In this book community organization is rooted in the overall orientation that is generally referred to as an anti-oppressive practice or perspective.

An Anti-Oppressive Practice/Perspective

Dumbrill states: "The term Anti-Oppressive Perspectives (AOP) refers to the integration of a number of social justice perspectives that challenge isms and attempt to bring "social inclusion, which means ending the isms that marginalize or exclude some groups from full participation within society." While this is a useful characterization, it is only a partial one because it leaves out the vital aspect of action. "Isms" are important in that they can underpin action, but by themselves they do not exclude or marginalize; rather, it is the actions of people that do so. Nevertheless, the centrality of social justice is key (Parada, Barnoff, Moffatt and Homan, 2010). In a little monograph that unfortunately did not get much circulation, Miriam Wolfson (2002) locates anti-oppressive practice as one of the many variants in a range of models that espouses a liberation or emancipatory focus. That is, they are fundamentally committed to the realization of social justice (Dominelli, 1998:4). Included in many of these emancipatory approaches is anti-discriminatory practice, which in social work literature is often interchanged with anti-oppressive practice. Although they share an ideological and theoretical framework that challenges oppression and discrimination, the social work literature describes anti-discriminatory practice as being primarily concerned with distribution of resources (Hopton, 1997). Some writers further suggest that anti-discriminatory practice has a narrower, legalistic perspective that does not take on broader sociopolitical concerns (Thompson, 1997). Others view anti-oppressive practice as being mainly concerned with the distribution of power – its use and abuse within the relationships at the personal, family, community, organizational, and structural levels. These levels, of course, are interconnected and they shape and determine social realities. Overall, many in the human service professions – particularly those in the social work field – tend to view the anti-oppressive model as one that is more inclusive and dynamic, and that deals with the interaction of many forms of discrimination and oppression, along with the manner in which they are expressed (Ward and Mullender, 1991; Dominelli 1998; Burke and Harrison, 1998). While there may be diversity of perspectives in attempting to describe anti-oppressive practice, there is common agreement around its central themes of power, social justice and inequality, as well as its values of equality, freedom, individuality, collectivity and cooperation.

These ideas are reflected in two important definitions. Anti-oppressive practice is a form of social intervention which addresses social divisions and structural inequalities in the work that is done with people, whether they are users of service, (so-called clients) or workers. Anti-op-

practice aims to provide more appropriate and sensitive ser-
responding to people's needs regardless of their social status.
ppressive practice embodies a person-centred philosophy; an
_g _arian value system concerned with reducing the disastrous effects
of structural inequalities upon people's lives; a methodology focusing
on both process and outcome; and a way of structuring relationships
among individuals that aims to assist people in empowering themselves
through addressing the negative effects of social hierarchies on their interactions and the work they do together (Dominelli, 1996: 271).

In the second definition, anti-oppressive practice is a set of ideas
that, taken together, have the purpose of conveying and promoting
sound practice that concerns the promotion and maintenance of
equality, rights, equity, well-being, and interdependence through positive structural and personal initiatives (Mallinson, 1995: 67).

It is also important to note that anti-oppressive practice draws
on critical theories that are concerned with social transformation
aimed at freedom from exploitation, domination, and inequality
(Mullaly, 1997). Thus, anti-oppressive practice has an emancipatory
focus which has been designed with a practical intent to be critical of existing social and political institutions and practices. In this
critical role, the link between individual emancipation and social
and political change is a defining characteristic. For example, before individuals find political solutions, it is essential to develop
personal awareness and understanding of one's own reality in relation to structural forces. In other words, emancipation is directly
related to the notion of self-reflection, which in turn leads to critical understanding or consciousness of personal issues from a social, economic, cultural and historical perspective. Once individuals
have a critical consciousness they can engage in social action which
in turn leads to collective emancipation.

In summary, the essence of any practice that is supposed to be anti-
oppressive is based on the following:

- Acknowledgement of the effects of the structural dimensions of oppression, which cut across a number of social divisions including social class,
gender, race, sexual orientation, disability status, religion and age.
- Adoption of self-reflective and critical – i.e. self-questioning – stances
on the part of workers.

- Promotion of co-participatory, rather than authoritarian, practice relations. This involves workers, service users, as well as academics and practitioners as co-participants engaged in the change process.
- Commitment to working with and for the oppressed populations to achieve social transformation.

Clearly then, as an anti-oppressive practice, community organization will take the side of the marginalized and oppressed (McGrath, Lee, George, Moffatt, 2007; Lotz, 1995). There are a number of reasons for this. The most significant one has been mentioned: the unequal distribution of power in society. In this chapter we will look at how that distribution is arrived at, and consider the implications for people's everyday lives.

We live in a society, a world in fact, based on class, gender, race, and other differences. This is to say that in our world groups of people are defined and separated by the social, economic and occupational strata in which they find themselves (Curtis, Grabb, & Guppy: 2003; Bishop, 1994; Forcese, 1975). Given this state of affairs, we find that:

- Power is unequally distributed: a certain few individuals and groups have a great deal of influence over resources and decisions; larger numbers of individuals and groups have considerably less influence; and a smaller, though significant, number of people have virtually no influence at all.
- Because of the unequal distribution of power, opportunities to gain access to the benefits of this world are unequally apportioned.

These two facts combine to marginalize particular social, economic, or occupational levels. This results in elites having (or at least having access to) many benefits, while various marginalized groups are left with significant deficits or burdens. Freire (1970: 44) suggests that the very fact of having "more" leads people to define having more for themselves as the ultimate "good," even at the cost of the oppressed having nothing. "For them, to be is to have and to be the class of the haves." Thus, having and not having are related aspects of reality, part of a complex socio-psychological, political-economic dynamic. Having, or being advantaged, requires that others do not have and are disadvantaged.

Neo-conservative commentators (Murray, 2006 for example) will ask, is there really anything so drastically wrong with some inequality in society? Certainly right-wing conservative groups like the American Enterprise Institute in the U.S.A. and the Fraser Institute in Canada continually assert that the market brought us the marvels of western civilization. And if inequality exists is it not a small price to play? These are particularly pertinent questions given the present neo-conservative assault on the notion of a caring and egalitarian society which has been building in the western world since the 1940s. As long as there are relatively few abuses of power and our society builds "safety nets" – though according to Murray (2006) we have far too many of them – for those people who "lose out," then aren't things pretty humane and as they should be? After all, compared to the nineteenth century, modern Western society in general has achieved an enviable reputation for high standards of both living and individual freedom.

There are two answers to the question of inequality in contemporary Western society. Western post-industrial societies, while still better off than most countries in the Global South, are by no means egalitarian societies (Wilkinson & Pickett, 2010). An article in *The Globe and Mail*, hardly a bastion of radical dissent, had this comment on Canadian society:

> The earnings gap between the rich and the poor is widening in Canada, with incomes among recent immigrants showing especially dramatic declines in recent years, according to sweeping new census data.
>
> Earnings among the richest fifth of Canadians grew 16.4 per cent between 1980 and 2005 while the poorest fifth of the population saw earnings tumble 20.6 per cent over the 25-year time period, Statistics Canada said in its 2006 census release on income and earnings. Earnings among people in the middle stagnated (Grant, 2008: L1).

The fact is we do not live in anything like an egalitarian situation. Overall, in 2005, the wealthiest 20 per cent of the world accounted for 76.6 per cent of total private consumption. The poorest 20 per cent made up just 1.5 per cent (Global Issues, 2008). As Figure 1-1: "Distribution of Household Income" illustrates, in the industrialized and post-industrial nations the income of the wealthiest 20 per cent of the population is roughly four-and-one-half to eight-and-one-half times of that going to the poorest 20 per cent. To put it in starker terms, in the United States the richest one per cent of the population takes 25 per cent of the nation's income. In Canada, the top one per cent manages to accumulate 22 per cent. Evidence that the rich are getting even richer is shown in the following:

Percentage Share of Income Taken by Wealthiest and Poorest Groups in Each Country

	Poorest 10%	Wealthiest 10%
Australia (1994)	3.3	22.5
Brazil (2004)	0.9	44.8
Canada (2004)	2.6	24.8
China (2004)	1.6	34.9
France (2004)	3.2	22.1
Germany (2000)	7.0	40.3
India (2004)	3.6	21.1
Italy (2004)	2.3	26.8
Jamaica (2004)	2.1	35.8
Japan (1993)	4.8	21.7
Netherlands (1999)	2.5	22.9
Nicaragua (2001)	2.3	33.8
Nigeria (2003)	2.0	33.2
Spain (2001)	2.6	26.6
South Africa (2000)	1.4	44.7
Sweden (2000)	3.6	22.2
Uganda (2002)	2.3	37.7
United Kingdom (1999)	2.1	28.5
United States (2007)	2.0	30.0

Distribution of household income is one of the easiest measures of inequity (Central Intelligence Agency, 2007)

Figure 4-1: Distribution of Household Income

Benefits and deficits are not randomly distributed. The interests of some groups are achieved more or less consistently at the expense of others, usually unorganized groups. Under the U.S. social security system, for example, huge amounts of money are siphoned off to middle and upper-income Americans (Howe & Longman, 1992). McQuaig (1998) has pointed out how the elites of the world use unemployment, and the fear of unemployment, to put pressure on workers to "moderate" expectations regarding wages and benefits. In Canada, thanks particularly to the Conservative government elected in 2006, "With tax rates on people in the bottom 10 per cent now higher than the rates on the top 1 per cent, Canada's upper-income earners are not paying their fair share of taxes compared to 15 years ago" (Lee, 2008). Mackenzie (2007) reports that between 1992 and 2004, 20 per cent of the gain in income share went to the richest of the rich in Canada, the multi-millionaires in the top 0.01 per cent of the income scale. In other words, a so-called "progressive tax system" is now geared to ensuring that the rich get richer and the poor get poorer. Globalization, with all the outsourcing of high-paying industrial jobs to the low-wage Global South, has exacerbated the situation of working-class people. This helps the rich in an additional way, by keeping inflation down which allows them to make huge profits from their investments. This example is a clear indication of how the rich and working people have quite divergent material interests under capitalism; and it is also a clear indication of how the rich fear equality, and why working people need it.[1]

British researchers, Wilkinson and Pickett (2010), have produced a powerful study with data drawn from a range of industrialized and post-industrialized countries. Their analysis suggests that the more inequality existing within a country (measured in terms of income inequality), the more likely people will suffer high incidences of health and social problems. These social ills include, but are not limited to, higher incidences of poor health, school drop-outs, and increased rates of violence and crime. The authors go on to suggest that inequality causes problems throughout the whole society; but those at the bottom of the income ranking suffer far more.

Some of the groups particularly disadvantaged by this systemic inequality are:

---

[1]   For further discussion and more information regarding poverty, see: Ross et al. (2000) The Canadian Fact Book on Poverty - 2000 (Ottawa: Canadian Council on Social Development).

- working class people in general;
- women, especially those heading single-parent families;[2]
- senior citizens, particularly women;
- immigrants, particularly those from the global south as well as racialized minorities; Aboriginal people;[3]
- people with physical, emotional, or mental challenges.[4]

A second issue is that inequality involves more than the simple fact of having or not having money. Disadvantaged people have less power or ability to influence their lives than do the rich or middle classes. In Chapter 2, we will discuss the nature and sources of power, but for now, let us examine the social and psychological effects of being disadvantaged.

The Structure of Empowerment and Disempowerment[5]

Rich people and theorists, who are often rich people, think of poverty in the negative, as the lack of riches – as disease might be called the lack of good health. But it isn't sir. Poverty isn't the

---

[2] McDermott (1992) points out that neither the Canadian Human Rights Act of 1981, nor the Employment Equity Act of 1986, has resulted in any significant gains for women who continue to earn 35% less than male workers.

[3] Like Aboriginal people in many countries of the world those in Canada face huge challenges and incredible marginalization. Angell and Dunlop (2001) make the case that in Canada and the USA the state has utilized social welfare policies to maintain First Nations as dependent. The *New Internationalist* (2008) reminds us that Aboriginal people occupy the bottom rung on the Canadian economic ladder whether they live on reserves, in Métis settlements, or in urban centres.

[4] A report published by the G. Allen Roeher Institute (1989) pointed out that Canadians who are disabled are poor. They tend to be unemployed or underemployed, but "most need to spend more money on items or services they require for daily living; and incur costs simply as a result of their disabling condition," (p.3).

[5] For a more comprehensive and critical discussion of social structural issues, there are three books you may find useful: Ben Carniol's, *Case Critical* (Between the Lines Press); Ann Bishop's, *Becoming an Ally* (Fernwood Press); and Joan Kuyak's, *Fighting for Hope* (Black Rose Books).

lack of anything but a positive plague virulent in itself, contagious as cholera; filth, criminality, vice and despair as only a few of its symptoms."
      - *Burroughs the butler in the Preston Sturges 1941 film,*
                                              Sullivan's Travels.

Empowerment, in its most practical sense, means that we feel we have an ability to influence (not totally control) our environment so that we can have our needs met. This feeling, or what White (1959) calls a sense of efficacy, is mediated by three factors or elements (see Figure 4-2):

- Instrumental – dealing with concrete issues and needs, such as levels of employment; or access to nutrition, or to social, educational, or health services.
- Personal – relating to our emotional and relational life, such as the ability to communicate or to be mobile, or to have access to friendship or support networks. These factors may concern the ability to communicate or understand, or the access we have to communication and understanding.
- Structural – concerning the social, political, or economic institutions and their support or constraint for peoples' lives. Issues such as racism, sexism, or ableism would be found here. The degree to which people suffer from these oppressions profoundly affects their quality of life.

Of course, these factors do not operate independently. Our sense of efficacy is comprised of the complex interplay of our personal abilities and the quality of the environment – instrumental and structural – in which we live.

Let's think about some of the issues that we hear or read about in the media today:

- An urban centre has an issue with guns and gangs (Chutleborough, 2007), or people without housing and a high use of social services. Police, social workers, teachers, and public health officials all point to the apathy, resistance to outside help, and destructive behaviour of the locals.

- A Northern Canadian reserve community is known for its high rate of alcohol abuse, school drop-outs, adolescent suicides, unemployment, and cyclical violence. Officials, teachers, social and health services workers talk about the negative attitudes of the people, as well as the magnitude of the problems.
- Statistics on mental hospital admissions show that women have a far greater likelihood of being admitted to institutions than men. Poor people are also more likely to be admitted than those in the middle class. Statistics on prison populations in Canada show that Aboriginal people are vastly over-represented, while in the U.S., African-Americans are over-represented.

What are we to make of all this? Do we accept that women, Aboriginal people, African-American people and the poor are stupid, self-destructive, weak or evil by their nature? This social Darwinist perspective[6] has been accepted by a significant number of people, even by entire societies. The first Europeans immigrating to North America, Australia and New Zealand based many of their genocidal actions against indigenous populations on the assertion of racial and cultural superiority. Nazis murdered 6,000,000 Jews on the basis that they were non-Aryans, inferior and harmful to the economy (Kershaw, 2000 & 1999).

There are more humane views of social problems, of course. A second approach used to explain these phenomena is the humanist liberal orientation, often put forward in social work. People like Johnson and Yanka (2007), for example, suggested that the fit between systems and individuals is sometimes problematic. The definition of social work adopted by the International Federation of Social Workers mentions structural issues (see below) but puts far more emphasis on individual system interactions (International Federation of Social Workers, 2000). Whitmore and Kerans (1988:53) have noted, however, that:

> After generations of being excluded, people cannot simply be suddenly invited to become involved in decisions. The result of such exclusion

---

[6] Rushton, J. P., & Jensen, A. R (2005) in an article in the journal *Psychology, Public Policy, and Law,* put forward the theory that intelligence is related to race. This is a recycling of ideas that Rushton has been trying to get on the public policy agenda since the 1990's. They are old discredited ideas but still continue to find a small audience in North America and Europe.

will not be so much unwise decisions, but a profound reluctance to enter into any decision-making process.

This statement claims that disadvantaged members will not be able to cope and will become casualties who, rather than being punished as the Social Darwinists propose, must be cared for, cured or protected. The emphasis in this approach is on the individual (Camiol, 2005).

A third approach is structural anti-oppressive which asks us to look for "root causes" and is supported by writers such as, (Wilkinson & Pickett, 2010), Baines (2007), Dominelli (1999), Mullally (1997), and Carniol (2005). It suggests that conditions of poverty or racial or gender discrimination are structured in the society and are, by their very nature, destructive to human development. The economic system, and the acquisitive social relationships produced by capitalism and bureaucracy, is largely responsible for inequality and social injustices. As Swift and Tomlinson (1991) note:

> ...social, economic, cultural, and political needs arise in response to unjust structure of society; and therefore, development must ultimately contribute to the restructuring of social, economic, and political relationships. ... The issue of control over the development process, of how needs and solutions are articulated – at the local and national levels – becomes critical to a development model.

These issues are the key understandings regarding the nature, and underlying causes, of social problems. It is important to be clear that the position taken in this book is that of structural community organization. It uses an analysis of systems and relationships. What distinguishes structural work from other approaches is that we believe that all our activity needs to be grounded in the broad structural issues of class, race and gender. Furthermore, it sees the need to root its work in perhaps less obvious, but equally important, structural issues such as ability and sexual orientation – realities which define (most often in oppressive or discriminatory terms) the relationships of particular populations to the dominant society. This theory is particularly useful to community organizers since it is based on the notion that a crucial aspect of "what it is to be a human being" is the need to be able to act and exert influence on one's environment. (Biklen, 1983; Freire, 1970).

Environment and Human Agency

White (1959) theorizes that an important basis for individual growth is the development of an understanding that we are different from our environment. This growth is accomplished by experiencing the consequences of our actions. He also suggests that the development of a person's sense of self as an autonomous social player is based on "a growing sense of competence." White says that our ability to feel competent, and thus behave in a competent manner, rests with our ability to actually experience competence. Martin (2002) as well as Hustedde and Ganowicz (2002) stress that autonomy requires that we be able to act in our own interests within our environment. The environment then, as well as our own talents, has an important impact on our ability to feel and be successful. It must be amenable to our activity.

Maier and Ellen applied the theory of frustration instigated behaviour (Maier, 1961) to human conditions. They suggested that if people find themselves in situations where their ability/opportunity to influence the course of their lives is sufficiently severed, and if this lasts a sufficient length of time, that eventually a "frustration threshold" will be crossed and the inner tension of the person will become the dominant cause of behaviour:

> Such behaviour is determined largely by conditions inside the organism, so that the expression of emotions and feelings, rather than what they achieve, characteristically accompany behaviour selected under conditions of frustration" (Maier and Ellen, 1965: 100).

In other words, a person who is continually frustrated will act, not to deal with actual objective conditions – which may not be amenable to action anyway – but with the anxiety associated with the frustrated condition. He will tend to act on whatever, or whoever, is handy.

Richard Ball (1973) became interested in frustration instigated behaviour and looked at it in terms of a community situation – areas where social dysfunction was reported to be high and of long duration. He focused particularly on some of the groups of southern Appalachia in the United States. He suggested that Maier's notions fitted these situations. The people had a long history of "unremitting physical, economic and social frustration, repeatedly blocked, pressured and defeated by their environment." He suggested that "self-destructive" attitudes of fatalism and apathy, or behaviour of intra-familial and community violence, for example, were actually frustration responses. "Such behaviour may be difficult for the motivation-oriented observer to comprehend, but it is quite likely to provide relief from the tensions of extreme and prolonged frustration." He explained that people, deprived of the ability to act effectively on their environment will become increasingly anxious over time. In situations of prolonged anxiety, they will resort to any behaviour that will provide even temporary soothing of the internal discomfort.

This is an important analysis with which to view the communities that have been marginalized with little or no resources to influence their lives or their environments. As human beings we strive to render ourselves and our environment understandable, predictable and manageable. When we think about it, that is why groups of people first came together to form primitive communities; individuals would perish but the groups offered physical protection, the opportunity to share difficult tasks and the possibility of social interaction. This striving can also be seen in the struggle to form trade unions to struggle against the socially dehumanizing and destructive force of the Industrial Revolution (Polanyi, 2001). To the extent that we experience our success in meeting our material, social, and spiritual needs, we experience feelings of competence and a sense of well-being as individuals and as group, which White (1959) refers to as efficacy and which others call agency. When we are unsuccessful – when things get out of our control – we experience feelings of incompetence, or non-efficacy, and lack a sense of well-being. If we think in terms of the empirical work of Maier and its application by Ball, we would refer to feelings of anxiety. There is a dynamic relationship among these three important variables. Our self-image influences our behaviour within our environments. This relationship is illustrated in Figure 4-2: The Structuring of Self-efficacy.

Likewise, our personal abilities, such as intelligence, are developed by our relationship with our environment. This relationship has an instrumental dimension (the actual access to the necessities of life) and a structural dimension (the degree of classism or racism or sexism, etc. which will have an effect on our ability to access necessities).

Thus, there is a dynamic relationship between our personal abilities and the environment in which they are activated and supported

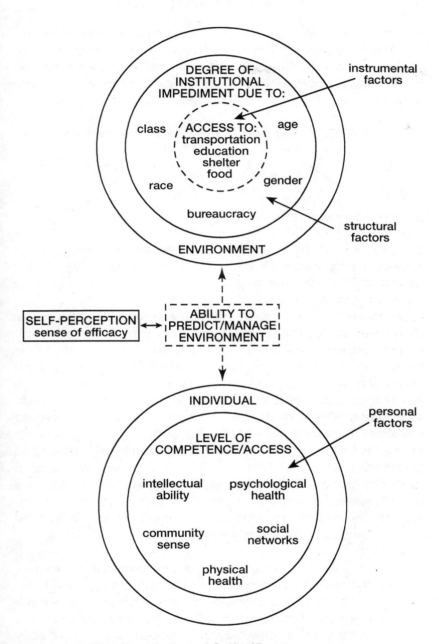

Figure 4-2: The Structuring of Self-efficacy

or blocked. This dynamic has an effect on how we perceive and understand ourselves; and this perception (of our ability to manage our environment) in turn affects how we try to deal with our environment. The positive side of this relationship is presented in Figure 4-3: Relationship Between Positive Self-image and Positive Outcome.

Figure 4-3: Relationship between positive self-image, a predictable / manageable environment and one's ability to act for a positive outcome.

If we live in a social environment that is predictable and manageable, we will generally be able to act within it to satisfy our needs. (This, of course, does not preclude struggle and resistance.) Further, we will be able to perceive and experience our success. This will lead us to feel positively about who we are and also about our environment, which we see as a relatively supportive place. The degree to which we develop a realistically positive image of the environment encourages us to act in and with it, perhaps rendering it even more manageable, and reinforcing the notion of ourselves as creative, productive individuals and groups – in short as human social agents (Hustedde and Ganowicz, 2002). The type of behaviour that is likely to emerge from this dynamic will, we suggest, be purposive and humane; that is, it will be shaped to attain the best results for ourselves and our environment in both the short and long term. As Langer states:

> "When people feel they can exercise some control over their environment, they seek out new information. They plan, strategize, and so on, behaving mindfully. As they engage in control behaviour, it is this mindful enactment of perceived control behaviour that yields the positive psychological and physical consequences described," (1983: 207-8).

What will occur, however, if this dynamic relationship possesses negative connections? What if the environment is unpredictable, and/ or unmanageable? What if our actions are unable to produce positive results for ourselves? Figure 4-4 suggests the result of this relationship.

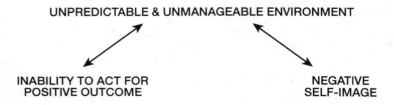

UNPREDICTABLE & UNMANAGEABLE ENVIRONMENT

INABILITY TO ACT FOR   **NEGATIVE**
POSITIVE OUTCOME   **SELF-IMAGE**

Figure 4-4: Relationship between negative self-image, an unpredictable / unmanageable environment and one's inability to act for a positive outcome.

Simply put, if we live in an environment that is socially and materially unpredictable, and unmanageable – one that is oppressive and blocks most of our attempts at meeting our needs – our activity within it will not be fulfilling. As we experience this lack of ability, we begin to feel hopeless both about ourselves as people and about our environment, perceiving it with dread as a malignant or dangerous place.[7] We begin to feel disempowered, over-stressed and/or anxious. Our negative image of the environment and our anxiety will discourage us from acting in any planned or coherent fashion. Our environment likely becomes less manageable, and our image of ourselves is one of passivity, powerlessness, and victimization. We become preoccupied, not with creation, but with survival – or simply with the relieving of stress and anxiety (Ball, 1973: 74). Langer, who reported on research with individuals who experience a chronic loss of control, states:

---

[7]   A most dramatic example of this effect can be found among torture victims *(Amnesty International Bulletin* December 1989/January 1990 Volume XVII, Number I). A remarkably consistent set of symptoms can be found among victims of torture. Psychiatrists call it post-traumatic stress disorder; it affects combat veterans, victims of natural disasters—anyone who has been placed under **great stress in a situation they have been helpless to control**. (Emphasis added.)

Here we consider situations in which people over time gradually and in-sidiously lose control. When people feel a chronic loss of control they don't take risks and they retreat into an all too familiar world (1983: 207).

The type of behaviour that is likely to emerge from this dynamic will lack an overall sense of purpose and will be centred on an immediate need satisfaction, which may involve the avoidance of internal pain or frustration. It will be shaped to attain quick, anxiety-reducing re-sults, relative only to the individual and his or her immediate feelings of anxiety. This response neglects long-term needs as well as the needs of other human beings and of the environment. [8]

A passage from Sennett & Cobb (1973: 22) eloquently presents the feeling of what it is like to be rendered marginal or ineffectual[9]:

> ... images in his conversation concerning the poor [including his father], both white and black, ... fuse material deprivation with chaotic, arbi-trary and unpredictable behaviour: he sees poverty...as depriving men of the capacity to act rationally, to exercise self-control ... [D]ignity means, specifically, moving toward a position in which he deals with the world in some controlled, emotionally restrained way.

It is important to note, of course, that the environment must be to-tally hostile to our actions for it to affect our self-image and our ability to act constructively. We refer to situations where we experience how our actions are irrelevant to a desired outcome; a situation where we can be sure of doing neither good nor ill. Such an environment might have benign aspects; for example, some nice people (teachers, social workers, politicians) might be doing some nice things for us, but it is

---

[8]   Maier & Ellen (1965) refer to this as the principle of availability. The individual vents feelings (anger or fear or frustration) at whatever or whoever is available, rather than engaging in behaviour aimed at solving a problem or removing an ob-stacle. (pp. 100-101).

[9]   A more recent British study (Charlesworth et. Al. 2004) provides a substantially similar perspective on how class differences are often experienced as punishing and life limiting by working and lower class people, and how this in turn inflicts violence on their ability to feel they can be agents in their own lives.

not within our power to influence them to our advantage, or to anyone else's. As Fromm (1964: 63) notes, even things can be treated nicely. *They* do things to, or for, us. Our activity counts for nothing, and we have no power. Fromm (1964: 57) states further:

> ... freedom from political shackles is not a sufficient condition. If love for life is to develop, there must be freedom 'to' – freedom to create and to construct, to wonder and to venture. Such freedom requires that the individual be active and responsible, not a slave or a well-fed cog in the machine.

Wilkinson and Pickett (2010) assert that the degrees of our physical and mental health are highly correlated with our sense of control, our ability to influence our environments. What else is mental health but a person's capacity to act according to his true interest?

This ability to act for ourselves has important implications for what community practitioners do, but as well as how we think about things. But before we get into those issues, we need to think a little about the actual entity that is community, and the process of how communities become dysfunctional for their members.

Some Practical Concepts

Community

A community is **a group of people.** It is also a complex concept. As such, it is subject to the various sociological and anthropological principles that have been discovered or constructed by social scientists to deal with how we organize our relationships. The principles may not always agree because, as pointed out by many – for example, Hustedde and Ganowicz (2002) and Warren (1983) – there are a variety of ways for understanding the notion of community. Boothroyd (1991) describes community as a human group engaged in free associations and distinguishes it from dyads, nuclear families, the state, large associations, and corporations. Boothroyd (1991) puts forth a normative understanding when he suggests that it is the freedom of association within a group that distinguishes community. He writes, "In sum, the essence of community is free co-operation in groups large enough to have variety, resilience, and capacity for complex work, but small enough for members to feel needed, recognized, efficacious, creative and unique" (Boothroyd 1991, 108). Boothroyd's concept of community recognizes the importance of identity and belonging as a key element of community. Brueggemann (2002) echoes this when he identifies a crucial aspect of community as, "...experiences in which individuals voluntarily attempt to provide meaning in their lives, meet needs, and accomplish personal goals (2002:110)."

More recent community-practice literature has attempted to define community in order to reflect its complexity. Communities can be imagined so that some factors, but not necessarily all, are present. Communities are defined so that at times they are conceptualized primarily by geography. Sometimes the communities exist as functional groupings, and at other times as associational groups tied to the identity of community members (Rivera and Erlich 1995; Wharf and Clague 1997).

Though we can think about community in many ways, here we are first going to focus on a way that allows us to understand the importance of community and community organizing.

Community as a Crucial Interface

This perspective, following on Karl Polanyi's analysis (2001) outlined above, focuses on the degree of complexity or sophistication that exists within the organization of relationships at various levels of society. For example, at the personal level we are individuals, complex beings, generally living in some sort of set of friendship and/ or family relationships. The institutional level of organization, which includes the state and the economy, represents a more distant and complex array of relationships. They are organized much more formally and impersonally, with relationships generally being contractual and legal. Figure 4-5: "Levels of Societal Relationships" illustrates that the lives we live "in community" represent a middle ground or interface between the personal areas of life, individual and family life as well as friendship networks, and the institutional level—the state and economic organizations and activity.

One definition of community (Ponting 1986:155) sees it as a network (or potential network) of reciprocal interpersonal and inter-organizational relations – made up of one or more groups of individuals, families and organizations. Within these relations there exists (or po-

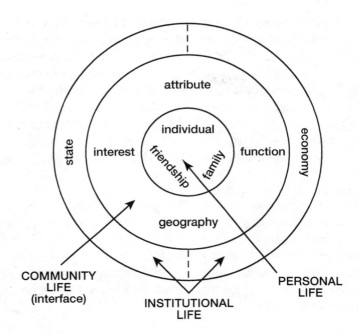

Figure 4-5: Levels of Societal Relationships

tentially exists) a shared sense of belonging. From this very general conception we can begin to see that community is an important focus for attention and organizing. It is neither as personal as family life, nor as impersonal or formal as institutional life, but partaking of both. It mediates the needs and demands of the personal on institutional life, and vice versa.

In practical terms there are essentially three types of communities: geographical, function (or attribute), and interest. There can be some overlap, but it is useful to think in the following terms:

Geographic - People living in the same physical area, such as an urban neighbourhood or a rural village. This is the common understanding of the term and the one that planners and theorists like Ross (1967) use. Other writers like Plant (1974) urged us to come to grips with other ways to understand community.

Function or Attribute - People who share or possess a common and essential factor, perhaps gender, race, religion, sexual orientation or socioeconomic status. Unions are found in this group, workers for a department store chain or auto workers, for example. Within this category we can include **communities of interest** (Fraser, 2005). This is really a sub-type of community "function." A strong common interest can be an essential defining characteristic of a group, such as people who band together to fight the construction of an expressway, to seek funding for some charity or special event, or to fight a polluting industry.

Boundaries - To be a community, the group will also demonstrate some sort of distinct boundaries. The geographic area it occupies or the attributes that members share will "separate" them from other groups. It must be recognized, or have the potential to be recognized, as having an identity of its own. For example, a group of people working within an industry may not appear to be distinct as a group. However, once they begin to unionize they become clearly visible as a specific group with loyalties and shared purpose.

Consciousness - A community will have some consciousness of itself, its boundaries and/or focus (Roberts, 1979:45). It may only be a potential consciousness, but members must ultimately recognize themselves as a distinct entity. A number of babies, three to ten months old, would not be considered a community; but a group of Aboriginal people would be.

Benefits or Deficits - Generally speaking, when we hear the term community we think of it as a positive entity, As exemplified previously when talking about Boothroyd's understanding, folks tend to define it in normative terms. Membership in a community however may result in members having particular **benefits or deficits**. For example, a single parent receiving assistance under a government social-welfare program (as a community of attribute member) can be seen as having the benefit of public financial support, (such as it is). At the same time, we know that this support is less than adequate to maintain that parent above the poverty line. In the fall of 1995, the Ontario Conservative Government cut the already meagre allotment by 21.6 per cent. The subsequent government has only reinstated a small part of that. Obviously, a person in this situation possesses an attribute that is a benefit and a deficit at the same time.

Community as a Political Entity

We need a politics that speaks more directly to the heart, and to the repressed need for social connectedness that lies there bruised and stunted.

-Barbara Ehrenreich (1993)

Keeping in mind that a community occupies the mediating site between personal and institutional life (Fraser, 2005), it follows that community should also be understood as a political entity (Moffatt et al., 2010). Any community will have a general self-interest, or set of interests, that correlates with some parts of its environment, and runs counter to others. For example, a housing co-operative – a community of attribute and geography – may have interests that correlate quite well with the municipality in which it exists. Good sewers, transportation, and education are examples of areas on which everyone would agree. However, if the municipality were to allow a polluting industry to be built next to the co-op – for tax and employment advantages – the members could find their interests very much at odds with other segments of the municipality. Thus, a community's political nature will be quiet and unseen at times and, by the necessity of its self-interest, be high profile at other times. Again, power is an important dimension (see below).

The political nature of community, and ultimately community work, has been particularly accentuated in the last two decades. The advent of five dynamics: diversity; globalization and technological innovation; the attack of the right or corporate interests on the disadvantaged and working / middle class; the strategy of selling the inevitability of these changes, which have had profound effects on community, whether geographically or functionally defined; and finally an attack on public space.[10]

1. *Diversity - within and among communities*

While a community has never been a single entity (Fraser, 2005) – there have always been sub-groupings of family, or interest, or class, or di-

---

[10] The framework that follows has been developed with three colleagues Usha George, Susan McGrath and Ken Moffatt – with whom I continue to work and learn.

versity – communities in North America have become increasingly diverse. Poverty, conflict, and oppression in many parts of the world, and recruitment from areas such as Asia, have brought a great number of diverse groups to North America. This has resulted in "racial and cultural diversity" becoming an increasingly important, and sometimes quite contentious, dynamic in community life. A second aspect is the increased number of marginalized groups (queer populations, and psychiatric survivors for example) that have found their voices, and wish to have their voices heard and respected in the mainstream of community life. Diversity has added complexity and stress to community life and work (McGrath et al., 2007; Lee et al., 1996). Some believe that it is dangerous and should be played down (Rubin and Rubin, 1986). The fear is that if we recognize the "identity" or "concerns" of specific groups, this recognition will sow division and injure attempts at building "community." Following this approach however would probably lead to the subjugation of important and legitimate "voices" which would simply reproduce unjust power relations. Indeed it could retard the effort to build realistically integrated communities. Of course we cannot, and never will, work with the "whole" community. No community worker tries to round up all the members of a particular community. We work with segments of a community, the leadership, emerging leaders, work groups and interest groups. Our efforts are with the people who are going to do the real work of mobilizing all the people they can in order to undertake the necessary change strategies. At the same time, while we look for leadership, interests, and issues, we must seek to understand the diversities that lie, sometimes hidden, within the community. We need to learn to deal across difference— to use the energy of diversity in positive ways (Narayan, 1994; Erlich and Rivera, 1995).

2. *Globalization and Technological Innovation*

As Rifkin (1995) has noted, technology – particularly information technology and the much freer flow of capital – has allowed many corporations to cut ties to local communities, and seek cheap labour and lower taxation around the world. This practice has undercut the material base of North American communities, decreasing the number of well-paid wage earners and tax payers which makes it more difficult for communities to "care" for their members. A powerful picture of the globalized economy is presented by Atkinson and Elliot (1998):

This is the 'New Command Economy' in which capital is free and working people have been nationalized. Unemployment is a fact of life; huge inequalities have opened up in income and in wealth, the private sector does what it likes and the public sector does what it is told. The very instability left by the rampaging wolf of global capital makes necessary much more stringent social controls; as jobs move out of the inner-city neighbourhood so the closed circuit cameras and 'zero tolerance' police move in. And the new culture of control is a make-work scheme for politicians and administrators; having abandoned any pretense at managing the economy, they channel their energies into managing the citizenry.

It adds a further element for consideration as we try to help people identify issues, and mobilize for action. The energy levels may be quite low in the face of real and severe crisis. As one community worker expressed: "People are feeling such desperation they want something, anything that will answer some immediate needs. They don't feel they can wait. They often don't seem to have the energy and patience for organizing." This is a dynamic that will have to be clearly understood by community workers, not so we will simply give up, but so we can work with people to help them develop energy and hope.

3. Attack of the Right and the Colonization of Community

"Capitalism is the extraordinary belief that the nastiest of men, for the nastiest of reasons, will somehow work for the benefit of us all." - *John Maynard Keynes*

"It can be readily seen that the market economy involves a society the insinuations of which are subordinated to the requirements of the market mechanism." - *Karl Polanyi*

This attack has three parts. The first is the assault on the idea of the welfare state which, whatever its faults, means so much to those injured by industrial capitalism. In 1944 Polanyi (2001) outlined the rise of the welfare state as an absolute requirement to save human society from the destructive colonization of community and the environment by free-market Capitalism. That is, that community and environment

are seen as valid only insofar as they serve the interests of so-called free markets.

The second is related to the first but is a more indirect strategy; a devolution of responsibility for services to the community. This is a delicate issue. Many, such as McKnight (1995) have argued that the community is the best place for dealing with local problems. The difficulty is that most of the devolution requires funding which only the state, through taxing authority, can provide. While companies and their money flee our communities – or threaten to unless given sweet-heart tax deals and low-labour costs – right-wing think tanks and corporate elites have mounted fairly successful attacks on important elements of the welfare state; like progressive taxation and the provision of public health, education and social services. The effects have been terrible. In Japan for example, community practitioners point to the increasing pressure on individuals to perform economically. Such pressure is resulting in serious problems in community and family life. Omatsu (1993) talking about the U.S.A. puts it this way:

> *The corporate offensive... brutally destroyed grassroots groups in the African American community. This war against the poor ripped apart the social fabric of neighbourhoods across America leaving*

them vulnerable to drugs and gang violence. The inner cities be-
came the home of the 'underclass,' and a new politics of inner-di-
rected violence and despair.

This author was perhaps unconsciously noting the same effect as that of the Industrial Revolution, as outlined by Karl Polanyi (2001: 173): "Only an overworked and downtrodden laborer would forgo to associate with his like in order to escape from that state of personal servitude under which he could be made to do whatever his master required of him." A more recent judgment has been delivered by Jim Laxer. He is quoted in an article by a business writer as saying that strategies like bankruptcy are part of a war on workers and a "gun to reverse the wages and benefits and working conditions painstakingly gained over decades by the Canadian Auto Workers" (Reynolds, 2009: B2). In essence he is saying that there is a struggle to turn back the gains made by the organizations of workers since the end of WWII. This is sobering. But if one thinks carefully about it, this is an accurate way in which to understand the current relationship of working people and elites. Organizing for power is thus even more necessary but we need to be ready for fierce resistance from existing elites and power holders.

A third part of the assault has been an increasing appeal to devolve "responsibility" to the community. A nostalgic notion has been sold that communities used to completely care for their members without the intervention of the state (McKnight, 1995). The fact of course is that while there is some truth here (there has been a decrease in families caring for elderly parents, for example) such a notion ignores the fact that historically the bulk of the caring was left to women, and that communities (particularly poor ones) experienced extreme variations in the levels and quality of services. It also ignores the increasing involvement of women in the paid workforce. As we have said, the communities we deal with today are not the homogeneous, place-based groups of the 1920s or 1950s. They have different strengths, different stressors, and presently are under attack from the very governments and right-wing interests that so hypocritically extol their merits. It is part of the community worker's assignment to be aware of this and to assist community members in reflection so that realistic objectives can be identified, and people can recognize the importance of joining with other communities to work for appropriate community supports.

4. The Myth of Inevitability

One of the most insidious parts of the assault strategy has been selling the notion that the trend of global markets (the domination of technological innovations and downloading of services) is somehow part of history's forces – a kind of social evolutionary process. Indeed as Polanyi (2001) has pointed out, this strategy has been utilized by free-market apologists since before the Industrial Revolution. We would think that this idea would have been discredited by the world banking meltdown (Chossudovsky, 2008) discussed earlier but we need to keep in mind that this is an ideological notion – what Polanyi (2001: 144) has called "the utopian springs of the dogma" and not one that is based in the way people really live. This is an ideology or dogma that obscures the fact that all these decisions are being made by human beings with particular interests in advancing these trends (Polonyi, 2001; Saul, 1995). We are urged to believe that the invisible hand of the "market" dictates that corporations move to areas where wages are low, and worker protections and civil rights are poor or nonexistent. This story obscures the fact that markets are human inventions (Polanyi, 2001) and liberates the corporate high roller from accountability. We are discouraged from thinking that any of us can, or should, do anything (Polanyi, 2001; McQuaig, 1998). An article in *Commonwealth* puts it nicely: "When laissez-faire economists believe in God, they are usually certain that he is one of them. The invisible hand of the market is, they think, also the hand of Divine providence, which anoints and protects those who manage to provide for themselves" (Sibley, 1908: 18). The idea that we are agents (citizens) who can act on issues is crucial to the health of a community. Remember Langer (1983: 207): "When people feel a chronic loss of control they don't take risks; and they retreat into an all too familiar world." If the idea that we can act is successfully undercut, much of the energy for progressive social change will disappear. As community workers, we must assist people in resisting the idea that they cannot act, and to search for the power to assert influence in their lives.

5. Attack on Public Space

A healthy society requires that the citizens have an opportunity to put forward ideas and concerns, and to discuss issues of interest to the public good. There has been a mounting erosion of public space so that citizen engagement becomes increasingly circumscribed. For example, "Police crackdowns on graffiti, postering, panhandling, sidewalk art, squeegee kids, community gardening and food vendors are rapidly criminalizing everything that is truly street-level in the life of a city" (Brenner and Theodore, 2002: 239.) Added to this is an increasingly hostile attitude from government and corporate elites on the right of people to occupy public space in order to protest conditions various constituencies see as injurious to their interests, or to the public good. As this point is being written, the Canadian government has just spent over 1.2 billion dollars on security for the G-8 and G-20 meetings in the Ontario town of Huntsville and the city of Toronto. At every protest during the period leading up to and including the meetings, there was an overwhelming police presence and a powerful media blitz suggesting that citizens who protested would be abetting "radical elements." Over 900 people were arrested for occupying city streets; the overwhelming majority released without charge. This one example of many suggests that those in power fear and wish to limit the use of public space where alternative voices seek to be heard.[11]

The Importance of Healthy Communities

Unless communities are viable and strong, the members that make them up (individuals and families) will face difficulty in their daily lives. Community depends on and reinforces supportive, complex and engaged human relationships. In a world of increasingly bureaucratized/managerially structured relationships, human beings are forced to follow imperatives of efficiency – the biggest material bang for the least use of resources – over effectiveness, the quality and process. New managerial strategies include a strong focus on the market, coupled with efficiency rather than effectiveness, as the main criterion of success. Within this managerial discourse, money and contracts rather than care and concern function as the foundation of relationships (Harris, 2003). This is both alienating

---

[11] It must be noted that while the power of the state was indeed arrayed in frightening power a huge number of citizens groups mobilized and refused to be scared away from their right to occupy public space and employ the democratic right to organize.

to individuals and families and to the quality of our general human relationships. It robs us of spontaneity and creativity. Authentic community life on the other hand is messy, spontaneous and creative. Healthy community life can nourish the individual and family. Healthy engagement in community life forces us to confront issues of what we value, what brings us together, how we share, how we deal with differences, how we deal with conflict, and how we understand relationships with other communities. Further, it has the potential to unleash creative energy for work that will humanize our lives in the economic and political spheres.

Implications for Community Practice

When considering the nature of community development, then the following things seem to be important to think about:

- Disadvantaged and marginalized people will have to organize – to develop, advocate and rescue themselves – because it is unlikely that they are going to be rescued en masse by those with the resources (Carniol 2005, Freire, 2000; Piven and Cloward, 1977). Relevant energy for change is only going to come from within disadvantaged communities as they use the awareness of themselves and their situation (Adamson et al. 1987; Bishop 1994; Freire, 1970); and the power of their belief; and their numbers in collective action (Bloomberger 1969; Antone et al. 1986). Numbers and conviction are often the only initial power resource the disadvantaged have but, as stated earlier, numbers are only potent if they are organized and cohesive (Alinsky, 1971). As Booth (1974) points out, numbers of organized people are the foundation and means of deliberate social change. Theorists may argue about why and how people act together (to alter the relationships of power in their society) as do Piven and Cloward (1977), but all would agree that large numbers of people are essential for a change process.

- Another apparent aspect of community organization is its healing or "therapeutic" quality. People who are organized and who organize and act to make their environment relatively more malleable (more just) are more likely to perceive themselves differently, as subjects not objects (Breton, 1995); as people who develop a vision of a bet-

ter world (a more long-range purposeful act) and who can act coherently to achieve it. Breton (1995: 6) asserts that "the process of
addressing individual and personal change or healing can be fulfilled
in the process of addressing environmental and societal change or
healing, and vice versa." The organizing endeavour can be seen as
the process of bringing people together to share their experiences,
create a vision, and develop means to act and to attain that vision.

- Community practice then must be prepared to take on a very complex mission: combating a widespread weakening of social·ties, and
  the shoring up of attitudes and skills that allow us to live a satisfy-
  ing community life. As well, community practice must see its roles
  not only dealing with issues of local importance (though that will be
  the arena of most of the action for community practitioners) but of
  examining them in terms of broad-based, social justice concerns.
  That is, the Right's attack is economic, national, and international in nature while we feel effects on the local scene. We must be
  prepared to seek out other communities and groups (social movements) who are acting on the larger stages and forge relationships
  of solidarity, so as to be part of strategies and solutions that get at
  root problems.

Example: Members of the Chetwynd Project in Toronto beautifully
articulated the healing potential of community development. They
suggested that understanding and sharing their experiences as single
parents, immigrants, or visible minorities had reduced their sense of
isolation. Becoming involved in action to improve their situation reduced their sense of isolation, and counteracted their seeing themselves as victims. They started to see their abilities and how they might
use them in other areas of their lives.

Power

*It is not power that corrupts but fear. Fear of losing power corrupts
those who wield it and fear of the scourge of power corrupts those
who are subject to it.*
- Aung San Suu Kyi (Freedom from Fear)

Power is a theme that is integral to community practice (Moffatt et al, 2010) and runs throughout every aspect of this book. As community development writers Hustedde & Ganowicz (2002: 6) note: "Power is about who controls or has access to resources ... If community development is about building capacity, then concerns about power are pivotal." In social work and allied social interventions, power often tends to be downplayed or if dealt with to be seen in a negative light. Power is defined here as the degree to which we are able to act to influence our environment – to get things done, or make things happen; or to keep things from getting done or from happening. Power is essential in bringing about positive change. A good way to understand its importance is to note what one-time New York State Governor Eliot Spitzer said. "[It is important to understand] that the exercise of power can be shocking and at times corrupting." But also, "power is absolutely necessary to fight the battles that must be fought. The trick is to fight these battles with humility and constant introspection, knowing that there is no monopoly on virtue" (quoted in Paumgraten: 84, 2007).

There are six elements of power: money, information, numbers, status, belief, conviction or hope, and legislation/regulation.

1. Money

When wealth and the wealthy are valued in the city, virtue and
     good are less valued.
What is valued is practiced, what is not valued is not practiced.

                                                  - Plato

Money is an obvious one. We see it clearly in the ability of rich multinational corporations to influence or control their environment. Some time ago, Speeter (1978: 52) made the point that "corporations can afford to lobby, influence the public through the media, and buy their way out of certain predicaments. The larger the corporation and its resources, the more resistant it is to attacks or reform." For example, the late Canadian columnist Dalton Camp (1998: F3) pointed to how powerful tobacco companies subverted the attempts of U.S. legislators determined to "address the problems of kids getting hooked on tobacco" by using the power of their political campaign contributions to dictate the way the elected representatives vote.

The American tobacco companies have once again cashed promissory notes and resumed their dominance of the Republican Party and its representatives in the United States Senate. The bipartisan bill aimed at the problem of kids 'getting hooked' on tobacco...has been sand-bagged by the ... usual coalition of tobacco pushers and free marketers. ... Pray observe this salutary illustration of Big Tobacco vs. the little man. ... The tobacco interests have spent 40 to 50 million (someone said 100 million) on television, trying to provide cover for the Republican effort to stop the bill's passage.

This power is in contrast with the ability of the poor to affect their environment. Bregha (1971:76) states that the inability of the lower middle-class "to secure proper housing, higher education, and better paying jobs is forcing it out of the so-called mainstream of Canadian life." As well, the poor have had little impact on our political system; they tend to vote in smaller numbers than do middle-class and rich people (Sigelman, Roeder, Jewell, & Baer, 1985) and Piven and Cloward (1977) have pointed out, they rarely complain en masse. Finally, if we think about the issue of diversity we must wonder why it is that so few "visible minorities" are seen in legislative bodies. Some argue that political science lectures on "the theory of representative democracy" (the familiar tale about how we elect the people who govern us) sorely needs updating. There is the question of who funds the parties, and what effect it has on the policies they pursue. Burris (2001: 361) speaking of the U.S.A. notes: "Through political contributions, members of this capitalist class are able to "exercise disproportionate influence over politics in the United States." Clearly things are not different in Canada (Dobbin, 2003).

2. Information

Information comes in many forms: technical, academic, "privileged" (from within an expert/elite system), and is a clear source of power in our "information-based society." Information issues occupy a central place in the public's attention, and are high on the agenda of business and government. There is an increased awareness that the role of information in the democratic process is being diminished. Paton (1994: 20) states, that "inclusion, participation, and open government are empty concepts." At the level of public policy, government has access to tremendous amounts of data that its departments develop. It is generally unavailable to ordinary citizens and, according to a series in the *Toronto Star*, (Champion-Smith, 2009: A10) is becoming even more difficult to access by investigative reporters let alone citizen groups and individuals. This is a situation that appears to have worsened with the passing of time in Canada. "Critics are alarmed at the growing trend to deny basic information that Canadians are entitled to, especially in the two years since the Conservative government came to power with a promise to be open and accountable" (Brenan, 2008). Citizens, particularly as individuals tend to be in a reactive position and, in effect, have difficulty challenging that which is inaccessible to public scrutiny.[12]

The relationship is one of power, and the power is potent when wielded by government and its bureaucracy. There is no room in this collectivity for the disadvantaged, the service receivers, or even the public. Most individual citizens have neither the information, nor the technical ability to digest the information that they may find. The implications are serious for all citizens, but as a Canadian social critic points out, they have particular relevance for the poor. Back in 1970, Ian Adams stated: "Ultimately, the confused multiplicity of bureaucratic systems keeps the poor on a treadmill of marginal living while simultaneously robbing them of pride and the ability to get back into society" (Adams, 1970: 67). As we have noted earlier, things have not changed in the more than three decades since he made this observation.

As we have seen, information is particularly crucial in the private sector. Large corporations possess massive concentrations of wealth, and are able to develop and exchange great amounts of data of which they become the sole proprietors. Recently, in the face of calls for responsible approaches to energy production, the oil industry in Canada and their government partners like the Province of Alberta, have been floating the notion of something called, "en-

---

[12]   Since implementation of the "Freedom of Information Act" requests for information are often met with delays; and when documents are released they are often incomplete and censored. Government departments can ignore deadlines. Practically speaking, a successful complaint to the Information Commissioner often results in only sympathy and an acknowledgment that the department in question is in the wrong (Webster, 1997).

ergy intensity," the amount of greenhouse gas produced per unit of energy (like a barrel of oil). And Suncor, Canada's largest tar sands exploiter for example, has trumpeted that the intensity of its operations was reduced by 51 per cent between 1990 and 2006. This sounds good to the average person. Difficulty arises however when we find that during the same period the company vastly increased production to such a level that its overall greenhouse gas pollution has increased by 131 per cent (The Ecologist in the Canadian Centre for Policy Alternatives of April 2008: 36). These are not isolated cases. The subprime scandal of 2007-08 in the U.S. showed how information was kept from the public until the money had been totally misspent and a bailout (costing the public purse billions) had to be developed. As well, many people were sucked into hopeless situations and lost their homes.

3. Numbers

We equate large numbers of people with power, most often as it is exercised through the vote. While this is an important and much-praised foundation of democratic society, it is only a token source of power that is used intermittently[13] (every four years in the U.S. presidential elections, every four or five years in parliamentary systems, and every two or four years for municipal councils). Macpherson (1977: 77) argues that our present system of democracy can best be termed a "pluralist elitist model." Our system is deficient in producing democratic processes, at least in Canada, in that there is a serious gap between how institutions operate and how well they are understood[14] (Campion-Smith, 2009).

---

[13] The British parliamentary system that allows a government to call an election at the most advantageous period for its re-election provides a ruling party a power which further undercuts accountability to citizens. Wide use of polls and the ability to distribute government largesse provides more tools to increase its advantage. A good example is the election called in 2008 by the Conservative government in Canada. Despite having passed a fixed election date law in the previous year, the Harper (Prime Minister) government called an election because it feared a coming economic downturn and believed that the electorate was divided on whom they should vote for: the New Democratic Party, the Green Party or the Liberals. The "Harperites" almost got it right and, though garnering less than 40% of the votes, managed a somewhat strengthened minority.

[14] This became glaringly obvious in 2009 when the Conservative federal minority government was allowed to get away with getting the Governor General to suspend

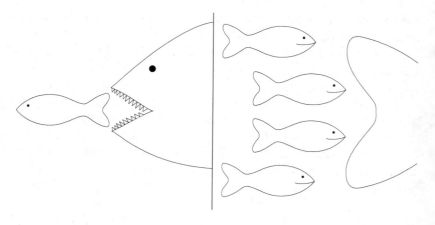

This is not to suggest that democratic institutions are without any use as expressions of their citizens' will. Clearly they are superior to dictatorships, but the vote does not and cannot represent a de facto reasonable exercise of power for the citizen (Fromm, 1955). It is important for citizens to organize to demand access to institutions which will reflect their genuine needs and perspectives – independent of powerful political parties (and their imperatives) – and of civil service bureaucracies (and theirs) (Adamson et al., 1988). Issue groups (for peace and life, women's rights, Indigenous Peoples' rights); service groups (women's shelters, housing or work co-operatives, daycare centres or senior citizen drop-ins); or even short-term lobby or pressure organizations (a group resisting an expressway or a specific piece of harmful legislation) are the life blood of a genuine living democracy. This type of political involvement potentially allows for people's power to result in empowerment and social justice.

4. Status

The power of status comes from a person's (or group's) formal or informal right to act in particular areas or on particular issues. Elected

---

parliament when threatened with being replaced by a coalition of more centrist parties. Not only Canadian citizens but the press appeared to believe that the idea of a coalition assuming the responsibility of government was somehow undemocratic rather than what it was, the working of the system the way it was designed. Actually it was the conservative government's actions that were undemocratic in that the parties that had achieved the majority of votes and seats were denied the right to attempt to govern (Campion-Smith, 2009).

officials are the most obvious examples, though they have another aspect of power, legislation and regulation (see below). We also have appointed officials who derive power from being placed in authority by elected officials. People can also gain power by acquiring some socially recognized credentials; doctors, lawyers and university professors obtain a certain power in their particular, narrow fields. We grant tremendous authority to these people. Often this kind of power can be used against ordinary citizens. While those in authority often deserve respect, authority must ultimately be granted by the people in a way that is not self-perpetuating and oppressing.

5. Belief, Conviction or Hope[15]

The most powerful social movements have always had a strong spiritual dimension.

- Jim Wallace

History says, don't hope
On this side of the grave.
But then, once in a lifetime
The longed for tidal wave
Of justice can rise up,
And hope and history rhyme.

- Seamus Heaney from "The Cure at Troy"

Deeply held beliefs (in a way of life, a transcendent spiritual reality, a just cause, or often a combination) have been a strong element of power for many community-based campaigns. Fromm (1961) refers to this as a spiritual aspect of life – a sense of purpose higher than simply accepting the circumstances of our lives. Another way of saying this is the notion of hope, the sense that our struggle for a better life has meaning beyond our immediate situation. Hope is often a major part of a strong belief system. Hope and belief can bring people together and provide us with courage to persevere in a difficult struggle. Indeed Freire (1994) argues that without hope we can achieve nothing. An Australian Aboriginal proverb says it nicely: "Those who lose dreaming are lost." But with hope we can generate the energy to overcome great

---

[15] The inclusion of belief as an element of power came out of conversations with community work activist and teacher, Gurpreet Malhotra. My thanks to him.

obstacles. Activist/writer/teacher bell hooks says, "My hope emerges from those places of struggle where I witness individuals positively transforming their lives and the world around them" (hooks, 2003: xiv). The majority of the organizers described in the first chapter, and the people with whom they worked, were motivated by the sense of purpose that transcended the rejections and disappointments that they encountered. In an ironic way, the importance of belief in community work is underlined by the way contemporary political and economic elites have tried to suggest that human beings are simply economic animals; and that the market, plus impersonal historical forces, are the last and best arbiters of our lives.

Belief in non-material values – spirituality, human brother/sisterhood, for example – is deeply threatening to a capitalist-materialistic position.

Clearly the power of belief can be misused. Fundamentalist movements like fascism (Kershaw, 2000, 1999) and some religious groups (Hedges, 2007) have manipulated and oppressed people, and have caused great harm. Thus we must make a point of reflecting seriously on what, and how, beliefs are being used in the communities.

Hope, or the call to be hopeful, can also be misused when it is confused with the notion of optimism. Freire (1994) suggests that optimism is a kind of passive assumption that "things will improve or somehow turn out alright." Aung San Suu Kyi, the committed and brave leader of the pro-democracy struggle in Burma, has stated she is concerned about the use of hope.

> I think by now I have made it fairly clear that I am not very happy with the word 'hope.' I don't believe in people just hoping. We want to work for what we want. I always say that one has no right to hope without endeavour, so we work to try and bring about the situation that is necessary for the country, and we are confident that we will get to the negotiation table at one time or another. This is the way all such situations pan out – even with the most truculent dictator

It may seem presumptuous of me to take issue with such an important worker of rights and freedoms for oppressed people, but it seems she has, in this quote at least, confused the notion of hope with that of optimism. In effect, if we look at her words carefully, she reflects a very practical understanding that people need to have a sense they can/will prevail <u>while</u> they seriously engage in the struggle for their own freedom. Whether we call it confidence as she does, or hope as do bell hooks and Paulo Freire, is perhaps not important. What is important is her admonition that work is important to actualize our hope, and that hope is important to underpin and inspire that work.

6. *Legislation/Regulation*

We typically speak of the power of government and sometimes of the government regulators. As Polanyi (2001) has noted, right-wing critics have for generations been heard decrying this power as it gets in the way of the so-called "free market." The power of government and regulators comes through the ability to enact and enforce laws. While we, as citizens, vote intermittently and in democratic societies, we speak of the "sovereignty" of the people, the fact is clear that this sovereignty is only wielded through the power of governments to legislate and regulate.

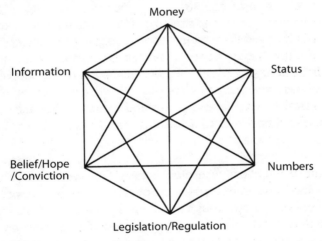

Figure: 4-6: Interrelationships among Elements of Power

Power is a complex phenomenon. It is not simply a matter of having it or not, but of what kind of power exists, in what quantities, and in what situations. Various elements of power can support or confront other forms (see Figure 4-6, above). If a group is able to raise sufficient funds they can enable themselves to cover the costs of research that is important to their issue and thus increase their information power. With this they can confront the power of legislation and regulation, though the power of organized numbers is also crucial in dealing with government. The ability to project a strong belief and hope in the efficacy of group action can bring more people into the cause and thus increase the power of numbers. Indeed, a strong shared spiritual belief can underpin group cohesion and thus add to the strength of their numbers. This is a dynamic that is particularly evident in the Aboriginal struggle where the reclaiming of traditional spiritual beliefs and practices has become an important aspect of both the healing journey and the practices of resistance and struggle. Power dynamics are not static but fluid.

Power vs. Privilege

Also, power can be compared to, and contrasted with, privilege. Power is active, the ability to make something occur or not occur. Privilege is, on the other hand, essentially passive. The categories of class, race, sexual orientation, gender, level of ability, etc., provide various levels of advantage or entitlement for some at the expense of others. The opportunities accrue to people who occupy certain parts of these categories not because of action but because of their status. For example the privilege inherent in whiteness is maintained because many white people enjoy privilege without personally being racists. The white, ruling class exploits both white workers and those of colour, and uses the divide and conquer strategy of racial privileges to sustain its rule. White workers benefit in comparison to workers of colour, while at the same time being exploited for their labour power. Clearly this maintains the social hierarchy, and points to the fact that ending exploitation, and the system of racial privilege that supports it, is in the interests of white working-class people as well as people of colour. Thus privilege is something that we can act against. But it is not a simple matter of those with privilege giving up their privilege. People will first have to recognize that class power and white privilege exist, and then we need to organize, educate ourselves, and gain some power to take action against it.

Organization Structure

Organization-building is an important aspect of furthering the cause of empowerment and social justice (Gecan, 2002; Kahn, 1982; Biklen, 1983; Roberts, 1979; Alinsky, 1971; Booth, 1974). Building a community organization that is consistent with the values of participation and democracy is important and difficult. The fall of the Berlin Wall, and the toppling of the dictatorship in Russia have shown that good intentions, or simply changing the people at the top, are not enough to bring about social changes that will guarantee genuine equality and liberation from oppression. Piven and Cloward (1977) argue that the act of organization-building may in fact retard and frustrate real change. It is hard, however, to imagine an increase in the rights of women, or of Indigenous people (for example), without strong organizations. Even Piven and Cloward agree that positive social change will not come about without some structure building (1977). They argue, however, that the vision and energy necessary to accomplish real social change can get drained off in the minutiae of system maintenance. Still, for most of human history it is difficult to find the achievement of real social change without organizations.

Models of organization that we have tend to come from the corporate sector (see Figure 4-7: Bureaucratic organization model). The image of the "lean and mean" capitalist bureaucratic pyramid is pervasive. People naturally tend to choose what they know, and what has been held up as successful. Important institutions, like the media, maintain this business hegemony, generally portraying capitalist business structures as efficient and effective. Institutions, such as the education system, structure relationships among people that mirror those in capitalist industry (Bowles and Gintis, 1976). The traditional organizational model has a powerful grip in North America.

It is not surprising that we tend to use the bureaucratic model despite the fact that it is both undemocratic and sometimes downright oppressive. Peoples' organizations desiring to "change the system" often develop bureaucratic structures and end up reproducing the traits of business and government structures; the exact traits which the people complained have been messing up their lives for years: rigidity, unresponsiveness and nepotism (Speeter, 1978). It is important to note that progressive groups – Aboriginal people and women, for example (Weeks, 1994; Gilroy, 1990) and people involved in worker co-operatives – are trying for alternative, non-hierarchic structuring of their organizations (Lakey et al., 1995).

Funding agencies, government or private, tend to demand the creation of familiar corporate structures before funding is granted. To access funding, the community conforms in order to satisfy the "ac-

PEOPLE AT THE TOP
make the decisions and
reap the benefits

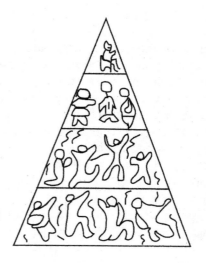

PEOPLE IN THE MIDDLE
see that the people at the
bottom do what the people
at the top want done

PEOPLE AT THE BOTTOM
implement the decisions and
reap the consequences

Figure 4-7: Bureaucratic Organization Model

countability" requirements of the funder. While the requirement for fiscal accountability is understandable from the perspective of funders, it works against the principle of democratic accountability to the people who are the foundation of any organization.

Power is a seductive commodity. As Lord Acton said, "Power tends to corrupt"[16]. As we gain power, there is a temptation to exercise it immediately rather than share it because that is the model of action that we have been taught. It is difficult to take "the long view;" that the organization is the message as well as the instrument of institutional change (Speeter, 1978). Freire (1970) points out how difficult it is for deprived people not to mirror their oppressors. There is a tendency to build organizations that are oriented more to controlling member behaviour than liberating the human spirit.

---

[16]   As Alinsky has stressed, Lord Acton did not say that power corrupts, but that it tends to corrupt. We cannot ignore power, or wish it away. As Joreen (1973) notes, power is always part of the equation. To try to deny it, and develop a "structureless" organization, will only mean that we have to deal with power in an unclear and disabling manner. The point is, then, not to avoid power, but rather to have its exercise transparent and appropriately dispersed, so that all people are able to act upon their environments.

Internet and Culture Transformation

There is a belief that internet technologies provide a forum for organizing, and new tools which can be used for organizing; internet culture can also create spaces for new forms of community organizing to emerge and, possibly, transform larger society (Martinez, 2001).

Three characteristics of internet culture – participation, permeability and transparency – are key, transforming organizing and larger society because they differ from and challenge prevailing ways of people working together (Kahn & Kellner, 2004; Martinez, 2001).

Participation is integral to internet culture. Participation can help people become connected beyond geographic boundaries, and network to share information, ideas and skills. The internet has created opportunities to involve and integrate organizations that couldn't easily participate in causes or collaborate with other groups. Online tools such as e-mail lists, e-newsletters (electronic newsletters), and blogs (web logs or online dialogues), provide various methods to take action (Surman & Reilly, 2003). Actions are 'user generated' and more organic and self-initiated; people can mobilize around an issue in which they are interested and decide on ways to respond to the issue.

The internet also provides a permeable space; whereby, people can choose when to participate and when to leave when they are no longer interested or able to be involved. Individuals can be involved for a short or long period depending on the skills they have to contribute and the time they have available. Participants at different levels, from the grassroots to leadership, can take action and control and voice their concerns on issues. Participation is flexible and open to anyone.[17] When information is shared in an online community, all members are able to see what decision was made, who was involved in decision-making, and what information was considered. Critical information and decision-making processes are not restricted to people who are executives, rather access to documents and information are made public.

The organizational culture of online communities is distinct from mainstream forms of organizations. Traditional organizations rely on hierarchy among staff, board-directed or senior management deter-

---

[17] Mark Surman of The Commons Group in an interview in Toronto on June 24, 2008.

mined activity, and careful controls on how information is disseminated and developed. Consider a community organization that is directed by a Board, has an executive director and senior management team who makes decisions on behalf of the staff team, decides what information is shared with the staff and what input from the staff and community they will consider when making decisions. In contrast, online communities do not typically have a Board of Directors, action is more self-initiated or grassroots, horizontal not hierarchical organization is the norm, and collaboration and exchange of information among all members of a community are essential for success. The internet also increases transparency. Transparency involves the openness in what information is available and how decisions are made, and the relative ease in monitoring.

Approaches to Community Organizing Practice

Traditionally there have been three ways of conceptualizing the manner in which community organization sets about its tasks. This three-way view is articulated in the classic article by Rothman and Tropman (1987) under the headings *Locality Development*, *Social Action* and *Social Planning*. While they make the point that these are abstract models and that in "real life" they often overlap, they suggest that community organization is essentially practiced within one of these frameworks (Rothman and Tropman, 1987).

Locality Development emphasizes broadly based participation, cooperation, voluntarism, education and community initiative to achieve community determined goals. The *Social Planning* approach focuses on professional expertise and technical know-how that operate out of a centralized planning context, to overcome designated social problems and "guide complex change processes." A *Social Action* approach aims to organize disadvantaged populations to make demands for "increased resources or, treatment more in accordance with social justice."

The focus of this book is on strategies that incorporate elements primarily of the locality development and social action models. The reasons for this will become apparent in the following sections. The approach suggested here will be referred to as a "pragmatic approach." (See Figure 4-8: Conceptualizing the Pragmatic Approach.)

MODEL	SOCIAL PLANNING	LOCALITY DEVELOPMENT	SOCIAL ACTION	PRAGMATIC
DESCRIPTION	experts using technical expertise identify & plan how to address designated social problems	community initiative to identify & achieve community goals	organization of disadvantaged to make demands for social justice	addresses complex organizational & developmental community needs & social/political constraints
RELATIONSHIP OF WORKER & COMMUNITY	people are objects of intervention	people are subjects & co-workers on problems	people are subjects & co-workers on problems	people are subjects & co-workers on problems
PRIMARY WORKER ROLE	expert planner	catalyst/facilitator	catalyst/agitator	facilitator/agitator & strategist
PRIMARY MEANS	statistics & reports	consensus	conflict, confrontation & negotiation	conflict, confrontation & consensus
ENDS	improved services	suitable sharing of community resources among members	readjustment of power between community & institutions	empowerment & social justice

Figure 4-8: Conceptualizing the Pragmatic Approach

A Pragmatic Approach

The three models, described above, have some important commonalities. They also have some key differences. See Figure 4-8: Conceptualizing the Pragmatic Approach. Social planning, in particular, we can see as "more different" than the other two. With its emphasis on central planning and professional expertise, it defines its relationship with its target population very differently than do locality development and social action models. For the social planner, the people and/or services are the "objects" of intervention. For the community worker, the people are "subjects" and co-workers on the problems. Thus a person employed as a locality development worker, or one working as an action organizer, is working with and among the people. A social planner, on the other hand, generally works with other professionals on behalf of a group. This difference is crucial because the worker's reference group will be quite different. Working day-by-day with a group of professionals who use statistics and reports gives one a different perspective on one's clientele than if the organizer is actually among them every day. Because of this, the social planner is more likely to see things from a so-called "objective" point of view, but also from the point of view of her professional colleagues. A locality development or social action worker on the other hand is more likely to have her professional view influenced by those of her clientele. It should be noted that there are risks and advantages to these situations of relative intimacy.

1. Risks of working in "relative intimacy"

There is a danger of losing perspective, of seeing things in a uni-social directional manner and missing an important part of the picture. This can lead to a loss of creativity, an inability to see various options. After all, if intimate experience with the problem were all that was required, disadvantaged folks would have solved their own problems long ago.

Intimacy can also lead to complacency (Lee, 2008), "if I'm with the people I automatically understand them, and what they need and want." Being with people does not guarantee that we will listen to them, or understand them or their problems (Narayan, 1994).

2. Advantages of working in "relative intimacy"

Paulo Freire (2000) has probably written the most forcefully on the importance of "relationships" with the people with whom the organizer is working. There are two essential points that he makes:

- Disadvantaged people have a particular view of their reality which must be used as a starting point for action. The organizer must be led by the people, and can only be led by them if she is with them in a very concrete way. The emphasis is placed, not on a doubtful objectivity, but on gaining an understanding of the client's perspective. A community organizer with a locality development focus, who was employed by a child welfare organization, stated:

  > The people who I took my cues from changed a lot once I came out to the community every day. After I was there a couple of months, I started to realize that I was defining problems differently than when I was working in a more traditional role out of the central office. Some of my social work colleagues charged that I was losing my objectivity. I saw it differently – that I'd exchanged the point of reference that informed my objectivity.

- Another notion crucial to understanding transformational social change is the idea that as organizers we are not "giving" people a "better life," but are assisting them to struggle and build it themselves. This notion of participation, of "building with" not "designing for," describes a profoundly different relationship with disadvantaged people than that which educators, social workers or politicians have traditionally attempted.

A close relationship with the people with whom we work allows us to be seen as human beings, and our techniques to be seen as human and fallible – not as some mystifying magic, but as a set of behaviours and instruments that people can themselves test. A crucial difference between the social planning model on the one hand and a pragmatic locality development/social action model on the other is the "immediacy" of the relationship. This immediacy might be termed solidarity:

the intimate identification of one's goals and actions with those of the members of the community.

Citizens and Victims

Although the pragmatic approach represents an attempt to integrate key aspects of locality development and social action, it does not use every aspect of each model. Rather, it creates the base of a model which will be useful with a wide variety of community groups, issues and situations. When a worker is acting in the community, however, she is not practicing a particular model, but attempting to deal with real people who are trying to get themselves together to influence some aspect of their environment. This requires the development of skills and strategies that can be general in their application.

The differences between locality development and social action appear initially to be difficult to reconcile, for they involve, in at least a general way, separate ends and separate means. The end for social action is the readjustment of power within society, such that the community is on a significantly more equal footing with major institutions of power. In contrast, the goal of locality development is the equitable sharing of community resources among its own membership. In the former, the community member is perceived as the victim of an invidious power structure, while in the latter he is seen as a citizen and member of a collective.

Out of these differing conceptions of membership and ends emerges a differing orientation to means. Social action stresses the need to engage in conflict with the oppressor, while locality development suggests that citizens use co-operative or consensus techniques among themselves in order to reach mutually advantageous decisions.

These differences, on the surface, are significant. However, if we attend carefully to Rothman's statement – that in practice there is much overlap – we can examine the "reality" with which the models deal and develop a pragmatic approach that has important implications for practice.

A community is not static. It has a history. People leave or join it. It can experience periods of internal conflict, as well as a degree of unity and tranquility. It can experience wins and losses. It has connections to its environment (Roberts, 1979). Thus, to view a community as only a group of citizens, or only as victims, is unrealistic. With groups of disadvantaged people, in particular, the structure of their lives demands that they be seen as both citizens and victims. People often have to deal with both the pressures of external oppression – unfair labour practices, racism, environmental pollution or sexism – and serious intra-group misunderstanding and conflict. It is not uncommon for a disadvantaged community to experience divisions of class or to have sexism or racism in its midst, as well as more personal problems of communication or personality conflicts. The interplay between historical development and contemporary interaction produces a complex set of dynamics that is not amenable to intervention based on one-dimensional thinking.

Example: A service provider, who became involved in the Chetwynd Project in one community, stated that working with some of the women had changed her view of them as being simply victims. "I know they still had difficulties with their kids, and many didn't have job skills; but they had ideas and they could get them across. Some could really organize an event. I can't look at poor people the same way anymore."

The pragmatic approach attempts to deal with the complex organizational and developmental needs of the community. It incorporates aspects from both of Rothman and Tropman's formulations: that change must be community-directed, and that the process of community-building is of central importance. However, the model presented here will approach the problem in a way that addresses an important dichotomy in community development: conflict versus consensus. This is rooted in a realization, addressed below, that disadvantaged or marginalized communities are dealing internally with a complex interplay of forces caused by the fact that they have two tasks before them: struggle and healing.

Struggle and Healing

Following on the notion of understanding community organizing as having to see a disadvantaged community as both a victim of oppression and a group of citizens, it is important to understand that this means the practice will have to take into consideration that a community is both struggling to overcome oppression while it deals with the injuries of oppression. Community life (See Figure 4-9 below) thus reflects and is partly shaped by the energy expended from dealing with the trauma that it has experienced. The effects of trauma can therefore be seen to affect aspects of community life (the dotted circle in the figure below). In our research my colleagues and I have looked at the notion of "collective" or community trauma (Lee, Moffatt, McGrath & George, 2007) and its effects on organizing. We believe that the same dynamics that affect community life in general and community organization are impacted by the twin issues of community healing and community struggle.

Many communities in Canada have histories that are affected by the experience of serious injurious actions, such as Aboriginal people, those in poverty, queer people, etc. That is, crucial aspects of community members' lives and identities have been shaped by injury. The injury can be physical, psychic, spiritual or all three. "What some call collective trauma impacts on the group's consciousness, and enters into the core of the collectivity's sense of identity" (Alexander, 2004:10). That is, injurious events or actions can leave scars that take energy to heal. Collective trauma can, therefore, be seen to damage the core life of the community.

A shared experience of discrimination and/or physical violence can be seen as a common, though painful, bond. As well, this pain may represent a key element in how community members understand their identity and their place in the global context. There is a clear trend for these communities to assume, and to be asked to assume, responsibility for providing supportive services to their membership. The community members collectively have a unique understanding of their history and day to day lives. In effect they are attempting to provide services that focus on healing but at the same time often are in positions where they must advocate for members. Thus, they must engage in two processes that are not necessarily seen as complimentary. They must involve themselves in processes of healing and resistance at the same time. For example, Aboriginal people in Canada have been developing their own community health centres—places where they can find the unique understandings and practices that will assist them in healing from the ravages of the colonial experience (residential schools, loss of land, attacks on their culture, etc.). At the same time they must fight for their rights for redress (getting long-ignored treaty rights recognized and the day-to-day racism that is part of their lives).

What is exceedingly important for us to understand is the two tasks, healing and struggle, are part of the same group of tasks. Struggle, resilience and healing are simultaneous processes. That is, organizing is undertaken by and with those who are living with the effects of the trauma, the effects of which they are attempting to overcome. These are not for the most part processes that are mutually reinforcing. If we are attempting to heal from any injury, it is difficult to find the energy to deal with ongoing or new attacks that have caused the injury in the first place. Yet, this is what disadvantaged or marginalized communities must do. This issue of healing/struggle will be referred to at various times in the rest of the book.

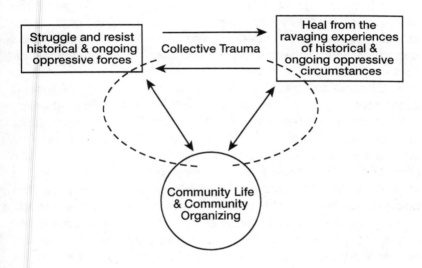

Figure 4-9: The Challenges Faced by Oppressed Communities

Example: A rather active member of a Central American refugee community related how she has noticed that at most large meetings many people will attempt to sit with their backs to the wall or a pillar or something. She's talked about her observation to other activists in the community and they have suggested that the years of being pursued or having to hide had made them suspicious of people they don't know.

So they are on guard until they feel they know the others. She said that "there are lots of trust issues for us because to survive we had to be very careful of others. It affects how fast we can get into an issue and come together."

Resilience

The picture painted so far is one that is accurate but limited. Communities that have been affected by serious injurious oppression do not simply give in. Sztompka (2004) argues that in the case of collective trauma, the experience is a shared one to which entire communities respond: they search for the means to mobilize, to resist, and recreate a sense of community (Sonn & Fisher, 1998). Indeed some research undertaken by my colleagues and I suggests that the desire to organize may come out of the experience of oppression, prejudice, and trauma (Moffatt, George, Lee & McGrath, 2005). Thus, responding to injustice may be at the heart of how communities organize themselves.

The importance of community as part of a healing process has been articulated in studies with Aboriginal communities (Abadian, 2000; Brave Heart, 1999), survivors of torture (Chambon et al., 2001), and the GLBTT communities (Lepishak, 2000; O'Brien, 1994). The concept of resilience is used to describe how people are able to live functional lives with a sense of well-being following prolonged or severe oppression (Hernandez, 2002; Weick & Saleebey, 1998). The notion of resilience is based on several theoretical approaches and practice models, including the strengths perspective and mutuality, and "self in relation" models (Weick & Saleebey, 1998). Community resilience is defined as the ability to "respond to crises in ways that strengthen communal bonds, resources, and the community's capacity to cope" (Chenoweth & Stehlik, 2001: 47). Thus, it is important to see that while the trauma of oppression runs through community life, so does the resilience of the community. The sources of resilience infuse community life with the energy to take on the tasks of struggle and healing that must go on in order to retain a high degree of community empowerment. Indeed resilience can probably be usefully thought of as being part of the energy that enables the tasks of healing and struggle.

Figure 4-10: Resilience in Oppressed Communities

Equity: Consensus and Conflict

Community problems are caused principally by the unequal distribution of power in society. Concern for a more equitable sharing of resources and power, both inside and outside the group, is essential. There is a tendency to think of co-operation and conflict as being two ends of some sort of ideological continuum. In the model offered here, they are seen in more pragmatic terms. We can expect to find situations, both internal and external, that require both consensus and conflict strategies.

A problem with some organizers is that they fail to take into account that they are building both communities and organizations. Without people organized and/or structured to work on their common interests, nothing can be accomplished. Organizers must be able to see members of the community as fellow human beings who can give more than merely political support on one or two issues. Like soldiers who may have joined the army out of economic necessity or because of their political ideals, they endure and persist because of the caring that they develop for each other. We cannot argue too strongly for the building of consensus, and for the fostering of networks of support within the community.

There are two reasons for stressing the notion of locality development within social action. The first is that in striving to overcome a "social wrong," or in building a "social right," a great deal of stress will be felt by the participants, as well as by the organizer. The establishment of positive human relationships (a major aspect of a sense of community) will alleviate the negative effects of stress (Speck & Attneave, 1973). The second reason for emphasizing locality development within social action is that there will be internal conflict as various individuals and interest groups – who hold divergent views – try to have their views prevail (see in Chapter 10: Dealing With Internal Opposition). Conflict cannot and should not be avoided. It can, and should, be managed. This is made possible by the development of an atmosphere of clear and direct communication and warm respectful relationships. This does not mean that community organization should become a series of therapeutic group encounters – only that organization development is not an end on its own. An organizer must attend to the personal, political, and organizational needs of her constituency or risk failure. If community work is transformational, it will change people as well as systems (Albert, 1993).

Example: Until it closed up shop in 2007, the Chetwynd Project assisted people to organize camp experiences for the communities with which it worked. One woman tells of meeting another at one of the camping sessions. She and this woman had had a serious conflict. "We had a chance to get to know each other and talk about [the incident]. At the end of the week we could trust each other. Now, back in [the project], we look out for each other. We can work together."

Intra-Group Considerations

With equity as a base principle, and the notion of democratic organization development as a major theme, locality development's emphasis on co-operation and consensus becomes central. Consensus has three values for the community. First, it can facilitate a non-bureaucratic approach to community interaction (i.e. decision-making) and development. The assumption is that deciding issues in a non-bureaucratic manner can lead to the formation of more egalitarian institutions. Second, consensus can operate as a binding force for the creation of "solidarity" within the community. With its emphasis on listening, and the avoidance of winners and losers, it has the potential to increase understanding and reduce barriers among members.[18] Third, a consensus approach reflects what Staples (1984: 4) refers to as a necessary prerequisite for effective organizational development: "real faith in people's basic judgment, intentions, abilities, and instincts."

While consensus is essential, the use of conflict or contest strategies is also important. There will probably be situations where the membership includes intransigent, destructive elements which no amount of cooperation or consensus can change. Strategies that recognize and deal with the conflict situation should be developed.

Extra-Group Considerations

A community that seeks changes in the way elites deal with change will rarely be able to use consensus. Quite simply, the power-holders do not have the same interests or the same views as the community; and until they do – that is, when power is more equitably distributed – strategies of a contest nature will be necessary (Touraine, 2002; Specht, 1969).

In dealing with institutions, however, consensus orientation will sometimes be appropriate. There may be powerful institutions that are quite sympathetic to the aims of a disadvantaged group. For example, some Churches are quite progressive, and occasionally progressive political parties or unions can be sought as allies. The "Days of Action" in Ontario in 1995 involved community groups, labour, and churches in confronting the Conservative government's repressive policies and actions. Indeed, as Moyer (1990) points out, we rarely try to directly change a powerful adversary. It is the wider public that we must "convince"; they will in turn force the adversary to alter its behaviour. It is important to be ready to listen, and to negotiate alliances that will further group interests. As a community is able to mount an effective campaign and power is achieved, the opposition will eventually have to be treated as an equal. In a sense, we use conflict strategies to obtain a situation in which equality is the basic condition for co-operation.

---

[18] See Schutt (undated) or Hogie Wycoff's *Solving Problems Together* for a discussion of consensus decision-making techniques and their value.

Reflection

"Community development is about redistributing power and re-sources. It is a political process, not simply a tool or technique for calming people or rubbing raw the sores of discontent."

                                                        - *Jim Lotz (1995)*

A major thrust of community organization must be to address the issue of power – the ability of people to affect their internal and external environments. This requires conceptualizing power and its elements, and focusing on coherent, collective action. It also requires considerations of external and internal issues, and their dynamics. Finally, it is crucial that the people with whom we work are seen as victims of an unjust social/economic/political system, and as citizens with rights and abilities. This leads us to view community organization as a conflict and consensus-oriented practice; which alerts us to the need to articulate objectives that are empowering, and oriented to progressive social change.

Chapter 5

OBJECTIVES OF A PRAGMATIC COMMUNITY PRACTICE

Unless we know where we want to go, we are in danger of ending up in the direction we are going.

- Chinese proverb

There are a variety of ways in which to define community organization practice. Some authors see it as planning and coordinating services to be more efficient and effective (Rothman and Tropman, 1987). Others see it as a means to redress power imbalances in society (Kahn, 1982; Rubin and Rubin, 1986). Still, others see it as a means whereby community members more effectively share limited resources to create a better life (Ross, 1972; Biddle and Biddle, 1965). In my own research (Lee, 1988) and experience, I have found that community practitioners tend to understand their work as framed by goals and objectives. The conversations, analysis and reflection that have come out of countless interchanges has led to the development of a practical – or pragmatic – down to earth model, of what community organization needs to strive for.[1] Over the years, countless conversations and reflections have deepened the understanding, and have firmed up the elements in the model which is presented below. The model presented here sees community work as a means of addressing

---

[1] The conceptions of the model have come out of discussion and reflection with community workers in a variety of countries, Canada, the U.S.A. Ireland and Australia in the Global North and Nicaragua, El Salvador, Nigeria, Uganda in the Global South.

the goals of empowerment and social justice; as well as having five specific objectives: citizen involvement; sense of community; organization development; concrete benefits; and social learning.[2] These objectives are thus deeply embedded in the need for both personal empowerment and the social justice.

The Goal: Citizen Empowerment

Empowerment is a term that carries a number of meanings. Some see it as something we undertake. In this sense, it is a process more than an outcome. Others see it as being rooted in what we can or cannot do. In this sense it is equated with actually having power. Community workers articulate the goal of community development as empowerment. (A goal is a generally preferred outcome that is expressed in terms that are global and carry a value orientation.) Empowerment is understood by many community work practitioners as a sense of agency (Hustedde and Ganowicz, 2002); the sense in people that they have the ability and right to influence their environment. This definition is also reflected in much of community work literature (Thomas, 1983). As such however, it is not precisely the same as possessing power. A person can have power but fail to realize it, and thus act in a disempowered manner.[3] That is, empowerment means people have the feeling within themselves that they can act on their own behalf to be able to meet their physical, spiritual and psychological needs. Some, such as Gutierrez suggest that while "...empowerment is most often expressed as an increase in personal power, it tends not to distinguish the individual perception and actual increase in personal power; and tends not to reconcile per-

---

[2] For other views and community work models see Checkoway's article Six strategies of community change. Community Development Journal. Vol.30: no.1 2-19; or Rothman and Tropman's (1987) seminal article, "Three Models of Community Organization Practice", in Cox et al. Eds., *Strategies of Community Organization* (F.E. Peacock Publishers).

[3] Michael Learner has written extensively on what he calls surplus powerlessness – the tendency to see ourselves as having less ability to influence our lives than we actually do. We can see how useful for it is for elites that the people buy into the notion that globalization, downsizing, and the triumph of technological change are part of "historical forces." To the extent we buy into this we acquire surplus powerlessness.

sonal and political power" (Checkoway, 1995). It is suggested by others that the goal of empowerment is not individual, but multi-level; and as such, it is not sufficient to focus only on developing a sense of personal power in working toward social change – that efforts for change should include all three levels: individual involvement, organizational development, and community change (Checkoway, 1995). Indeed, it is the position here that empowerment is both personal and political. We need to understand our abilities. Likewise we need to be able to recognize the extent to which the political, economic and social environments are amenable and support action. At the same time, we need the social and political environments to recognize the rights (social and legal) of citizens. More will be said about this dynamic at the end of this section.

Community Organizing Objectives

As well as this general personal goal, community work addresses specific outcomes or objectives that we can actually see in the communities within which we practice. They can be understood as the more concrete results that are expected to come out of a community development process. They have links to the more general concept, the goal to which they add concreteness or an operational sense, and from which they draw direction and meaning. As well as speaking in general terms about power and empowerment, community workers wish to achieve important kinds of specific outcomes in and for communities. (These objectives are outlined below, and are included in Figure 5-1: Community Organizing Objectives as Related to Empowerment.)

1. Citizen Involvement or Participation

Nobody makes a bigger mistake than he who did nothing because he could do only a little.

- *Edmund Burke*

As Saul (1995) and others (International Fund for Agricultural Development, 2007) suggest, active citizenship is crucial to the health of any society. Participation means that we make decisions and act on them, in an attempt to do something about the problems that are important to us, "to help others while being helped [our]selves" (Rice, 1990: 9). Another way of saying this might be engagement in a change process: citizens actually acting on their own behalf to bring about some positive alteration in their environment. Saul (1995) makes the point that the very essence of citizenship is our active involvement in the life of our communities. Citizens have both the right and the responsibility to act. To be able to act, however, people must see themselves as citizens; with rights and abilities to express opinions, and to acquire the resources they need. The link to empowerment is obvious: for a group of people to feel positive about their ability to influence their lives, they must actually take action. Simply "believing" like Peter Pan, will not make it so. If we never act we will never gain, and we will tend to lose the sense that we can act. Participation or action can be expressed at various levels: voting; attending a meeting; or joining a self-help, advocacy, or social action group, for example. If people take up leadership responsibilities in community organizations, their participation deepens. The point of participation, however, is not simply leadership. It is **participation in action.** Action can have a positive effect on how we see ourselves; and how other people see us, and/or the issues for which we advocate. Problems are often ignored when we are not active in bringing them before the policy makers or the public.

It is important, as Bloomberger Jr. (1969) has suggested, promoting collective, as opposed to individual, action. That is, widespread participation of the citizens in the attempted change process. Even the World Bank has come to examine the merits of participation in decision making (Herz & Ebrahim, 2005). But participation can be, and often is, a catch phrase that means both everything and nothing (Fraser, 2005; Arnstein, 1969). The notion of participation for this book reflects four assumptions:

1. The participation of the people must be meaningful, not token activity or simply for the benefit of decision-making elites (Arnstein 1969).
2. Decisions made with the serious and meaningful input of the people – who are both to be affected by them, and who implement them – will tend to be better, more realistic decisions.
3. People who feel they have been part of a decision have more at stake in seeing the decisions implemented well.

4. Participation of people, in the decisions that influence their lives, is healthy. People will tend to act better, more logically, sanely, and humanely, if they have a sense of influence over their lives.

2. Sense of Community

It's brought the community together. Before, no one got together much or knew each other. It's a real neighbourhood now – a community.
  - Karen (Youth activist; Chetwynd Project, Jamestown)

As we have seen in the previous chapter, community is a term which is used with a variety of meanings. We can speak of geographically based groups like urban neighbourhoods. We even speak of virtual communities (Fraser, 2005). Community can also refer to people who share common attributes like race or culture. Whatever the bonding factor, however, it is important for the members to have a positive sense of themselves as a distinct group. They must believe in the validity of their perceptions about their experience. Members must also possess a realistic satisfaction with their culture and traditions—not that these are superior to all others, but that they are valid and useful to them. Oppressed groups, such as Indigenous people in North America and Australia, invariably re-establish connections with their traditions and culture as a crucial part of their organizing. These are all important factors in overcoming the experience of victimization, and in establishing an image of themselves as people with a capacity and right to act.

We live in an alienating, and alienated, world dominated by technical efficiency and bureaucratic procedure (Napier, 2002) and inequality (Wilkinson & Pickett, 2010). Boothroyd (1991: 84) has put it clearly:

> The price we have paid for the material progress, personal liberty and cosmopolitanism enjoyed in (modern society) is a deep sense of aloneness, anxiety and impotence. This sense comes from the realization that ultimately only we or our immediate family cares about our economic fate, that our lives have no meaning outside that which we invest in them...

Wilkinson & Pickett 2010 suggest that communities have become increasingly "atomized." The separateness that people feel not only leads to loneliness but also to feelings of confusion and impotence. Alienation is disempowering. We need solid social relationships. As lone (and alone) individuals we cannot hope to influence the powerful systems that exist all around us. Indeed, we may feel that they act on us in the most oppressive ways. To feel powerful we must also experience some connection to others. The rediscovery and re-establishment of a sense of community – our common experience, common dreams – can reduce the sense of powerlessness and is a necessary component in any struggle to achieve social change (Hustedde and Ganowicz, 2002).

3. Organization Development

You can have all the people on one side for whatever you want to do, but, unless they're organized, nothing will happen.
- Chicago neighbourhood activist

This category refers to the building of a new organization, or the improvement (for example, gaining resources, and increasing participation) of an already existing one. A key element of power is having a large number of people on our side. Many writers (Rubin and Rubin, 1986; Alinsky, 1971), however, point out that numbers only lead to power when they are organized. One crucial aspect of empowerment is the establishment and strengthening of civil-society organizations representing the interests of the marginalized (International Fund for Agricultural Development, 2007). An organized group stimulates energy in the form of cohesion and status. Local organizations provide opportunities for local governance (International Fund for Agricultural Development, 2007). An organized people can share information (on the problems they face), resources, or their own skills. They can divide tasks that need to be done to achieve their objectives, in an efficient manner. Further, the image of a strong community organization raises the status of the community in its own eyes, and often in those of the bureaucracies with whom it must deal (Alinsky, 1971). As noted in Chapter 1, there are difficulties associated with organization. Still, it is clear that for people to feel that they can achieve what they need, they must have an effective organization that can mount strategies over a significant time period.

4. Concrete Benefits or Resources

If I leave a community and people like me, and people have partici-
pated, and people feel good about themselves, that's important. But, if
they have not achieved some good resource, well, I leave a failure.
                                   - Barb Hanson, Toronto community worker

"A key requirement for any escape from poverty and hunger is access to productive resources" (International Fund for Agricultural Development, 2007). Community practice often begins with the hope for the acquisition of: a specific resource; a right; an increase in service or access to credit or even land; or the development of a new facility of some sort (for example, a health centre). As Thomas (1983) has pointed out, there is a clear connection between lack of power and a people who are denied access to basic resources. Aside from the usefulness of the actual resource, community workers see a connection to empowerment. As one community worker put it, "people need victories to prove to themselves that they really are capable." It is much easier to believe in ourselves if we are part of a successful attempt to have a particular need met. If we understand that we have achieved one thing, we can believe that we can achieve others.

5. Social Learning

To develop an active and healthy community we must have the opportunities, and means, to learn. Social Learning is linked with the development of power. Knowledge is one of the five elements of power. This objective has the following three facets:

(a) Skills - One refers to people in the community acquiring new skills. To know that we have the skills to accomplish something – that we are not simply wishing that we could do it – is a crucial determinant of our self-image. People's feelings of self-esteem are often influenced by the realization that they have learned how to do something, such as: chair a meeting; write a news release; research some information; or deal with a bureaucracy or a complex situation. Community workers spend considerable energy helping activists as they learn how to operate their own organization and develop strategies to influence "city hall" (Alinsky, 1971; Rubin and Rubin, 1986;

Godard, 1991). Shragge (2003: 135) interestingly uses the language of the Pragmatic Model (1999)[4] and refers to this as the: "pragmatic practice of community organizing. The goal here is to help people learn how to get things done, how to mobilize resources within the existing limits of power."

(b) System Knowledge - The ability to use the complex system of regulations, laws, and public organizations is important to our ability to influence our environment. It is something that all of us have to learn. As indicated in Chapter 1, information is often difficult to get or shrouded in technical jargon. Yet, with focused effort most of us can acquire the ability to negotiate these systems.

(c) Structural Analysis - Social learning also refers to people gaining a new and useful analysis of themselves, their community, the larger society, and/or the problems with which they are faced. As the Women's Movement has demonstrated, having an understanding of the social, political, and economic factors that shape the conditions of our lives can help to free us from self-blame and debilitating guilt over our inability to be as successful as we would wish (Adamson et al., 1989). Analysis is a crucial aspect of recognizing and utilizing our own experience. Community organization experience, when it is engaged in popular education activities, provides opportunities in which participants at all levels can learn to use experience to contest their social situation and engage in a variety of new activities in order to build social solidarity, and to act in a collective way to promote social change" Shragge (2003: 134).

Interrelationships among Objectives

There are interrelationships among community development objectives. Participation can obviously be linked to the attainment of a concrete benefit, or the development of an organization. As the International Fund for Agricultural Development (2007) notes, "community partici-

---

4 I do not mean to imply that Shragge has used the language without reference. Indeed there is no sense that he ever read earlier editions of *Pragmatics of Community Organization*.

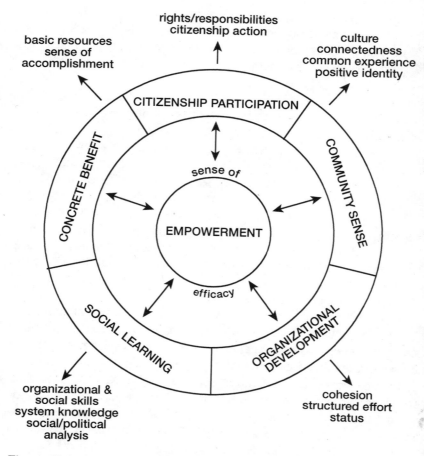

Figure 5-1: Community Organizing Objectives as Related to Empowerment

pation can contribute to ... the development of other forms of local institutions." A viable organization, as we've noted earlier, is necessary to form the members of a community into a coherent force for the attainment of benefits. Social learning is a crucial element in that it stimulates and informs our actions as citizens. This objective is crucial to citizen involvement. Learning the workings of an organization, as well as the workings of the social-political environment, is required to make the organization successful. A positive sense of community identity can result from the successful work of its "own" organization. At the same time, the development of a sense of pride and of the connections among people should shape the nature of the organization, and provide a sense of vision for its work. As well, a sense of community, in the sense of mutual emotional identification, can be seen as a key aspect of citizen participation (Hariman & Lucaites, 2007). Folks who see each other as occupying the same historical, moral human space are more likely to see themselves acting together. The following description by Alinsky (1972) is a good example of the interrelationships among objectives:

> ...But perhaps our most important accomplishment...was intangible; by building a mass power organization, we gave people a sense of identity and pride. After living in squalor and despair for generations, they suddenly discovered the unity and resolve to score victories over their enemies, to take their lives back into their own hands, and control their own destinies.

It is important to be clear that the exclusive pursuit of a single objective would not be reflective of a community development process. Indeed, such a course of action might be harmful. For example, the development of a sound and efficient organization without reference to the objectives of community sense or citizen participation, can lead to power struggles, unnecessary internal conflict, elitism, and alienation of those not involved with the leadership. The temptation to formalize, or professionalize, an organization can lead to alienation of the community it was set up to serve (Cain 1993). Focusing solely on the acquisition of a concrete benefit can lead to co-optation – where people are "bought off' by some individual "goodie" that makes them feel they no longer need to struggle (Piven & Cloward, 1979). If we are only interested in one issue, a failure to achieve it may sap energy from carrying on with other objectives. Social learning is crucial if we expect people to continue the struggle of development when the worker has left the scene. If we do not develop a critical analysis of what we are doing, what we are attempting to do, and the environment in which we are striving to do it, we will probably develop very naive strategies that could lead to defeat, disillusionment or co-optation.

An important reason for considering the five objectives as a kind of package deal is because working for change in and for communities is a long-term process. Thus, we need to note achievements when they are accomplished at different times. To see only one objective as important – for example, a concrete benefit like the passing of progressive legislation – can be counter-productive. Folks need to have a sense of achievement to keep them in the game, in the struggle. For example, Aboriginal communities in Canada worked for years to see the issue of residential schools addressed and redressed by the Canadian government. Along the way, they found themselves bonding within the struggle, developing a sense of community and a sense of learning the system. They achieved things on the road to the larger victory, which were important to their pride and who they are as nations and as communities.

Integration of Empowerment and Objectives

Good power distributes itself and makes others strong; power is empowerment.   *- Dorothee Soelle, activist and mystic*

Empowerment can be seen to exist when people believe that they possess the ability, opportunity and the right, to act effectively to influence their environments – to use Freire's (2000) language: a sense in people that they are subjects of the world, rather than objects. Another way of saying this is that empowerment is the recognition of citizenship of our ability, our right and our responsibility to act. It is clear, however, that empowerment is not something to be brought about in a simple way, or as something that can occur in isolation, unrelated to concrete objectives. It emerges from, and contributes to, the objectives. It is both dependent on them, and energizes their achievement.

Empowerment in development is a complex phenomenon, something that must be examined critically, relative to its rootedness in the concrete experience of people. It has to be actualized through the achievement of specific objectives. In this sense, empowerment is something that informs objectives and tasks, and in turn is informed by them. The goal of empowerment – the feeling in people that they can influence their environment – is an intimate part of the objectives, and the objectives are intimate parts of empowerment. (See, once again, Figure 5-1.) The concept of empowerment is not one of a state of mind that arrives after, or is caused by, the attainment of the objectives. Empowerment is reflected in, and experienced in, the actual achieving of the objectives; and the achievement of any of the objectives can be empowering.

Empowerment cannot exist outside of the striving. This is why the objective of citizen participation is so important. That is, as we begin to strive for the accomplishment of one or more of the objectives –as we find that we can participate in a discussion, or that by making our voices heard we begin to be listened to – we develop a sense that we have the ability to influence our lives; that we are truly citizens. In this way, community development becomes "an empowering process," the aim of which is to see people gain a greater sense of their ability to affect their environment. We can reflect on the success of community-development projects by examining the extent to which there is evidence that any of the objectives are present, or are increased or decreased.

Community Work and Social Justice and Citizenship

Injustice anywhere is a threat to justice everywhere.
- Martin Luther King Jr.

Community workers, while focused on issues of a local or community-specific nature, must be very aware of the broader social and political context of the problems people face. Assisting a group to obtain a stop sign, produce a community newspaper, develop a women's shelter, or get a polluting industry to clean up, is important. On the other hand, none of these necessarily have the effect of eradicating, or even challenging, structural power imbalances. Adamson et al. (1989) point to the difficulty women activists face when trying not to have their work become solely focused on small institutional changes rather than structural change. Indeed some authors (Mowbray, 1985; Repo, 1977; Mayo, 1975) claim that community workers actually contribute to the acceptance of society-wide oppressive systems by focusing on local or community-specific issues. Piven and Cloward (1979) worry that community workers will encourage people to focus on building organizational capacity when they should be pressing their demands for change. Most community workers, however, reject the notion that we are unaware of the potential for co-optation, or the "band-aid" nature of our work. We tend to see our work as part of the patchwork quilt of action and reflection that can contribute to positive social change and the development of citizenship (George et al., 2003). Certainly no "revolution" is in sight. The promise of a truly egalitarian and empowering society often seems to recede into the distance. Still, we need to be aware of the hard and important work community practitioners put in every day assisting marginalized people to form themselves into support organizations and citizen advocacy groups that make changes which do improve their lives. (George et al. 2003). As activist/popular educator Robbie McGregor put it (in a conversation we had in 2009):

> I really believe that only by getting into individual and group action can people motivate themselves to tackle big social issues. If we just keep sharing our observations, values and ideas, without doing something, it all just blows away in the wind.

We also need to remember the work of the social activists who have gone before us, leaving us a legacy of hope and some concrete changes, which clearly have made the world a better place. Without the organizers in the Labour movement assisting in the struggle for decent working conditions in individual factories, workers would not have the benefits – safety standards and minimum wage legislation, for example – that they have today. Without the organizers in feminist communities, women would be without many of the very important benefits and services that exist today, such as shelters and equal-pay legislation. The co-operative movement – housing, credit unions – owes its existence to the local struggles waged by its early organizers. In this way community organizing can be seen as an empowering process, and as a process of social change. Fromm (1966) reminds us that social change is a slow process with radical improvements taking generations to achieve. We must be honest and clear about this. Those of us who involve ourselves in community work with the assumption that we will be involved in immediate fundamental change are sure to be disillusioned and will burn out very quickly. Acting on this kind of assumption will endanger the achievement of what is possible, and may indeed retard the struggle for long-term fundamental change.

An important concept that is crucial to framing community work in social justice terms is that of citizenship. A key writer on citizenship is Marshall (1950), who proposes three areas of rights of the modern citizen: civil, political and social. Civil rights concern individual freedom, including freedom of speech, thought and faith, the right to own property and the right to justice. The political aspect includes the right to participate in the attempts to influence political processes. It is in his identification of social rights, however, that distinguishes Marshall's definition from previous understandings. He argues for a range of rights, from "the right to a modicum of economic welfare and security, to the right to share to the fullest in the social heritage and to live the life of a civilized being according to the standards prevailing in the society" (1950, 10-11). So in seeking social justice, community practitioners may find themselves working to help people gain any or all of the range of rights suggested by Marshall. This is a very large agenda.

Alinsky (1971) has said that a "realistic radical" – one who can approach the world the way it is and not the way one wishes it – can further the struggle by helping to establish powerful popular movements and organizations. It is important that community practitioners help the people with whom we work to reflect on how their particular struggle connects with the "larger" issues of the day – how the "local" strategy meshes with, or runs counter to, the flow of a "movement" (Moyer, 1990). It is equally important for community workers to help their groups look for coalitions so that they can become stronger, and the larger issues can be tackled when opportunities arise.

Social justice can be understood as a goal, like empowerment. However, while empowerment is a personal objective (an internal emotional and cognitive state in people), fundamental social change is found in the societal dimension. As with empowerment, social justice is a valued end state, difficult to define in concrete terms. Also like empowerment, it cannot be understood in isolation; it is only furthered in terms of the achievement of the development objectives in the community. Figure 5-2: Dimensions of Community Organization represents the interconnectedness of the three dimensions of community organization: the personal, societal, and community.

Figure 5-2: Dimensions of Community Organization

A Definition of Community Organization

Now that we have discussed the things that community workers are trying to achieve, we can try out a definition, and examine a few of its implications.

> **Community organization is a social intervention which seeks to maximize the ability of oppressed or disadvantaged people to take action and influence their environments; by facilitating a growing understanding of their social, political and economic environments and of themselves as citizens. The aim is to develop power to: acquire resources; change inadequate institutions and laws; or build new ones,**

more responsive to their needs and those of all human beings.

Importance of the Local

The only way anything serious will ever get done is by community movements. Governments are so co-opted and pressured or in bed with lobbyists and all kinds of special interests that we can't look to governments to solve these problems.
- Henry Mintzberg in conversation with Toby Heap,
Corporate Knights, Issue 31 Spring, 2010

Comments on Terms

First of all, what do we mean by "local" when we talk about community organization? Traditionally we have meant neighbourhood or at least a slice of real estate. Any contemporary practitioner however, must be aware that notion of community of function, identity or interest group is just as important as neighbourhood, perhaps more. So when we use the term "local" we are including the notion of smallish groups of people who may be linked by identity or interest, as well as or rather than geographical location. Second, we must think about what we mean by change. Indeed change, fundamental or otherwise is important but so too is resistance. In community and social movement work, the struggle may be to resist, as well as achieve, change.

Over the years, many writers in community practice (Shragge, 2003; Mowbray, 1985; Repo, 1977) have raised concerns that local community work tends to aim and achieve small gains for small groups that may ameliorate problems for some people, or they may achieve short-term gains; but, may also actually harm work for widespread and fundamental progressive change. Obviously there is truth in this concern. Community work may indeed result in a group of people getting some social good that is useful for them, and then withdrawing from the struggle for more widespread change. Small changes may be sold by power holders in terms that suggest that "the system works" and no structural change is necessary. Thirdly, a community project may get captured by elite elements within a community so that gains for people are unequally apportioned, even within the community. These are serious concerns for community work and as indicated above, not ones that have gone unexamined. At the same time, many of us understand that community work does have a utility both in its "local" focus and in its potential as part of efforts for widespread structural change. Del Morel (2005) forcefully sums up this position:

> But the idea did create space for people to approach the problems of need and oppression from a different angle than philanthropy and charity. The radical grassroots strove to improve the whole of a person, not simply the basic materials of food, clothing and shelter. It also created space for issues that are less urgent to industrial workers like environmental integrity and human rights of others. The concept of community, not only worker, empowerment was able to grow from this new space of activism.

Community Change or Resistance is Important

We need the affirmation that gains made by our local group can provide. People need the experience that they can have some influence in their lives, not simply a voice but a voice that is seen and felt to obtain results (Ulbig, 2008). Conversely, to not assist people in making gains at a "local" level leaves people suffering, and undercuts energy for widespread involvement. As Diski (2000) said in an article of the *London Review of Books*:

> Two people in pain are not nearly as likely to ...found a religious community or become comrades in battle as they are to curl up silently in separate corners ... to suffer alone.

Organizing locally on issues that are immediate or have local significance can be empowering experiences for those involved. Progressive (or negative) change doesn't come all at once as a result of some grand scheme. Developing analysis, strategies, and tactics that are spread throughout other centres of activity depends on local experiments (Tarrow, 1994).

Example: Robbie McGregor an adult educator working with the people of Sambaa K'e, a Dine community in Canada's Northwest Territories, comments on how proud the people there were of their organizing accomplishments. "A small group of 90-100 Dene people organized themselves and took action when confronted by multi-national and other resource-extraction projects. They used a community research process they called 'ground truthing' in which the local people inventoried the natural features and ecosystem of their territory and articulated traditions relating to them. This resource enabled them to make representations that resulted in the relocation of a pipeline path and the refusal of a gravel "borrow pit" that would have violated land that was sacred to them.

Local gains can provide beacons of hope for other local communities. We have to start somewhere. Moffatt (2006) suggests that the queer community has utilized local struggles as such beacons. We experience and understand deprivation and injustice locally, not as a mass. A struggle for specific local change can be the beginning or a part of a larger engagement through growth in consciousness and confidence acquired in the struggle. Most of the Native activists I know are people who began in local work.

Engagement in struggle is a long-term and wearying experience. Local victories can help us maintain hope and energy in a process that provides relatively few grand triumphs. Indeed sometimes people only have energy for local work, for them there is no alternative.

None of this is meant to suggest that local struggle is superior to work on fundamental social change. There are lots of pitfalls and frustrations in community work; the point is that the two should not be thought of as separate or antagonistic to each other. My concern with the critics of community work's so-called local orientation is that it is often arrogant and dismissive in tone, and confuses challenges and pitfalls for fundamental fatal flaws. It reminds me of my early days in community work. Lots of my colleagues (and I) accused caseworkers of simply putting on band aids and not attending, like we were, to the large wounds of social and economic injustice that underpinned human misery. While there was some truth in our position, we ignored the positive work that was being done by caseworkers, and alienated a good percentage of people whom we should have been recruiting as allies. There is danger of that dynamic being repeated in the interface between community and social movement work. The tendency to dismiss community work as part of social movement struggle therefore weakens them both.

Reflection

Community organization is an ancient, and persevering, human endeavour. In some ways it is the most natural of human activities – getting together to make necessary changes in the way we live together or to challenge the status quo power structures. At its best, it promotes equity, and liberation of the spirit of humanity. It is also, however, personally demanding, a time-consuming, threatening (to some) and very complex bit of business. It requires dedication, energy, and a rigorous analysis of situations, events, and people (from ourselves, as well as from those with whom we work). The rest of this book attempts to come to grips with the pragmatics of how our dedication is put into practice.

Chapter 6

ROLES AND SKILLS IN PRAGMATIC COMMUNITY PRACTICE

Right away I began to see that organizing was difficult. It wasn't a party. I began to see all the things that he did, and I was amazed – how he could handle one situation and have a million things going in his mind at the same time.
- Dolores Huerta on Cesar Chavez (Levy, 1985)

The overall role of the community organizer is extremely complex and sensitive (McAuley, 2007; Staples, 2004; Gecan 2002). As indicated earlier, when we speak of a pragmatic model of community work we are talking about a melding of locality development and social action. Very simply, the approach here is that the building of community capacity (developing and sharing resources, building consensus, etc.) cannot be undertaken without attention to issues of class, race, gender, etc.; as well as power and conflict – all social-action concerns. The notions of role and skill then are based on this analysis of pragmatic community work. We work with people who we understand as "victims" of an unjust social order; and as "citizens" with rights, responsibilities, and abilities to work for a just one. We are not able to do this unless we collaborate – work with the people as partners – in transforming the social reality in which we all live. To do this we must have some sense of what behaviours will be useful, i.e., what our role or roles will be in the process.

The Notion of Role

Strean (1979) notes that role can be seen from a number of perspectives. The one used here is that of "a synonym for behaviour." This is different from simply looking at activities however or a list of what workers might do. Rather it is a "pattern of behaviour" (Strean, 1979: 386). That is, the key roles in community work will be discussed as sets of behaviours. But how is the idea of role useful to community workers? Very simply, if we see and understand that role is a set of particular behaviours it can provide us with a sense of the range of activities we need to be prepared to undertake.

Two major points should be made before the discussion of roles. First, no role can be thought of, or utilized, without reference to others. Second, all core roles imply the development of trust – they are part of a relationship that is built up through the enacting of each role (Jeffries, 1993). The five roles discussed here will be: initiator (catalyst/ agitator); encourager/supporter; popular educator; mediator; and planner (strategist/advisor).

1. Initiator *(Catalyst / Agitator)*

People who are disadvantaged – particularly if they have been marginalized for a long time – can become "stuck"; either in inactivity (even apathy), or in repeated behaviours that are not getting them out of their predicament. (Remember "frustration instigated behaviour.") They may have all sorts of strengths and resources, but these can become dormant either in the face of serious, long-term oppression (Kretzman & McKnight, 1993); or because they face sudden and complex threats to their living conditions (Ball, 1973). The situations of Aboriginal people in North America and Australia or of people in the African-American ghettos of the U.S. can fit the former dynamic. Communities like Walkerton in Ontario, that had to face the crisis of their water system failing and the resulting serious illness and death (National Union of Public and General Employees: 2008), are suggestive of the second. Thus, the community worker will often be required to assist community members in getting started – i.e., be the person who asks the first question or gets the first meeting called, etc. *The Social Work Dictionary* (1991) puts it this way: "The social worker-community organizer's function of creating a climate of introspection and self-assessment for the ... community, and facilitating communication, stimulating awareness of problems, and encouraging belief in the possibility of change" (p.30). This initiator role is clearly central, and related to other key roles.

2. Encourager/Supporter

The community worker – because he is often working with people who have been alienated and deprived of the opportunity to influence their environments – will need to be able to encourage people to believe in themselves, their abilities, and their ability to learn (McAuley, 2007). This has obvious connections with the catalyst role but is broader. Many times, as a community pursues its struggle, a worker will find people doubting themselves personally or as a collective. Dealing with this insecurity requires taking time to listen, and assuring those involved that they have been heard. It also includes validating the understandings of the people and that they have had disempowering experiences in the past. Organizers in the women's movement provide lots of examples of this. It involves further assisting people in looking for and finding their strengths. More and more in social work today, we are being encouraged to develop a "strengths perspective" (Saleebey, 2006) to counter the long experiences marginalized folks have had being discounted. Disadvantaged folks have often been taught to see themselves as weak or as victims; and to dismiss or at best take for granted the abilities and positive qualities they have. It is important then to take the time to notice and share with people our sense of their strengths.

3. Popular Educator

As Colorado and Collins (1987), Illich (1972), and Freire (2000) have pointed out, education is a critical instrument or process that can be used for either subjugation or liberation. This is why the government and churches attempted for so long to deprive Aboriginal communities of their education function (Lee, 1992). The community worker's education role however is not one of a formal teacher—where it is assumed that people are more or less empty vessels into which the bounty of knowledge is poured. As indicated above, oppressed people have been taught to devalue their own experience and knowledge, and not to see the processes that have made them the objects of oppressive systems (Friere, 2000). Thus the community worker, as well as helping to provide new information and/or analysis, must often assist people to examine their old and new experiences. They do this so that they can identify: where the roots of problems lie; the things they know already; and what they need to learn in order to come together, and/or confront oppressive systems and processes.

4. Mediator

In western mainstream society we are encouraged to see each other as individuals first and people in relationships second. As Freire (2000) points out, we are taught (particularly where power and resources are concerned) that for one person or group to have more means, others must have less. This has clear ramifications for Aboriginal communities who have been stripped of many resources, and have little power at this time. Individuals, families, and groups then often wrestle for whatever resources and power that they perceive to exist within their borders. The resulting tension and conflict can be debilitating. Note the factions that we see in many Aboriginal communities and in others such as women's groups and housing co-ops. Thus the community worker must at times play the role of mediator. The Social Work Dictionary (1991) – unfortunately limiting it to family therapy – characterizes it thus: "...sometimes acts as a go between in getting various members of the [community] to communicate more clearly and fairly with one another" (p.141).

Mediation however, is actually far more complex then helping people to communicate clearly with each other. After all, if we are clear in our communication we actually may be clear about how much we cannot stand each other or how far apart we are in our competing demands. Mediation, at least in community work, must include assisting people to see, at best, their common humanity; or at least their common interests. Certainly that involves clarity, but it also involves reaching an understanding of their legitimate needs as well as those of others. This does not necessarily mean that those involved must come to like each other; it is about working on building mutually respectful and trusting relationships so that we can move forward on issues of common concern.

5. Planner (Strategist/Advisor)

Strategy or planning requires a set of activities: research, issue identification, and prioritizing. The worker – while looking to assist community members to understand their own strengths and identify targets for member action – must be clear that she brings a unique and valuable expertise to the community. One of these skills is the ability to plan a course of action, whether for internal development or external campaigning. This means that the worker must assist members to acquire these skills as well, of course. However, sometimes the best way to "teach" strategizing and planning is to be involved in a real process. Thus, initially, the community worker may have to take the "lead" in planning or strategizing, but in a collaborative manner in which people are able to learn to do it for themselves. As longtime organizer Mike Balkwill has stated: "That is what organizing is about, finding opportunity doorways, but not slipping through them alone. We have to build a path with others, so we can go through these doorways together." Again, there is a connection with other roles such as popular educator and catalyst.

Core Skill Requirements

We now turn to the area of the major or core skills that are called for when working within the pragmatic model of community organizing. What skills are required by the basic roles that have been described? While community work writers (Abrams et al., 1990; and Rothman and Tropman, 1987, for example) point out that the skills required are quite complex, there are some very important basic skills that are necessary for the community worker to have. Some are from the affective, or communication and interpersonal area (Kahn, 1994); others are more instrumental, while others are more political. Further, some will be more important to certain roles than others, but like much of community work, these skills are pretty much interactive. One last point is that, while we talk about skills as if they were single bits of ability, they usually require a number of interrelated behaviours. What is presented below is probably best understood as skill sets which include: listening; information gathering; analysis; facilitation; and negotiation. This can assist us in thinking about the broad core abilities that the basic roles require for useful intervention.

1. Listening

Listening is probably one of the most important skills to have for any person involved in the social services. Gecan (2002) sets it as a crucial aspect in the beginning phase of organizing. It is said that Barack Obama, the 44th president of the United States, is a great listener, and that he gained that skill while working as a community organizer in Chicago. The ability to listen to community members – to hear what they are really concerned about, and the emotion with which they say things – is a crucial skill and basic to any social work. It is particularly important when working with those who have a long history of not being listened to, or of being discounted. As such, there is no role that does not require the worker to be a good listener. If, for example, one is going to initiate reflection or action, or encourage people, appropriate listening is crucial. A mediator must be able to understand both sides of a dispute in order to be able to frame an appropriate and useful intervention.

2. Information Gathering

Information gathering – about the community, individuals, or issues, for example – is also basic. While it may have less relevance to the encourager/supporter role, it will be used in others. Information is like energy – a source of power which fuels one's activities in getting things started and in strategizing. A popular educator needs basic information to help people structure their learning experiences. A mediator must have information about the basics of the situation, and about the history of a dispute.

3. Analysis

Analysis is the ability to take information and make connections or put it together in some meaningful or whole picture. It is the creation of meaning out of separated parts. The ability to analyze situations and problems is key to three of the roles: popular educator, mediator and strategist. The popular educator is someone who helps people to develop their own meanings out of their own experiences. The mediator must help people find their common interests within what may appear to be a very badly fractured community relationship system. The strategist / planner must be able to help people build a coherent picture of their situation and of their options.

4. Facilitation

Facilitation is defined here, very simply, as the ability to assist a group in achieving a purpose through working together. The worker is not doing the group's work, but acting in a manner that helps them do it well. This may involve helping to set up meetings and agendas; or encouraging participants to listen carefully to each other at a meeting; or supporting a leader who is chairing a first meeting. Much of the work of community development is based on productive and smoothly functioning groups, so facilitation can be seen as basic to all the community development roles.

5. Negotiation

Negotiation is bargaining in order to help people attain some form of benefit, or to resolve a dispute. Negotiation may take place within the community, between two groups that see their needs or interests differently. In this case it is a skill likely used in relation to the mediator role. The worker is more or less disinterested (not on one side or the other) and assists people in coming together in order to find their commonalities. On the other hand, negotiation is a skill required when representatives of the community are attempting to gain something from an outside body; the worker is likely playing the role of strategist / planner: the worker is on the side of the community people, using negotiation abilities to help the community achieve its goals.

Reflection

It is useful to make a couple of observations as we leave considerations of roles and skills.

Being Self-aware[1]

These roles and skills are ones basic to community organization; but they are not the only ones a worker will require. We always need to be prepared to reflect on our abilities in order to grow, and to improve ourselves. As well as understanding the various contexts that surround our work, we must have a handle on what we are about – our own values, biases, and analyses.

The worker is not merely a programmed automaton. We take on, consider, react to, and discard any number of values and perspectives

---

[1]   Alan Kaplan offers some thoughtful perspectives on the use of self in his book *Development Practitioners and Social Process: Artists of the Invisible (2002) London, UK: Pluto Press*. Earlier books, by Katrina Shields, *In the Tiger's Mouth* (1994); New Society Publishers) and Len Desroches (1996) *Allow the Water* (editions DUNAMIS publishers) provide some useful tools for self-reflection.

we meet as we grow and develop. What is important is to understand how we see and understand the world; not so as to force it on others, or to keep it from contaminating them, but so that we can be clear, honest, and direct when we are doing things. If we don't know how we see things (and obviously this can and will change with experience) it will be hard to answer the questions that people invariably ask: "What the hell are you here for?" or " What is your stake in this?" As Bishop (1994) notes, we all occupy different points on the various continuums of privilege. As well, we have all been touched by racist, homophobic, or sexist ideas. None of us is perfect, and part of ourselves may be working on this stuff for a long time. We have to possess some self-knowledge, such as what things bother us, motivate us, or make us angry or sad. We don't want emotional imperatives to motivate our reactions to people and situations.

By being clear and honest with ourselves we are in a position to be more pro-active with the people with whom we work. For example, if an organizer understands that he has a need to be personally very well or-ganized, he is less likely to see that attribute as absolutely necessary in others. Or, if he is aware that it has taken him effort and time to be able to confront difficult people, he will more likely be able to demonstrate patience with his community members as they struggle to develop the skill. We will be more comfortable in making demands of people and encouraging them, if we know that we are doing so not out of some personal need or bias of our own, but because of their needs and those of the situation. Understanding ourselves also includes being aware of what we are good at and where we have to improve. This keeps us from getting into situations that are over our heads, and assists us in know-ing when to ask for help. Ultimately it will help us to be more secure.

Diversity Issues and Being an Outsider

Earlier it was mentioned that community organization is often prac-ticed by people from outside of the community (Cruikshank, 1990). Sometimes that simply means that we don't live in the same commu-nity. Increasingly, however, we will probably find ourselves working with people who are of a different culture than we are, or have profoundly different life experiences than ourselves (Narayan, 1994). We may have ways of seeing situations, or of communicating, which are different from those of the people we are working with. Not only that, but more importantly, if we are carrying essentially mainstream identities (white, male, middle class, straight, credentialized – a post secondary degree or a professional one – or abled) we will also carry more privilege than folks from marginalized groups (people of colour, female, working class, queer, those with little education or folks who are in some way seen as disabled) (Mulally, 1997). This obviously does not mean we are smarter, more experienced, stronger, etc. It does mean however, as discussed earlier, that they have less access or opportunity to exercise agency in their own lives. This will impact on how (and whether) we take on different roles, or use particular skills. For example, it can be tricky for a white person who is attempting to play the role of advisor to an Aboriginal group; who may reasonably be sensitive to the issue of "advice giving" (given the paternalism many Native people have experienced from members of the dominant society). A similar dynamic can exist in situations where males are working as advisors among women.

Example: A community worker with an Australian development organization was stationed in the small South Pacific nation of Vanuatu. Her first assignment was to give some workshops to local women on how to conduct meetings. She was worried that this might appear presumptuous, but was not sure she could confront the funder at such an early time in the project, and did not feel that she could turn down the opportunity. Her strategy was to emphasize the popular education role. She facilitated the sessions in a way that encouraged the women to reflect on how they were running their meetings already. Occasionally she would raise questions that helped them reflect on how they could improve things. The development organization was happy that the event had taken place, and the women were very pleased with the process and with what they had learned (Miles, 2006).

A similar issue can exist in relation to communication. Hall and Hall (1987) make the point that some cultures (Euro-North American for example) are contractually oriented. That is, there is a tendency to want our working relationships to be very clearly spelled out—very "product oriented." Efficiency is valued, and a preference for written contracts. Other cultures (Aboriginal folks or some immigrant/refugee groups from Latin American or Africa might be examples here) tend to prefer the work relationship to grow out of personal relationships.

There is less dependence on contract, and more on understanding where people are coming from and who they are as people. Process tends to be more valued than efficiency or strict rules. Time might be viewed as something to use to first foster relationship and later focus on "product."

Now clearly these are generalizations. We need to be careful not to fall into the trap of essentialism (Todd in Lee, Sammon & Dumbrill, 2007: 12-13), the belief that certain cultures and or experiences brand a person with only one way of looking at the world or one way of acting. Aboriginal people and women are not automatically going to reject advice from a white male. Neither will queer people automatically reject advice from a straight man or woman. And Aboriginal folks understand the nature of the world they live in and the utility of having written contracts. Being born into a culture does not necessarily mean that one will not take on attributes of others with which we come into contact. Many Euro-North Americans can be very concerned about and adept at relationship building for example. The point here is not to put forward "cultural laws," but to suggest that we need to think about how different groups might respond to different roles, and how skills may have to be tailored to unique situations. An important rule in community work is never to take anything for granted, but let our actions emerge out of our experience and reflection.

While there are particular challenges and struggles to being an outsider, there are also important positive aspects:

a) Fresh Perspective

The outsider may bring some fresh perceptions and thinking to situations. As long as we are respectful of people's experience, this can be a valuable asset to a community. An outsider can ask those "dumb" questions that insiders may not think to ask because for so long they have been part of the community or are so deeply involved in the issues.

Example: A female Native community worker tells the story of going into a small community and quickly realizing that the reserve was being run completely by men. In going around the community, she was told about how the women felt shut out and disrespected. The women kind of deputized her to raise the issue at a Band Council meeting. She was nervous about doing this, but felt she had built some trusting relationships among the councilors. She decided to do it by asking the men why no women were on council, or in any leadership positions in the community. While there was some (not unexpected) resistance from some of the men, the majority found that it was an interesting issue. One pointed out that, traditionally, women had occupied places of respect in Native communities. This was the start of a process – not always an easy one – that brought more women into leadership roles in the Band.

b) Perception of Impartiality

As suggested above, communities often find themselves dealing with splits and alignments within their membership. A community organizer from the outside may be seen as someone who is not connected to one group or another, and be more able to bring people together in an atmosphere of safety.

Example: I was hired by an Aboriginal community which had an acknowledged history of factional conflict. As part of building a community analysis, I facilitated a series of popular education workshops. Representative people from different segments and factions in the community were brought together to work on a coherent community vision, and to identify some of their key problems. At the end of each two-day session we engaged in feedback rounds to evaluate the process. In every case, participants talked about how nervous they were in coming to the sessions, and how important it had been to have an outside person there as a guide. They also spoke of how good it felt to hear some of the "different ideas" in the community, and to be able to express their own. I didn't bring the new ideas; rather I had offered a framework and a "safe" place to talk and do some thinking.

Being an Insider

It is tempting to think that being an insider would be an easier situation. In many ways, this is accurate. Issues of identity do not have to be negotiated. If we are "from" the community there are things we can take for granted. In some cases language may be one area where an insider has a clear advantage. Working through an interpreter is fraught with the possibilities of misunderstanding and confusion. Some of the issues of power may be mitigated as well, as a community worker from the group seeking community-practice assistance probably bears the same stigmas and disadvantages (and thus understands the pain). Less time might be spent working out the relationships. On the other hand, as I and my colleagues have discovered (Lee, et al., 2002), an insider does face some issues on which we need to be clear. One of them is boundaries. In our study a woman who worked with refugees spoke about how her status as a community member rubbed against that of her role as a worker.

> ... it's hard for us to put our boundaries in certain areas because of – I work with [them] and they are part of my community. And they don't see me as a worker. They see me as a friend. But because I have to put my boundaries and say now I am a worker and have to do certain things, but the people don't see it – and then it's hard. ... because you are part of the group. You cannot isolate yourself from your own community (Lee, et al, 2002: 12).

In the same study an Aboriginal practitioner once told how

> Folks who wouldn't think of calling a worker who was from outside the community, think it is fine to call me at any hour of the day or night. I always have to figure out if I need to talk about some issue at 11:30 at night or while I'm trying to get my kids off to school in the morning.

Another issue is that situations which affect the community can also affect the insider practitioner in a very personal way that can be very emotional for him or her. One worker in the study mentioned earlier gave a good example of this:

> Women I've known for years that I never expected to be working the streets, I see that now. ... The cuts to welfare have meant that most of people's money goes directly to rent and there's not much left over for other things that they really need. It pushes people toward more stress, alcoholism, and like I mentioned, I saw a woman on the street just recently who I thought would never ever do it – she's in her mid-30s; she had no choice. It was hard because she is sort of related to me and I know that there is nothing I can do directly (Lee, et. al, 2002: 11).

A worker from "outside" a community dealing with issues like this would certainly be moved by the plight of community members. On the other hand he probably would not have to deal with the emotional energy required if a relative was being so deeply affected.

Being an outsider (Cruikshank, 1990) or an insider varies with difficult issues that need to be negotiated. Each brings its own pitfalls, stress and opportunities. It is important to be aware of them, and not to try to be perfect wherever we come from. We are going to make mistakes. If we know this, and know that we are not the only ones to face these dilemmas, we may be able to take these opportunities to grow and develop as community workers.

IT IS IMPORTANT FOR THE COMMUNITY WORKER TO:

- be able to work with small groups & individuals
- understand & work with political power
- understand & have a sense of social & economic justice
- be able to work with large groups & coalitions

In conclusion, the relationship between the organizer and the community must frame the professional use of roles and skills. That relationship, if it is to be one that assists marginalized groups to empower themselves, must be one rooted in an anti-oppressive approach to practice. This requires that we have an authentic respect for the people with whom we work, and in practical terms, understand the need to see community practice framed by a conscious, balanced understanding of the resources which the community and the practitioner bring to the experience of community organization. They form a whole; if one side is missing the whole enterprise will ultimately fall apart.

Figure 6-1: Community – Practitioner Balanced Interface

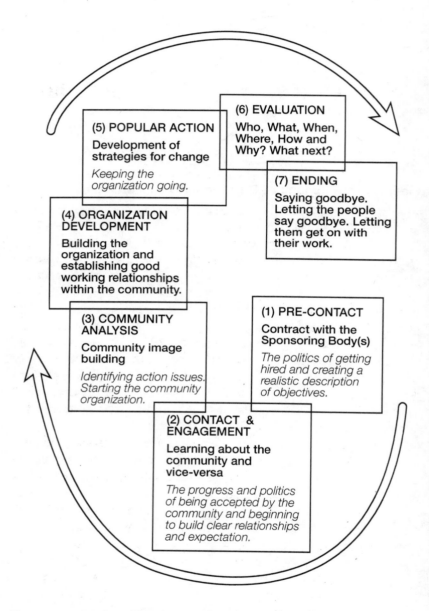

Figure 7-1: Phases of Community Organization

SECTION III

Phases of Community Organization

The process of community practice may seem in some ways a chaotic one. That is, we choose objectives, make plans, enlist folks, and suddenly the situation changes. Funding doesn't come through, or as often happens, is delayed, or someone important to the work becomes ill, etc. The point is that we have to be prepared to be reactive as well as pro-active. Nevertheless, it is important to understand the practice and the journey of the practice. While things never work out perfectly there is a trajectory that is important to understand so that we can be sure that we are not overlooking issues or questions that will be important. Thus the practice of community organization will be discussed in terms of phases and will be outlined in a kind of spiral fashion (See Figure 7-1 opposite). This of course does not reflect the real complexity of what will happen. It is difficult to represent a phase process, as the real world is not two dimensional. So the phases are presented here in an overlapping circular fashion as an attempt to try and capture the interrelatedness of the action.

For example, development of a community analysis process will contribute substantially to the creation (or re-creation) of an organization. The same is true of popular action. Evaluation may go on formally at various times in the life of a community project, not just at the end. On the other hand, the people involved will constantly be reflecting (informally) on (evaluating) the things in which they have been involved – meetings, actions, negotiations – so that they can repeat the good things and eliminate unsuccessful behaviours. This being said, we begin this section by examining the issues and tasks in the first phase of organizing: Pre-Contact. (At the end of each chapter, you will find a chart that summarizes the key aspects of each phase.)

Chapter 7

PRE-CONTACT

As an organizer I start from where the world is, as it is, not as I would like it to be. That we accept the world as it is does not in any sense weaken our desire to change it into what we believe it should be – it is necessary to begin where the world is if we are going to change it to what we think it should be.

- Saul Alinsky (1971)

As we've noted earlier, more often than not, community organizers are not hired directly by the people they are supposed to help organize. Communities which are in most need are usually the least likely to have the money on hand to invest in this kind of professional person. Often they will not even see the need for hiring an organizer. Community practice is not the most well known branch of the human services. A public institution (like a government department) or a private one (such as a church group or a foundation) may do the initial thinking, advertising, and hiring.

Kramer (1970: 222) makes the point that: "Formally, the sponsor serves as the legitimizer and sanctions his change agent role." Even when community leaders do the hiring, many of the issues raised here will be relevant. Leaders are not always well connected to the people. As well, leaders are often using dollars from outside – government, foundations, and church groups for example – and this will impact on the nature of the development program for which they are hiring. It is crucial that the potential organizer gain a clear and definite contract with the hiring/funding body. Further, it is important for the potential organizer/employee to understand the sponsor, the sociopolitical context, their structural interrelationships, and the ways in which they can affect the objectives, methods, roles, and outcomes of the organizing endeavour (Kramer, 1970).[1]

If there are people within the organization who are cool to the project, or to some of its objectives or are merely ignorant of the community organizing process, the worker can end up spending a great deal of time later on educating people, or on mending fences. We have to learn who are the program sponsor's internal advocates and (as much as possible) leave them with the responsibility of handling organizational questions. If this responsibility for keeping her sponsor base strong is left vague, or solely with the organizer, she has to divide herself in two – half for the community, half for the funding organization – in order to maintain her credibility with the latter. With these questions on the table, the worker can make some decisions about how (or if) to proceed; and, at the very least, the potential for unforeseen events may be decreased.

Internal Political Situation

It is a good idea to try establishing contacts within the funding/sponsoring organization so that we can gain the most realistic perspective possible. These are a few of the initial questions we should be asking:

- Who, in the funding/sponsoring organization, is advocating the program?
- What is their status?
- Do they have good links to the community?
- Who, in the funding/sponsoring organization, is resistant to the program?
- Why, and for how long?
- What is the status of the person resisting the idea? It is important to know whether this is someone who is "noisy" but not influential, or a person who's "yes" or "no" can make a real difference.

---

[1]   Ben Carniol's *Case Critical* 4th Edition,(2005) Between The Lines Press, offers a solid critique of the way in which social agencies can constrain work for social change.

External Political Situation

What kind of credibility or clout does the funding organization wield in the larger community? What kind of credibility or clout does the organization wield in the particular target community (for example: an urban Native population, a certain neighbourhood, or a group of disabled people)?

Example: It is no secret that many Canadian institutions have historically had a destructive record in Aboriginal communities. This is particularly true of the Department of Indian and Northern Affairs (DIANA), and the churches involved in the residential school system. It is important that a person wanting to do development work in these communities be aware of how individual communities, or organizations, feel about accepting money or other resources from such mainstream institutions. Many refuse to accept funding from DIA (for example, the First Nations journal "Beedaudjimowin") because of the institution's records or from churches (a southern Ontario Native organization was offered the use of a local church hall, however, it could not accept the offer because many community members, who had experienced the residential school system themselves or through family members, were outraged and refused to attend events held there). On the other hand, there are Native communities which are working closely with churches and using these institutions' resources to develop healing programs and in their own communities' social justice initiatives.

Therefore, it is important to be aware of the political situations and feelings of the particular community with which one is working at any given time.

Who, or what, does the organization represent? For example, who is involved on its board or policy-making body? This question can be related to the first two. Persons possessing power in the overall community and in the organization might have little or even negative influence within the target community and vice-versa.

Are there groups or institutions likely to resist efforts which would help members of the target community become more influential in their own lives? How powerful are these groups?

Does the sponsoring body have particular enemies within the proposed target community – or the community at large – who tend to react negatively to any attempts at change supported by the sponsoring body?

- What are the dynamics involved?
- Are they based on personalities, or principles?
- What is the history of the conflict? What were the major events? Who were the major players?
- What are the prospects for resolving the enmity?
- If no resolution is in sight, what other possibilities exist for dealing with the problem?

Example: Until it ended in 2007, the Chetwynd Project in Toronto followed Alinsky's principle of requiring an invitation from the communities with which it works. Part of the selection process is to sort through those applications received, for those which seem the most appropriate. At one point two communities applied. While both seemed to be ones which could benefit from development intervention, one had supporting letters from two major social agencies, while the other did not. (Both agencies had extensive involvement in the two communities). This was significant in that Chetwynd depended on the cooperation of agencies for its work. The staff had to ask whether there was a message there: that the agencies would not be cooperative unless "their" choice was selected; or was it simply that the other community had not asked for the agencies' support? The staff also wondered if the one community wished to have nothing to do with these two powerful agencies. Whatever the answers here, it is important to get good, clear information, so that no nasty surprises come up that may damage the work carried out.

Sponsor's Vision/Ultimate Interest

What is the sponsoring body's **ultimate interest or vision** in having this particular community become organized?

- To get people to utilize the services of the funding body more fully?
- To create a new and better image of itself within a certain segment of the population; i.e. public relations?

- To get in on the latest fad? Though many governments in North America are touting the John McKnight (1995) idea – that the community is the best place to handle social problems – unfortunately there is little commitment to the necessary level of funding.
- To tap some new money that has appeared on the funding horizon? Though government funding levels have decreased, certain areas might have money on a project basis. For example, disability rights education has been identified as an important issue in some parts of Ireland. (Thanks to the organizing of disability activists.)
- Altruism or ideology? Are those advocating the project interested in empowerment and social justice?
- What are their critiques of poverty or racism, for example?
- Anything else we may think that is relevant to the particular sponsor and/or community?

Sponsor's Concrete Objectives

Does the sponsoring body have a clear, and definite, conception of what the "organized" community might actually look like – an informed and active citizenry, or simply a program with a nominal community board? Is there an interest in really developing the community? (Remember empowerment, and social justice, and the five objectives.) How influential have community voices been in creating the picture? How rigid a mandate will the organizer be given, and how does that fit with your own principles and style?

It is important to have clearly defined expectations in order to avoid misunderstandings or arguments, which could sap time and energy at a later more crucial time.

Example: A small foundation funded an organizer to assist small citizen groups to be more effective in challenging various environmental issues. Difficulties arose fairly quickly however. There was an assumption – though not clearly stated – that a whole bunch of groups needed only a bit of help from a skilled organizer to get some serious action going. Indeed, it turned out that the funder had hoped to see lots of media coverage stimulated by militant action. But in actuality, the organizer found most of the organizing that occurred was not nearly ready for militant action. In fact, he discovered a deeper problem: there was no coherent overall strategy to deal with the environmental crisis. The organizer and foundation had to spend a great deal of time reaching an understanding about what kind of work could and should logically be done.

Taboo Issues

Are there any **particular issues** the sponsoring body will not want the organizer to touch? If so:

- What are they? For example, are there any subtle messages that diversity issues should be played down?
- How public is the organization about this?
- To what degree is this stand congruent with the stated mandate of the organization? For example, one would expect that a Roman Catholic funding body would object to pro-abortion involvement. On the other hand, objection to involvement in anti-land development activities would not appear logical, though it might exist for other, less public, political reasons.
- Why does it want these issues avoided? What relationship do these issues have to the organization, to members of its board, or to its funders?

Example: Over the course of the last 40 years, a social planning council in a major Canadian city has often run into trouble with its major funder, the United Way (McGrath, 1998). The latter, dominated by large corporate interests, objected to the council becoming involved with policy advocacy around progressive issues. When the Council becomes too "radical" the United Way has invariably tried, often successfully, to move it back into a less controversial line.

- How does this stand fit with our own value position? This may require some careful thought and self-evaluation. (Remember our discussion of the importance of being self-aware in Chapter 3). It is dangerous to avoid dealing with an uncomfortable fundamental question at this point. Trying to figure things out in the heat of the moment can drive us crazy and/or lead to indecisive and ineffective action.
- Is the stand of the organization negotiable?
- What about our own stand?
- Any other possible reason? Think about it.

Taboo People or Institutions

If contest situations develop, are there special people or institutions which the sponsoring body will demand we or our group not confront (e.g. social agencies with financial or legislative ties to our outfit, or companies who have contributed to the coffers of the sponsoring body)? Alternatively, are there folks who are expected to be kept out of the organizing project?

Example: Many members of a social planning council in Ontario told the people they worked with that the environment needed to be raised as a social issue; that poor people, for example, would be more adversely affected by pollution than middle-class or well-to-do folks. Initially there was good support from the executive director for some initiatives, so they pushed ahead with ideas. Soon, however, the director began to receive calls from board members that this organizing would not sit well with some of the industrial businesses in the city. He let the workers know they would have to be very careful but he was still supportive. They all knew that the plan was going nowhere however when an idea for the organization to name an "Environmentalist of the Year" was shot down by the Board. It was seen as an initiative too high-profile for an organization that depended on corporations for some of its core funding.

- Who are they?
- Why are these people special – positively or negatively – to the funding body?
- Are there organizational interrelationships?

These questions may not always be easy to answer, and we are not suggesting that we need to become investigative reporters. On the other hand, it does make sense to look at the various "boards of directors" (in both the business and the voluntary sectors) and see what overlap exists. Talk to friends in the area, look through relevant documents, and try to get a sense of these "policies."

Time Frame and Funding

Is there a guarantee of funding for the total projected period?

- What time period does the funding cover? Is there a projected time span for the project (which may in fact reflect the funding body's conception of "the organized community" or its ultimate goal? See above).
- Are the funding and the time frame realistic? People often believe that things can be achieved far more quickly than they can. Remember, community is complex and so is community work. It takes time.
- Can this time frame be elongated later—is there a provision for the project to be renewed or extended?

It is worth considering Piven and Cloward's assertion that the majority of citizen organizations will receive continued funding not because they fulfill a primary need for people, but because they have a payoff for the elites (1977, xxi). More recently, del Moral (2005) summarizes the dilemma:

> The reality is that many problems we work to uproot will not be eradicated in the near future. And if you have the resources to create financial stability for your organization, your work will probably be more effective. As any nonprofit employee will attest, a lot of time and effort goes down the money-hunting hole. This is the catch-22 for social justice advocates working within the nonprofit structure. You work to solve the problem at its source, and therefore make your work obsolete. But you also want to be able to stick around long enough to actually do that, so you need to work in a way that promotes longevity, skill building, social networks, and organizational stability, so that the movement grows and people don't burn out. Depending on immediate but precarious sources of money, such as foundation grants available through nonprofit status, does not do this. To what extent do we pursue financial relief now, and to what extent do we work for the long-term goals? Within nonprofit structure, the two aims frequently conflict.

Of course, the needs of one are not always diametrically opposed to the other. Kramer (1970: 223) suggests that it is legitimate for organizational needs and interests to be accorded some recognition. Still, it is an important caution for an organizer to keep in her head when considering continued funding.

Is There a Definite End to the Project?

There are some groups that have successfully planned and campaigned over the years to maintain their funding and thus their existence, eventually to become organizations without a foreseeable end. The problem therein is that a lot of energy and creativity has to go into the fight to keep them alive – energy which might have been better utilized to carry out their mandate. On the other hand, very few projects ever will be funded "for life." Really understanding the ideas about the time frame of the funder at the beginning makes it easier to strategize extending a project's life if it becomes logical and necessary to do so. It is important to remember that community development is a process. The dividends usually do not come early. In the world of commerce, good companies will invest resources over a number of years before expecting a return on their investment. This is one area in which we should follow a "business" model. We need to consider the results of community work more in these terms. If we expect quick results, we may be setting our communities, and ourselves, up for failure. This may lead potential funders to cynicism and negative reaction.

Take some time to think and talk about the time frame in terms of what has to be done. If it appears to be unreasonably short, we should ask ourselves:

- Can it be lengthened? If so, how? If not, why?
- Is the funder expecting quick results? Often it is.
- Does it have any understanding of the process? Often it has only a limited one.
- Is education needed?
- Does this reflect a fad which may fade in a year?
- Is there any way of negotiating a compromise?
- Is there provision for lead time? (See below)

If it can be done, it is a good idea to negotiate sufficient lead time (See Chapter 8: "Contact and Engagement Phase") to "de-cobweb" our own brains; that is, to get rid of any pre-conceived ideas of the target community, and begin to gain an understanding of what it's really like. (The importance of reflecting on our pre-conceived ideas can be appreciated if we remember our discussion of being "outsiders" in the communities we are often working with. See Chapter 6.) Paulo Freire states the case nicely: "One cannot expect positive results from an education or political action program which fails to respect the particular view of the world held by the people. Such a program constitutes cultural invasion, good intentions notwithstanding" (1970: 84).

This does not mean that we must strip ourselves of personal beliefs and values; but rather that the community must be seen through the context of the lives, situations, and consciousness of the citizens we will work with (Alinsky, 1971: 70).

Accountability

Accountability refers to who has the right and power to ask questions, demand answers, and evoke sanctions regarding the quality, effectiveness, and relevance of your service or practice, and the method of delivery.

- How much of the organizer has the funder bought? To whom do they think we are accountable? Or do they really see the money as buying the organizer for the community? Again, it is a matter of values and consistency. If we believe that power relationships need to be altered, it would be a bad precedent to have a project where the organizer's ultimate accountability lies outside of the community she is organizing.

- Ideally, the funding should go through the group to which the organizer will relate. In some cases, however, the community is not sufficiently "together" to be able to apply for and administer funding for the employment of an organizer (at least not at first). A good question to consider would be: "How soon does the sponsoring group see the structure of financing being altered?" Many funding or sponsoring agencies – given a basic bureaucratic distrust of non-hierarchical control and perhaps of people in general – may cast a jaundiced eye on any such funding transfer. For example, it took one community worker, her supervisor, and her community in Toronto over three years to convince her agency that the community organization could be entrusted with the funds to actually hire her itself.

Approximately one year after that, the sky had not only **not** fallen, but the people in the organization began thinking of how they might eventually be able to survive, and do well, without the community worker at all. In another two years, the worker was able to leave a strong viable organization standing on its own.

- In cases where the organizer is being asked to "develop" a role, the issue of accountability transfer (from the funding source to the community) must be thoroughly hashed out, understood, and agreed upon. Obviously the role to be developed cannot, and should not, be completely predicted or predetermined. However, there needs to be a clear sense of what the organizer's parameters are, while at the same time an assurance that not too many options are closed off.

- At times it may make sense to have accountability within the sponsoring institution spread around (or spread among various sponsors). This allows for some protection for the community and the organizer in that no one person can exercise the power of life or death over the project.

Example: A small social planning council in southern Ontario had managed to get funding from three organizations funded by the United Way, as well as from their regional government. When the Region objected to some of its action research in the community, it told the council that this was seen as "perhaps causing confusion" around issues of race in the community. The council had to spend some energy and time to successfully rally the other funders to its position. The Region then backed off from its objections.

The less positive side of this approach is that it increases the number of people we must keep informed. On the level of multi-institutional funding, it can rob the organizer of valuable time that gets siphoned off into fund raising, reports, and other administrative necessities.

Example: A neighbourhood organizing project in Toronto had a number of funders—child welfare agencies, parks and recreation department, a local church group, and the social housing authority. There was often confusion around goals, and how much funding each agency would provide. Though ultimately, the project consolidated its funding, and now feels more secure, the organizer and some of the key activists were forced to spend a number of months and valuable energy working to clarify the overall agenda and strategy to mollify the various concerns of the funders.

Bureaucratic Imperatives

Another issue to be aware of is that often a particular agency will have bureaucratic rules specific to itself. These can be obvious ones, for example a union contract specifies a certain rate of pay for anyone employed by that agency or institution. On the other hand, they may reflect various elements in the organization – departments and/or individuals – attempting to protect specific turf. Thus, a particular part of the organization may attempt to insert duties into a contract that will enhance its standing or increase its access to resources.

Example: A team of social work academics at a university managed to get some funding to a community for a participatory action research project. They worked with a community worker in the area. The university was of course the agency that would administer the funds. A whole series of difficulties arose when the Public Relations department of the university kept demanding that they make PR announcements involving university administrators. The purpose of the project was, on the other hand, to highlight the community leadership. The friction between the academics and the PR department carried on throughout the life of the project taking valuable time and energy.

Evaluation

This is an issue linked strongly to accountability, as well as to concerns of productivity and efficiency (Fraser, 2005). Data gathering and reporting should be planned flexibly so that they can be of use to the community. Evaluation should be built in from the moment a project is conceived. The original objectives should be clear, and accounting and statistical procedures should be in place. More will be said about this in Chapter 12 but it is worth mentioning at this point that the timing of evaluation should be related to the process of organizing.

- Who does the evaluation: is it community self-evaluation; the sponsor; staff; or is it contracted out to someone else?
- To what extent will the funding body, the general community and the community organization be involved:
  - In the data gathering?
  - In the formation of the questions?
  - In the consideration and analysis of data?
  - In sharing in the formation of strategies?
- When will it be done? How often?
- Is the evaluation seen as an integral part of the total community development program? Is it action-oriented? Can the process itself assist the community to identify and clarify objectives? (See above.)
- Is there funding provided specifically for the evaluation (and for the needs that cannot be specifically planned for, e.g. training)?

Reflection

These questions suggest that a lot of work is required during this phase. This can appear daunting but in fact we may already have a good idea about the answers to some or many of them. As well, we may find some issues of greater interest (e.g. having a particularly strong value stance) while others may be less important.

If the pre-contact phase is completed positively, we are in a better position to present ourselves, and our overall task, to the community. This is all that a well accomplished pre-entry can do – it offers no particular expectation for succeeding with the community. It will not keep surprises (good or bad) from occurring. On the other hand, a well-founded contract with the funding body does two important things: limits unexpected behaviours by the sponsors and the organizer, and; provides the organizer, sponsor, and ultimately the people of the community with a foundation and framework within which to discuss the contentious issues that invariably arise in any change process.

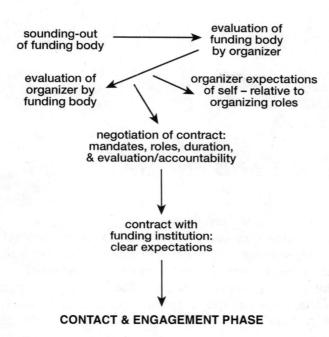

Figure 7-2: Pre-Contact Phase Summary

Chapter 8

CONTACT AND ENGAGEMENT

Intervention that is defensible on ethical grounds must always be paradoxical. One acts for others only to the point of initiating a symbolic gesture of genuine concern and respect. This is the first overture. There is further action if, and only if, the other responds positively. The response is much more than consent as we usually think of consent. After this accepting response a spiral of action, reaction, and interaction can result between the two. In the final act of love, who is to say who [is] the helper and who the helped? The notion of help is finally irrelevant.

- R.A. Sim (1969) in Lotz, 1995

In trying to engage a community, the first thing any potential organizer must do is establish contact – i.e. get to know some of the people in the community who understand it and care about it. There are two fundamental ways in which to do this. First, if the community is already somewhat cohesive – and has some sort of formal or even informal leadership – we can make contact with that leadership. For example, if workers are attempting to organize themselves at their workplace, the organizer might first approach the people who have the most visibility and apparent credibility. If a worker is being hired by a housing co-operative there will already be a Board of Directors running things. Various diverse communities have organizations that provide space for their members or have even developed social services (Lee, et al., 2002). Of course, if a community is already organized in some fashion the worker may be invited in by a leadership group. For example, a housing co-operative may be looking for an organizer to assist the community in dealing with some internal strife and/or increase participation, etc. In these cases many of the same questions raised in Chapter 7 should be addressed such as, the reputation of the groups' members, their particular connections in the community etc.

Second, where the community appears to be less organized (for example, around environmental concerns), or where there is little information – we may be asked to go into an area where there is a high rate of vandalism to see if we can help a teenage population organize and channel itself into constructive change – a good deal of low-key familiarizing may be necessary until credible or relevant people appear. In a geographical community this may take the form of walking around the area, or establishing oneself in places like restaurants, taverns or shopping centres frequented by community members.

Example: A colleague and I were hired by a group of Aboriginal agencies to do some action research with Aboriginal people living on the street. We took some time to talk with some experienced workers in the field and mapped out where they would find people, drop-ins, shelters, and popular street corners. When we went out and started talking to people we had to spend little time looking for people to interview. Also, the fact that we had spoken to some of the community leadership gave us a little bit of credibility when approaching the street folks who could naturally be expected to have a bit of suspicion about white guys asking questions.

Example: Molly Bannerman who works with street sex workers in Toronto found it useful to hang around drop in-centres and places where the women came for a respite. "Sometimes it took a long time before anybody would talk to me but eventually one by one the women started to talk to me and trust me with information."

If there is no geographical centre to the community (like there might be in a social housing development, for example), it may simply be a matter of door-knocking or phoning. This is done until we achieve a sense of the people, and hopefully discover some informal leadership. Then, more formal contact can be made. Nicholas von Hoffman (an Alinsky organizer in Chicago) gives some of the feeling of the contact and entry phase:

I learned more during those weeks than I ever learned in my life. I really think I did. It was day after day of going out and finding out about other people and other things, taking it home, putting it down, thinking about it, trying to make sense out of it. Day after day after day, making the connections and trying to understand people's motives and activities. I cannot think of anything I have ever gone through that was more valuable (Horwitt, 1989: 276).

Third, a worker may need to contact people through existing organizations. This is particularly important in situations where minority and/or marginalized groups are involved. It is often these community-based organizations that provide the major assistance to newcomers for example; in Toronto and Hamilton there are a number of organizations that serve specific groups such as Aboriginal people, refugees, and immigrants. Not only are these groups important in sharing an understanding of community issues, they can also be the conduit for a worker, helping to bring folks together to form a larger mass-based organization (see Chapter 3).

Example: In Toronto, a federally funded project to develop an advocacy organization for immigrant seniors operated through a local women's centre. Its worker first attempted to go around to various recreation centres and churches to make some contacts. This was obviously time consuming and not very effective. Instead she began making appointments with various ethno-cultural groups and developing initial relationships with them. They in turn (after getting a sense of what the project was about) assisted her in connecting with various individuals. In many cases they helped her by arranging meetings where she could greet a number of people. This proved highly successful in two ways. First, as mentioned, she met a number of people, and some became interested in the project. Second, by going through established agencies she was able to gain some credibility and did not have to deal with the suspicion that naturally would have been present otherwise.

However an organizer decides to make contact, there are questions and principles that should be kept in mind.

Introductory Questions

What is the image, if any, of the funding body in the community? Obviously this is not something that we are going to ask directly but it is something to be sensitive to. Often an agency will have a long history of intervention with a particular group. This reputation will influence the initial attitudes of members once they are introduced to the agency-funded organizer.

Example: A CIDA (Canadian International Development Agency) funded, university-sponsored water project in northern Nigeria hired a colleague and me to do a small survey in the target village. We were to get some basic demographics, and attitudes toward the proposed intervention (which was to assist the people in sharing knowledge about the use and storage of water in times of drought). One of the first things we discovered, however, was that there was cynicism and distrust of the project. This stemmed from two dynamics. First, government and university officials had been coming to the village for years promising help with water and electrification. They had asked a lot of questions, had gotten a lot of data for themselves, but had done nothing. None of the workers in the current project had any connection with what had gone on before, but the information that we turned up suggested the need to slow down the project and spend some time gaining trust in the village.

What is the image, if any, of community workers? Have there been bad, or good, experiences in the past that will influence community attitude? Some disadvantaged communities, for example, have been so "used" by researchers and student social workers (counsellors and organizers) that any outsider coming in has to live down a great deal. On the other hand, a bad intervention image can be used by people who want to resist change, or who wish to guard their own advantaged position. It is tough for an organizer (and ultimately the organization with which he's connected) to always have to fight a rearguard action against a negative image not of his making.

Example: A co-op housing project was having difficulty in getting itself organized. Members were particularly concerned with a lack of participation. Unfortunately, one of the high-profile members had a bad experience with a very new community worker some years previously in another co-op. Thus, he was extremely suspicious of the community worker who was hired to assist the co-op. The fact that he wished to maintain his own power on the Board of Directors was also a factor – he didn't relish people participating in ways that would make him more accountable to the residents. For some time he was able to frustrate the work of the organizer by linking her activity with the legitimate concerns about the person he had known several years earlier.

Are there aspects of the community that require particular attention? Are there particular experiences or attitudes in the community which we should be prepared to deal with? Some communities (because of the experience of their members, or attitudes related to ethnic tensions) have particular issues that a community practitioner will have to be cautious of, and which will frame what she does as she seeks to make contact.

Example: A worker was beginning her work in a large nonprofit housing project in Mississauga, Ontario. The Board of Directors of this building had sent a flyer to all tenants introducing her, and indicating that she would be knocking on doors to introduce herself personally. The great majority of the tenants had come from Croatia in the former Yugoslavia and their first language was not English. Fortunately the worker had a chance to examine the flyer before it was sent. Being somewhat familiar with eastern European languages, she checked it over and found it was written in a Serbian dialect. The flyer would have been a terrible beginning for her, as some Serbs and Croats had imported their disputes to Canada. Since this approach would have made people quite distrustful, she got a Croat friend to translate the flyer into the appropriate dialect. Matters were even more complicated, – she was of Ukrainian descent and she had a name that looked like it might be Serbian. Again this would have caused initial distrust. She solved this problem by making it a point to speak some Ukrainian (who naturally talked to their neighbours about the new Ukrainian-Canadian community worker) to people as she did her door knocking.

Principles to Guide Engagement

Ordinarily, this work is difficult because it involves engaging people who may feel quite alienated by formal politics, have internalized responsibility for the injustices they suffer and/or react with hostility towards others who foster hope for ... change.

- Heather Fraser

The organizer, from the moment of first visibility, is modeling his future behaviour to the community. As Speeter (1978: 21) says "You as an organizer will be looked upon as model communicator, co-worker, and risk-taker, whether you want that or not." Winning trust is very important here. The organizer must be prepared to immediately demonstrate personal qualities and skills of confidence, tact, empathy, ability to listen, and accountability. The principle of **beginning where the people are** is crucial (Alinsky, 1971). Their value system must be quickly learned, and respected, so that we can dialogue with them (Freire, 2000).

We should be prepared to understand (and so should the agency or funder) that engagement takes time. The folks with whom organizers work have often been marginalized and hurt by society's negative attitudes and even discriminatory treatment. The whole community can often be seen to have sustained an injury, one that is social in its dynamic (Alexander, 2004; Burstow, 2003). This does not make for a trusting and open population, particularly with outsiders.

Molly Bannerman, the worker with street sex workers who was mentioned above, notes how careful she had to be in making contact:

> I think it took about three months to connect with this one woman. Every week I'd show up at the centre and she'd see me. After about three months, one day she said 'Hi'. The next time she saw me she said 'Hi Molly.' And the next time she asked to talk and a flood of stories came out. It took time but it was worth it.

From my own practice working with Aboriginal groups, I can identify with Molly's strategy of taking her time and letting folks make their own decision on whether or not it's worth their while to invest in some sort of relationship.

Contacts should be broad. This is not necessarily easy. When we first make contact with the community we may find that we are dealing with a narrow range of people. Usually, the people privileged by their race, gender, ability or education levels are the ones who have the higher profiles. However, try not to stay with an "elite." Find out who has power and credibility, and who can mobilize others, and who does not, and why. There has been more than one organizer who became attached to an initially attractive, or noisy, group only to find out later that the members were narrowly representative. Also, when a citizens' group is seeking funds for a project, or confronting a bureaucrat or politician, the question will invariably be asked: "Just whom do you represent? How broad is your support?" Speeter (1978: 33) offers the following list for types of people to look for:

- those interested in positive community change
- those who will work to get others involved (door knock, phone calls, etc.)
- youth leaders
- senior leaders
- leaders of local groups or organizations
- people who can speak in front of large groups

We would add:

- leadership among women or members of any groups of diverse people
- not only existing leadership, but individuals who indicate potential in the community
- those with good listening skills
- those interested in learning
- those who can work cooperatively with others
- social networks. One way to approach this is to develop an informal map of the social networks that we become aware of. To do this it is easy to simply keep track of names that keep popping up in conversation. Who are the folks that are often mentioned; in what context? Who seems to be connected to whom and are there folks that seem to be spoken of as being important in some way – are they leaders, folks whose opinion is valued, those who seem to be "doing things"

for others, etc? Take a look at how these names are clustered. These are social networks (Freeman, 2006) and gaining a beginning understanding of them will provide a sense of how the community is informally structured.

A few other things to look for when contacting and engaging:

- potential for economic benefits – unused or underutilized resources
- issues that people are likely to coalesce around (either positive or negative)
- functioning groups or organizations (formal or informal)
- things and processes that show ability – though people may not always be aware of that ability
- signs of hope – little things that people have accomplished themselves
- human resources – skills and energy, or connections to power outside the community
- economic/philanthropic – business/entrepreneurship, etc.
- people working to help each other

All of this should be done carefully, however. It is important to remember that simply because something works well in one setting does not mean that it will work well in others. While we must always be prepared to be sensitive to local conditions, it is particularly important in this beginning phase.

Example: A worker was hired by a teachers' union to do some organizing with parents concerned about education issues in the county of Peel in Ontario. The first meeting he organized with these groups went extremely well – the participants were able to identify concerns, issues (in this case, concerns about the quality of resources in local schools) and tasks. They immediately started work, and began suggesting other areas where meetings should be organized. Unfortunately, the next couple of meetings were not as successful. People came out but showed a lot of hesitancy in getting to specific issues, and reluctance to getting involved in action. After some reflection, the worker realized that the success of the first meeting was linked to specific local conditions. Many of the parents had known each other from various community and school events. One of the teachers involved had actually known the organizer from a project he had been involved in several years earlier. Here there was a bed-rock of familiarity and trust.

In the other groups, these conditions did not exist; the people were new to each other and to the organizer. It was not that parents were less concerned – indeed, there were good turnouts – but the pace of getting people involved had to be slower so they had time to get a sense of each other and the organizer. The organizer needed to attend to initial, local conditions.

Motivations for Involvement

Before we leave the topic of people becoming involved in community endeavours, one more issue needs to be addressed: the motivation of wishing to become involved. There are a number of reasons for someone wishing to become involved in a community project. We are going to look at four important ones. This isn't to suggest that the organizer should see herself as the "gatekeeper" of who becomes involved, but it is important to have a sense of what is motivating people and how this might affect the way the process may play out.

Those Drawn to the Idea of Action. Some folks are drawn to a community project because they like the idea of being active. For the most part, this is a great quality. Folks like this are likely already aware of the need for action on particular situations and thus prepared to work hard. The bad news comes if someone is interested in action only for action's sake; if they are hoping for a bit of excitement or simply want to distract themselves from other personal issues. If they are not tying action to a clear goal and specific objectives they may have problems in working within the discipline of a collective enterprise. This isn't an easy issue to spot but we can look for a sense that they appear to be more excited in the idea of "going to battle" than being able to articulate a sense of what they hope to see come out of the action.

Those Drawn to an Issue. Obviously our work in the stage of organizing is to find folks who can articulate the issues they care about and which will benefit the community. Again, this is a strong motivator, particularly if they are able to identify their own self-interest. As Rabbi Hillel famously asked, *"If I am not for myself, who will be for me?"* We also hope however that people will be able to see that there is not simply one issue for a marginalized community to take on; as the Rabbi also said, *"When I am for myself alone, what am I?"* So we are looking for folks who are interested in hearing about what others in the community think and need. A person who is committed exclusively to his own position or interest may bail out if it does not appear to be the number one thing that a community as a collective needs to organize around.

Example: Activist Marnie Cuff tells of how this kind of issue can affect a campaign. "We were fighting a serious environmental issue in our local (agricultural) community which involved the powerful energy company Hydro One. This kind of thing is always going to bring in people with somewhat a mix of views on whether this was a local issue or a grander social justice/global issue (in fact it is both but one member kept trying to make it a particularly a global environmental battle for our group rather than focusing on the local issues). The local issues we are addressing were of course social justice/global environmental issues. But she spent more time trying to contact people like Al Gore and David Suzuki than addressing the tasks at hand, which was fighting the immediate threat of uncompensated land expropriation and pollution. It impacted whether/how some in the group viewed our wins/losses as well as draining energy in fruitless discussion.

Those Looking to Connect with Others. This is a perfectly legitimate reason for folks to become involved in community organizing. One of the objectives of community practice, as pointed out earlier, is the reduction of alienation. Individuals with this kind of motivation will often be eager to undertake outreach and will be prepared to come to meetings and involve themselves in the work groups that are so necessary as part of community organizing. If it turns out to be the only interest however, it can be a problem for the project. People have to be able to work beyond friendship; we cannot always work with only people whose company we enjoy. They may object to working with folks that don't want to be friends. Also, a person who is getting friendship needs met only in the organization can become a kind of "poor soul" who other members begin to resent as they require too much social energy. The organizer may find that he is spending an awful lot of time helping the person with relationships rather than getting on with the project.

Those Looking for Personal Growth. Community organizing projects are excellent places for citizens to learn and develop knowledge and skills. Again, social learning is a key component of community practice. There is potential to learn communication and research skills for example. There are opportunities for coming to a more sophisticated understanding of political and social issues as well. So this is a great motivation and eager learners are the life blood of an organization. It is unfortunate however when some folks simply see the opportunities within a community organization to hone skills and then utilize them for their own private purposes. The example below of this dynamic is rather an extreme one.

Example: A young woman with very good basic skills became involved in a complex community project in Hamilton. It involved, among other things challenging the local housing organization as well as the regional welfare office. She had the opportunity to gain a lot of experience and expertise in both areas. After about eight months however, we found out that she had applied to the region as a welfare officer and utilized her experience to gain the job. There was a sense of betrayal and it was terribly frustrating a year or so later for organization members attending meetings with the welfare department to find her sitting on the other side of the table.

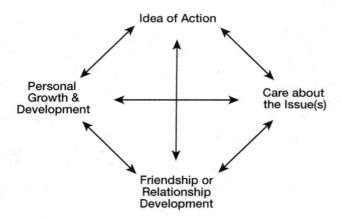

Figure 8-1: Why People Become Involved in Community Action

To be fair, the concerns raised above tend to reflect exceptions and certainly not the rule. The point is that recruiting people to work in community projects has to be taken seriously. As much as possible, we need to work on assuring ourselves we are being as rigorous as possible; that we have been reaching out to sufficient numbers and varieties of people; and that we have listened carefully as they discuss the issues and their interests. Once the organizer feels he has contact with reasonably representative and credible people, the interest of the funding institution (in providing a community organizer) can and must be shared publicly. Sometimes, however, funders or sponsors are not aware of the complexity of community work. This does not mean that the organizer has been secretive about this up until now; nor does it mean that he must now call a meeting, or make some sort of public announcement. He may simply start making it more clear to people "why" he is there," what" the mandate is from the sponsor, and "how" people can begin to get together.

Example: A worker was hired by a women's centre to do some organizing around the needs of immigrant seniors (predominantly women). The centre had gotten a sense, through its drop-in and settlement services, that elderly folks were feeling quite isolated and lonely. The response of the administration was to develop an undertaking that would be aimed at linking people with resources – such as, public health and recreation. It was thought that this would be a fairly simple project. The worker, however, quickly found that she was confronted by a complex grouping of eight cultural communities. Initially it was thought that she would go in and ask some nice clear questions about needs and resources. What she found was that she would need to take time to get a sense of the cultural mores, where people lived, how the various groups received information, and what relationships existed among the groups. She had to do some education with the centre's director.

Reflection

Entering and beginning to connect meaningfully with people is a crucial element in the organizing process. It can also be one of the most confusing times in the project; the organizer doesn't usually know many of the people, and the community may be quite diverse and dispersed.

Things may seem (and probably are) quite complex. This is a bad news/ good news situation. Most of us like a little control in our work, but this is a very fluid time, with new people and perspectives coming at us all the time. The good news is that we are capable of recognizing this, and of reflecting on the fact that it is not we who are causing the complexity. We have no responsibility for knowing it all, let alone understanding it – this is the beginning of analysis. There is strength in seeing ourselves as being at the beginning of a journey, one in which we will learn, and in which we shall become more deeply involved. At this point we are looking for people who wish to travel with us, and for things that will assist us along the road.

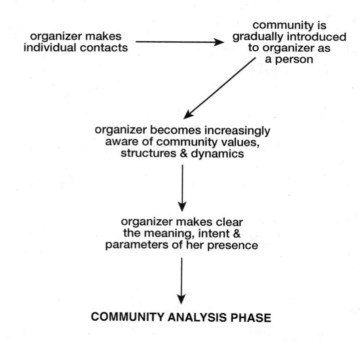

CONTACT & ENGAGEMENT PHASE SUMMARY

organizer makes
individual contacts

community is
gradually introduced
to organizer as
a person

organizer becomes increasingly
aware of community values,
structures & dynamics

organizer makes clear
the meaning, intent &
parameters of her presence

COMMUNITY ANALYSIS PHASE

Figure 8-2: Contact & Engagement Phase Summary

Chapter 9

COMMUNITY RESEARCH AND ANALYSIS

Critical investigation helps people to look at social problems in the light of what they wish to achieve as self-reliant and self-determining social beings.

- Susan McGrath (Teacher and Activist)

We talked earlier in the book about understanding community as something that is dynamic, fluid and, organic. Meaning, it is complex (has parts that are interrelated), and is in flux (the parts are moving). It is important as an organizer begins acting in the community, that she attend to this notion of dynamic organism. It is important that community members understand this as well. Remember that social learning is a key objective of community development. Freire (2000: 71) says that it is crucial that the people "come to see the world not as a static reality, but as reality in process, in transformation." An important role for the organizer, at this stage, is facilitator of learning.

In some respects, community analysis is a continuation of the contact and engagement phase. The organizer is becoming more visible, not as a leader, but as someone who cares about the people and the issues, and who appears confident that the citizens can work together and produce something of good quality. Members in turn are forming clearer conceptions of her. The important difference is that previously, while the organizer was getting information primarily for her own use, this phase involves information gathering and analysis for the community's self-development[1]. While in the entry phase, the organizer was the primary investigator. In the community analysis phase, community people must begin to question – and gain an understanding of – their own community. The objective of community sense comes into play here; they must begin to get a sense of themselves as a distinct group with particular problems and strengths (Speeter, 1978). While there are standard types of information that need to be gathered, questions generated **within and by the members** will also be very important.

At this point we can make some assumptions:

- the organizer has spent some time "in" the community
- she has some notions about the values and the people
- she has made a firm link with a group of people, probably small, and her presence is known by a reasonably wide range of community members
- the small core group may be formal or informal, but the members have some credibility, and can likely wield some clout within the community
- if the community already has a leadership structure in place, the worker has a sense of others with leadership potential
- she is beginning to have some conception of the problems faced by the community
- she has some awareness of the diverse interest or reference groups in the community
- she has taken the opportunity to "test" some of her conceptions or assumptions with community people

Example: Judith Dunlop, community practitioner and academic tells the story of working with two assisted-housing communities that on the surface seemed to be very similar. Each had concerns about the prevalence of gang activity and drugs disrupting the lives of the residents. In the first instance Judith and her team found that people

---

[1] There are a number of good books and monographs on research for people's organizations: *Community Research as Empowerment* by Ristock and Penell (1996); *Participatory Action Research* by Fals-Borda and Rahman (1994); *Research for Change* by J. Barnesley and D. Ellis (1992). Another is Australian activist Yoland Wadsworth's *Do It Yourself Social Research (1984)*.

wished to have much improved lighting in the neighborhood and the removal or cutting back of various shrubberies. This would significantly cut down the opportunities for illegal and dangerous activity. They received help getting in touch with the municipal utility company and were able to get the work completed, and indeed the illegal activity was curtailed. Subsequently she was involved with the second community with similar problems. There was a not unreasonable assumption that they would wish the same strategy. When the folks were contacted and had an opportunity to indicate their sense of what needed to change in their community their ideas were quite different. They actually wanted a well-thought out plan of "greening up" the area. It turned out that their concerns were influenced by their surroundings. They were situated in a highly suburban residential area and a plan of bushes, grass and trees would help their housing fit in and reduce stigma. A very different city department (Parks and Recreation) had to be engaged to implement this community strategy which was accomplished in sequential steps. The importance of checking out "where the people are" was strongly affirmed here, as well as the importance of paying attention to community "uniqueness" even though neighbourhoods may be close together in the same urban setting.

At this point it is tempting to launch directly into action to solve some obvious and serious problem. Be careful! There are some major pitfalls to this approach. For example, the base of support or action is small and needs to be broadened. Action (even on a most important issue) without consensus and a broad base of support tends to be short lived, frustrating, and leads to burnout. It can be divisive as well.

Example: A new worker in an inner-city neighbourhood knew that an obvious problem there was high unemployment. When he was approached by a small group of people to help them organize a local economic development project it seemed to make sense. Difficulties quickly arose however, when some other groups in the area raised questions as to whether the project would primarily benefit just that particular group, but not help anyone else. As the issue became more public, serious opposition arose, and community divisions (already existing) became worse. It wasn't that the original idea was a bad one – it had simply moved too quickly. The project never got off the ground, and the worker had to spend a lot of time mending fences.

There may well be other issues that are seen as more important, or at least linked to the ones that first appear. There is not likely any community consensus at this point. **Action without a community consensus leads to division and failure.**

It is necessary to create a strategy (remember the difference between strategy and tactics indicated in Chapter 3) to avoid these pitfalls. The strategy must include:

- the development of **clear problem definitions** meaning the what? where? when? who? how? and why? must become clearly understood so that appropriate strategies and tactics can be developed (Stinson, 1979);
- the development of a solid **community consensus** around those problem definitions;
- the development an understanding within the community of itself—a **community image** which will include strengths as well as problems and deficits (McKnight, 1995); and,
- the development of an **organizational base** from which to deal with the problems. This involves the development of:
  - *Participation* - committed, animated people prepared to work on specific concerns
  - *Leadership* - confident, sensitive people with vision prepared to work and involve others
  - *Coherence* - focused and relevant analysis plus effective use of human resources

Community-based Participatory Action Research

A Health Canada document provides a general orientation to this kind of research:

> Members of the community play an integral role in the research process, by determining what research is relevant and ensuring the results will have a useful, practical impact. In addition, community involvement

in the research process will help increase participation rates among hard-to-reach populations and ensure the research is sensitive to ethical concerns such as confidentiality, voluntary participation, and consent (Health Canada, 2002).

There are a variety of ways, however, to approach the objectives noted above. What we are going to talk about here is the mounting of a community research project. All varieties of community research are complex and demanding (Lee, 2008). This kind of strategy will be a complex, comprehensive and lengthy process; it can take eight months to a year to complete. It is nevertheless one that, if well-thought out and implemented, can pay large dividends. The kind of research suggested here is linked to a variety of structural traditions; the main ones being feminist and participatory action research. Reinharz (1992, p.175) describes feminist research as being inherently linked to action. The purpose of feminist research must be to create new relationships, better laws, and improved institutions.

Participatory action research focuses on the following principles: "...the people studied make decisions about the study format and data analysis...the research ...adopts an approach of openness, reciprocity, mutual disclosure, and shared risk" (Reinharz 1992, p.181). So essentially we are talking about a kind of research that is political, and geared toward popular control and social transformation.

Among other things there are two key ingredients invariably missing from communities which have experienced marginalization/oppression: information and analysis. Solid information is an important underpinning for a community to analyze itself and its situation. Information which people can share is necessary to enable them to see their commonalities, and to become involved in a process of consensus, action and change. Analysis is a process of reflection, during which time members talk to one another in a manner that enables them to learn about their situation and themselves, and to appreciate their own understanding and analysis of their experience (See Figure 9-1: Action/ Reflection Spiral).

To facilitate community involvement (remember the citizen involvement objective), a participatory action-research methodology can be really a powerful tool. People, particularly those who have been marginalized, often have a deep-seated distrust of any kind of research

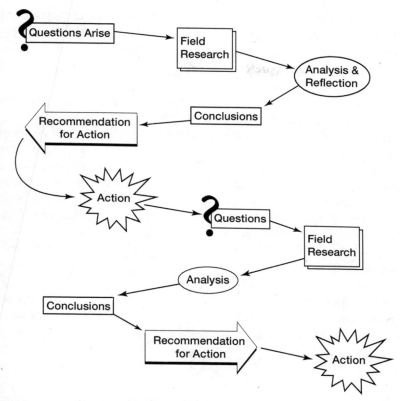

Figure 9-1: Action/Reflection Spiral

Adapted from *Do it Yourself Social Research* (1984) by Yoland Wadsworth, Victorian Council of Social Services, Melbourne: Allen & Unwin

and/or of getting together with others. This is legitimate, in that it is often a reflection of their experience. Folks may say: "Why bother? Nobody really cares anyway; it won't work, we tried it before; or, this will only benefit those in power or some academic!" In working with Aboriginal communities I have often been challenged with examples of planners or academics or government bureaucrats who have come in, collected a bunch of information and departed with no value being produced for the community. It is an issue that needs to be understood and managed.

Participatory action research is a process that needs to be experienced if people are to develop confidence in themselves, or faith in the procedure. Part of the process is learning about, and understanding, their community history; and how such a history may affect how people see themselves and their environment. This means that the people of the community should be deeply involved, not only in giving information and hearing about results, but also in developing the questions to be asked, and in doing much of the questioning themselves. They must be in charge. Action research has another important aspect which is: **a question should stimulate a question**. This **analytical process** should, in effect, never end. Through it, the community begins to know and feel itself, to develop a sense of community, and to engage in some social learning. It may be that there is little or no community identity feeling prior to this process. Often this is true. Ideally, the people raise their consciousness of themselves as a collective, and begin to specify objectives in relation to a particular situation or problem.

As well as being useful for a community that is developing its self-concept and raising important issues, participatory action research can help highlight the people with leadership potential – persons who show particular interest, creativity, or charisma with respect to the issues that arise. Finally, an action-research effort can help to de-mystify research and assist members in developing their own research skills.

An Open-Ended Process

It is important to remember that this whole analytical process will likely continue for some time, somewhat loose and unstructured. It can lead, in the short run, to blind alleys. It can also drive us crazy if we expect results quickly. Hang in there, and try to move with the grain of the community as it raises and drops, and raises its issues at its pace; as new people become involved and as leadership develops and broadens.

Example: The action group "Single Mothers Against Poverty" in Hamilton, used the organizing assistance of students, and a faculty member of McMaster University School of Social Work to do an action-research project. This group of individual single mothers on Family Benefits Assistance grew from a nucleus of five people to over twenty members. They were able to produce two research reports dealing with the experience of single parenthood and poverty. For over five years the organization was a significant player on the Hamilton scene. It was instrumental in affecting changes in local welfare administration concerning single mothers. The initial organizing strategy was that of Participatory Action Research, which helped them identify issues, and helped motivate these single mothers to take action.

Participatory Action Research[2]

We create knowledge so that we can better understand the meaning of our own experience and identity, and the complexity of the society in which we live. It is a process of understanding who we are, and determining how we want to be. Knowledge should help us to understand our current experience and to develop alternative ways of living that respond to the issues identified.

                                    - Susan McGrath (Teacher and Activist)

Step I

A group of representative community members (people whom the organizer and trusted community members perceive as having potential to work together, and provide broad leadership) are invited to meet to discuss things they think they know about their community and want confirmed, as well as questions they want answered about their community. In a community that is relatively cohesive and structured, the worker may have to ask the formal leaders to invite the people. This provides legitimacy for the endeavour, though there may be a problem of the group being less representative than we would like. This issue would have to be raised as the idea is presented to the community leaders. At this point, the group has at best an unclear and diffuse concept of what the important issues are, and how they are generally viewed. They may have some ideas, but little precise data to either back up or contradict their thoughts or ideas. There will likely be a good deal of disagreement, or contradiction, or at least a

---

[2]   The model suggested here was first used in housing co-operatives by Mike Balkwill and in anti-poverty work with women by Sharon MacQueen. Mike has subsequently utilized it with homeless folks in Kingston, Ontario and I have used it working with the Indian Friendship Centre in Toronto. It is a comprehensive model aimed at developing a good deal of information, and at building a strong, organized, and informed citizens group. Circumstances may dictate an alternative or scaled-down approach. That's ok. However, keep in mind that this is first and foremost a community and organization building tool. As long as we are clear on the implications of what we do, the benefits will turn out to be largely what we expected.

wide range of ideas about the community. (This is true even within an established group.) This situation is not a weakness, but is actually a strength (Freire: 2000).

During this stage the organizer must assist the group to use this diversity of concept to get all the possible aspects of the community. In fact the community worker will want to model a stance of acceptance of diversity. The first task of this step, then, is to help the group to brainstorm around what elements make up the community – physical, social, psychological, political, etc.

An approach which can be very useful here is the use of popular education approaches. Some organizers have done some interesting and very useful work using popular education techniques, drawings, maps, cartoons, etc. (Hope & Timmel, 1984; Barndt & Freire, 1989; Lee & Balkwill, 1996) and it is one that I have found very productive in a wide range of community projects. It allows for more intuitive, less structured conversations, and draws on the innate creative ability of folks in group process. As well it can be very helpful where we need to be attentive to those people for whom English is not their first language, or where the culture of the people privileges oral and pectoral communication.

Step II

The second task is to construct some sort of survey instrument or process out of the brainstorming that will enable the group to begin querying the community. The organizer will want to make sure that particular standard areas and methods are covered. A non-exclusive list of important areas is offered, but first it is important to remember that different groups have different ways of understanding, valuing, and sharing knowledge. The format for collecting information from members should be sensitive to specific community ways and needs. Several workers have shared stories of how questionnaires had sometimes proven to be an inappropriate means of gathering information in some groups. In particular, these workers referred to their work with homeless people, and with Aboriginal folks. In both situations it was found that knowledge was shared as "stories," not as responses to specific questions. And while many of these stories may have initially appeared to be irrelevant, or not directly connected to the issues being addressed, careful listening and discussion reveals them to be dense with information – especially those issues of importance to community members.

Instrumental Issues

Economic
* Income range of the population
* Occupation inventory and the number of members involved in each type. Among other things, information of this type might highlight particular skills existing in the community.

Demographic
* Age ranges
* Family size and make-up (e.g., the number of single-parent families or the number of female-led families, etc.)
* Gender ratio
* Range of people with disabilities and their types

Education
* Levels
* Types: technical, professional, on-the-job training and workshops, life experience, and traditional (from Elders)

Geographic
* Where members live: social classes, age groups, racial groups, ethnic groups, or disabled people
* Important geographical features
* The physical placement of important institutions or services (e.g., churches, daycare centres, businesses and shopping). It can be fun and instructive to have people draw a large organizational map of all the institutions that impact in/on the community (Lee & Balkwill, 1996). The exercise can get people talking about how they feel about the organizations. This information is just as valuable as the locations and sizes of agencies.

Resources
* What kind and range of economic resources exist to serve the community? For example, in many neighbourhoods where there is a predominance of poor folks or rent-geared-to-income housing, people find themselves without banking services.

- What kind and range of social and health services are available? By available we mean things like appropriateness (culture, for example) and accessible (not simply for people with disabilities but for other sectors like single mothers or seniors).
- What kinds of schools are available to the community members? This also involves issues of access and appropriateness of curricula.

Affective Issues

Strengths and/or Assets
- What kind of strengths do folks see in their community?
  - Leadership?
  - Sense of community?
  - Resources?
  - Allies?
- Is there a sense that they see these strengths as contributing to their taking on the problems that have been identified?

Emotional Tenor
- How is the community or various parts of the community feeling? Are there feelings of:
  - Contentment?
  - Anger?
  - Hope or despair? (This will in part depend on the extent to which people have a positive vision of themselves.)
  - Apathy? (i.e., a sense that things can be done but the effort isn't worth it? Again this might be linked to vision.)
  - Energy for action?
- Are there different segments or constituencies within the community that appear to have differing emotional tenors?

Vision or Visions for the Future
- What are the ideas (hopes and dreams) of what the community should look like in the future or how it should operate? Do they tend do be in the area of resources or are they more focused on community relationships or issues of citizenship and social justice?
- Is there a reasonable amount of consensus, or are there competing visions that will need to be negotiated?

Religion or Spirituality
- Formal
- Informal
- What are the relationships, positive or negative, among groups?

Culture Issues
- Tensions between or among cultural groups that make up a community
- Fears or concerns around participation by a particular group
- Opportunities for members of cultural minorities to provide learning for other community members

Structural Issues

Power Structure
- What constitutes power – money, information, numbers and status – within this community, particularly in relation to attacking possible community difficulties? Can a force-field analysis exercise be useful here?
- Splits and alignments. Who lines up with whom, or against whom, on what specific issues? The construction and use of a sociogram or force-field analysis can be useful (Lee and Balkwill, 1996). As with organizational mapping, a good conversation and a sense of feeling will likely emerge here.

Problem Definitions
- How do people see the problems?
- Do they see any as interrelated? For example, "There is a lot of apathy around here [first problem] because a few people run everything [second problem]." To what extent do they feel personally affected by the problems? How deep or sophisticated are the analyses? Are they connecting local or specific problems to structural issues, like unemployment or some form of discrimination?

Other Considerations
The way these questions are asked, the amount of stress placed on the various areas, and the language used must be that of the community. Watch out for technical terms – e.g. validity and reliability – which we may (or may not) understand well, but which may not be familiar to the people. Also, some subcultures have particular ways of

expressing themselves—everything from slang to the use of stories and concrete examples. This must be considered as the instrument is constructed. Remember there are two objectives to building such a survey: first, to come up with an instrument that will provide clear and honest responses; second, to begin to involve people in their own process of analyzing: i.e., in "understanding" their own community. It is crucial then to make the survey-building process public (Warren, 1977) and invitational. This can be done by getting the core group to:

- Ask members at large to suggest questions. People on the survey committee should approach friends and acquaintances and invite them to think about giving them questions they would like to see added.
- Check out various aspects of their developing survey instrument and process with others in the community (i.e. the language, timing, etc.)
- Invite people who become interested by the questioning activity to join the core group.
- Invite people to volunteer for short periods of time to do small tasks that they might be interested in doing, like delivering and picking up questionnaires.

What you are attempting to facilitate is not only a generalized knowledge and involvement, but the creation among all community members of a real stake in having the process come off as successfully as possible (Warren, 1977). This survey instrument, which is to be an accurate and valuable document for the community, must in every sense belong to it, and not just to the original survey committee.

It is one thing to develop a questionnaire or interview schedule. It is another thing to have it completed successfully; that is, have a high degree of returns and have good information to analyze.

We are probably going to be asking personal information or at least information that people perceive as personal. It is important that the group, from the very first moment, stresses that all responses are completely confidential. As well, groups of people who are disadvantaged are often justly suspicious of people who ask them to fill in forms or ask them questions. Thus, it is worthwhile to take some pains not only to treat the information with great care, but to **show** that you do so as well. Intra-community trust is one of the things your group and you as an organizer are trying to facilitate, so everything that relates to that dynamic is important.

Step III

An interim report will have to be made to the community in some way – a couple of "fact sheets" may be all that is necessary. As well, a community meeting should be organized to present the report (more on meetings in the next chapter). The completion of the survey, and the analysis and sharing of the results will provide the community with a much clearer image of itself. Some old ideas will have been confirmed, others will have been shown to be untrue or exaggerated, and finally, information about the community that no one expected to find will have been invariably uncovered. Most important, however, is that the image that develops at this point will be commonly held and based on facts. This allows the members to talk about their community, using the same information.

Questionnaire or Interview Schedule

1. A questionnaire can be sent out or delivered to community members. There is minimal or no personal contact. In a questionnaire we are not attempting to get a great deal of, or very sophisticated information.

2. On the other hand, with an interview schedule we are getting people to sit down with each other, probably because the information desired is a little complex and participants may need some help or encouragement in giving all the information required.

3. Some general rules to use when trying to decide which is best for our group are as follows:

- The larger the population we need to question, the more likely we will have to use a questionnaire because of the difficulty of meeting everyone.

- The more complex the information that we want, the more likely we will want to use an interview format. This will allow the volunteers to help people interpret the questions and encourage them to be complete in their answers.

- Obviously, with an interview schedule we are going to have to have a large number of volunteers to contact and to sit down with people. These volunteers will have to be trained - either by the organizer or by other members of the survey team - in how the questions are to be asked and how to answer any questions that participants may have.

- Be sure that we are clear on what kind of instrument we are constructing – interview schedule or questionnaire. Depending on the people involved and the kind of information that we are trying to get, you will want to do one or the other. In one Native community, a group of people developed a very interesting interview schedule. They hoped that, in the process of the person-to-person contact, some community building could go on. Unfortunately, their system of training interviewers was not very rigorous, and many of the people who volunteered lacked confidence. They simply handed out the interview schedules to people and asked them to fill them out, like a questionnaire. Not surprisingly, much of the information gathered was superficial or not very clear. The exercise had been designed as an interactive one, and failed as a simple questionnaire.

Step IV

The fourth step is, ideally, a second round of questioning. As presented here, it is in the form of an individual questionnaire. It is possible to combine the interim report meeting and the questioning session. In this case we would want to use a small group format and choose and train facilitators. The advantage of this is that the process is quicker. The disadvantage is that we may not get to nearly as many people.

As we have discussed before, a community is a living thing and is in constant motion. The first survey is probably going to miss things; some information that was turned up may be confusing to the members; or some things may have changed. Thus, a second round of questioning can be very useful. This does not mean that, if some extremely clear issues have emerged in the first round, no action should be planned.[3]

---

[3]   In some ways this step can belong to the chapter on Popular Action because it is very much action-oriented. It is presented here, however, for reasons of simplicity and coherence.

In fact, these are the very issues that should form a major focus for the second round of questioning.

Another aspect of this step is that it should be more personal or immediate than the first one. There should be more interaction between those seeking the information, and those giving it. Thus an interview, as opposed to a questionnaire format, should be used. This can be done partly because we are now working on the highlights raised by the first round, and there will be a much shorter schedule of questions. This more personal approach is necessitated by the fact that:

- We are going after more subtle types of information now—feelings, detailed opinion and attitudes, etc.

- We want to make the process absolutely as open as possible. It is important to try to capture every nuance; not only do we need answers to questions, but a sense of how people felt about the questions and answers.

- Organizing is a human endeavour. Making this an interview format stresses the human, face-to-face nature of what we are doing.

- We are really trying to flesh out concrete action targets now, trying to instill a sense of immediacy (even crisis if there is one) so that people will be motivated to get involved to take action. This step cannot be executed at long range. Only people interacting with each other can achieve this.

The process of constructing the interview guide, popular education exercise, or whatever kind of process the group decides upon, is identical to that used to come up with the first survey. It will obviously take less time the second time around, though just as much effort.

Note: Be prepared. The people may want to construct another questionnaire or interview guide. They've just come through a successful experience with questionnaires or interviews. They feel that they have become good at it. It is natural for all of us to want to do the things that we are good at; nevertheless, they must be helped to further develop their abilities, and to get on with taking action on, and using, the knowledge they have developed.

The actual format might look something like this:

1. A limited number of statements (no more than six) are made based on data from the first survey. The respondents have all seen the "interim report" so that statements aren't new. (For example X per cent of people feel that there is a big problem with the absentee landlord; or Y per cent of the population are children between six and 10 years of age).

2. The interviewer elicits opinions and feelings about the statements. For example:
    *   Is the respondent surprised by them? Why or why not?
    *   Is she happy or angry? Why or why not?

3. If the respondent appears really interested in one or more of the issues, the interviewer asks her if she would be interested in:
    *   Receiving more information?
    *   Finding out how other members feel about the issue?
    *   Coming to a meeting with other members, if one were to take place?

Note: Remember our strategy objectives from page 155.
1. Problem definition
2. Consensus
3. Realistic community image
4. Building a community organization
    *   Participation
    *   Leadership

This part of the strategy is focused on getting things off the ground and on the way to achieving solutions to those identified problems. Thus, the people recruited to do the interviewing are taking on a special responsibility, and will probably need some group meetings to provide them with:

1. Training - from the organizer and/or each other (remember to be open to the strengths the community possesses);

2. Group Support - from each other. This can be an issue for groups that have experienced long-term injury (remember our discussion of the possible effects of oppression in Section One. The ability of community members to trust each other may have been damaged. This may be reflected in a generally low community confidence.

3. Encouragement - from the organizer may therefore be a very important component in this phase of things.

All three aspects are necessary because most people are not used to doing this kind of thing, and need to have some reassurance. In effect, what we are hoping for is that the citizens of the community will begin to organize themselves. They are going to need help from their organizer, but the community should really be in control.

Step V

The point of all this activity is to assist the community to get a solid sense of the issues which its members feel they should, and can, work on. Thus, it is important to disseminate analysis throughout the community. This can be done by compiling a final report and getting it out either through a series of meetings, or mailings, or drop offs. Even people who were not involved in the other processes might find themselves interested if they can identify with any of the issues and recommendations for action in our report.

Reflection

Example: A small, inner-city neighbourhood association had been dormant for some time, and the community had been experiencing a number of problems: vandalism, booze cans, poor city services to the area, etc. Five local women along with a volunteer organizer had been trying to get people together for about a year, without much success. Finally they did a small action research project. They talked to people about what they were finding, and were able to identify some key issues for residents and some ideas around strategy. They finally called a meeting to check the interest. To their delight they got a large turnout of local residents who responded strongly to the range of issues, and the strategies that had been identified to the small group of activists.

This example shows that people need some leadership, and clearly focused information that is relevant to their experience before they come to feel that they want to get involved in a community change process. The community-analysis phase is a crucial step in the development of community capacity.

We are addressing the issue of knowledge creation, or social learning. Also, in the identification and involvement of new leaders, and the identification of action targets, "organization development" is being addressed.

Learning is one of the central objectives undertaken with a popular education approach. It contributes to other objectives, such as sense of community and participation. Indeed social learning should become a habit, and the action/reflection process can contribute to the long-term development of the community.

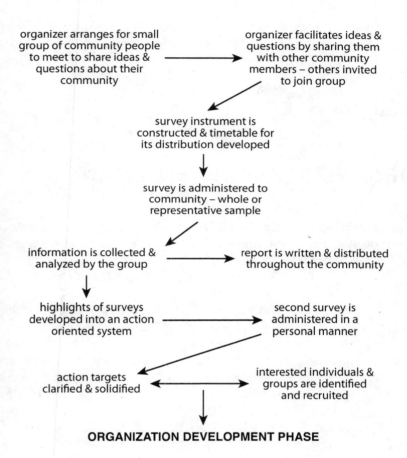

organizer arranges for small group of community people to meet to share ideas & questions about their community

organizer facilitates ideas & questions by sharing them with other community members – others invited to join group

survey instrument is constructed & timetable for its distribution developed

survey is administered to community – whole or representative sample

information is collected & analyzed by the group

report is written & distributed throughout the community

highlights of surveys developed into an action oriented system

second survey is administered in a personal manner

action targets clarified & solidified

interested individuals & groups are identified and recruited

ORGANIZATION DEVELOPMENT PHASE

Figure 9-2: Community Analysis Phase Summary

Chapter 10

ORGANIZATION DEVELOPMENT

Our success with social change depends on our ability to implement our visions within our own organizations, even as we work toward them in the outside world.
- Duane Dale and Nancy Mitiguy (1978)

The title "Organization Development" is used because it is in this part of the process that specific issues begin to appear publicly as targets for action. As noted previously, group power can only come into play if we are organized, that is, if we have structures and processes to marshal community resources over time. The major organizing effort must now go into building structures and strategies that can tackle the targets. Activity should become less diffuse and more concentrated on particular issues and associated tasks. Also, the project should be quite well on the way to being the "community's project" as opposed to the "X Agency Community Project." This means that if leaders were not visible when the organizer began, they should be emerging sufficiently to take on major initiative and organizational responsibility. If leadership was in place prior to entry, it should now look broader and increasingly more skillful and thus the organization should be "more developed."

The creation of an organization is important because it is the centre of action; often the first thing that a community does as a collective enterprise. It is thus an important concrete expression of the hope that people can develop the power to change their lives (Ganz, 2005).

The Importance of Communication

As Gandhi said so many years ago, communication is fundamental for the building of community/peoples' organizations. It is crucial that organizers be in a position to assist the citizens who involve themselves in organizing to identify issues they face, the resources they possess, and the resources they need. Communication is the key. There are many aspects of communication that we will discuss, from meetings to newsletters, to outreach, to internet use.

Meetings

Action-oriented people like activists often find it hard to think about meetings as important elements in community organizing. The fact is however, that meetings are important for many reasons. Meetings are where plans are laid, discussion is held and ideas exchanged. It is important that the community reinforce the habit of consulting itself regarding its objectives and the strategies for reaching them – this is part of "citizenship." It also builds an organization that can tackle serious problems affecting its members. It is essential that this organization be an open, democratic people's organization (Alinsky, 1970). Meetings are a major tactic for informing, involving and mobilizing citizens.

After an action-research process, the problems have become reasonably well perceived and understood by a majority of members. The community is now ready for a variety of meetings: general community, task groups, committees, etc.

First meetings are particularly important to get things well off the ground. Particularly at the beginning of an organization's life, some "pre-meeting" meetings may have to be held. These should include the formal leaders and other key actors; and might focus on important individual positions, internal disagreements, building confidence and enthusiasm; and agreeing on general, but flexible, directions for the first general meeting.

This first meeting is a model of how well the people can do something together. It is not necessary (or possible) to have all the answers right away. It is necessary for the leadership to be prepared to lead the people in the direction they see as most likely to provide answers. At the same time, leaders must be prepared to:

- listen to the membership;
- offer what suggestions they have;
- accept criticism and the shaping of their suggestions or the building of new ones.

This is no place for an ego trip (especially the organizer's), though it is reasonable and important to feel good for any job well done, and to be recognized for it.

It is very important that the people leave the meeting knowing that something is going to be done, and that specific members have volunteered to take on the tasks. This sets some reasonable expectations, and suggests that this organization is for action, not just talk. This is an early period and people are new to this, so the organizer must be prepared to help this along.

Example: An organizer in a downtown Toronto neighbourhood was present as the group was just coming to the end of its first meeting. The two women co-chairs had done a great job of setting the agenda, encouraging constructive discussion, and helping people identify some important issues. There was a good feeling in the room. At this point however, he noticed that both the women began to look a little distressed and seemed a *bit lost*. He also noticed that no committees had been struck to take on the issues. So he raised his hand for permission to speak. He suggested the meeting strike about five committees to cover the issues and take some initial action. Almost immediately people started volunteering, and a little later the meeting ended on an upbeat note. During a "post meeting" meeting with the co-chairs, the two women thanked him for his timely intervention; they had gotten temporarily lost in all the information that had come out. They then reflected on all the good things they and the members had accomplished that evening.

1. Major Objectives of a First Meeting

a) To present a clear picture of the problems as analyzed up to this moment.

b) To take a general issue and turn it into a specific action target.

c) To serve notice to the community and others that some members of the community are prepared to work to solve a particular configuration of problems and issues.

d) To begin recruitment of workers for the problem-solving efforts.
e) To offer tentative or beginning strategies – not a grand design – for people working together on the common effort.
f) To mobilize volunteer efforts.

2. Raising Issues

a) Any issue that is chosen early in this phase should be clearly "do-able" or winnable. Remember, a community that needs a community organizer may not have a great deal of confidence. A quick loss could destroy the credibility of the leadership and the organizer; and the organizing effort could be set back.
b) It should be possible to link sub-issues to the major one: e.g., "Not only is there a drug problem in our neighbourhood but the police are slow to react to a call from residents. Have you noticed that we seem to get inferior municipal services here?"
c) The leaders, or most of them, should be associated with the issue (i.e., have a stake in the problem).

3. Post-Meetings: Debriefing Each Other

Equally as important as a "pre-meeting" is a "post-meeting." The meeting has hopefully produced some desirable results: clarified issues; increased and broadened participation; outlined objectives; and set priorities. Now it's important to have those involved (including new activists who have emerged at the meeting) take a look at what has gone on. Alinsky suggests that an organizer must assist the citizens in learning through their experiences. This is a crucial technique that the organizer must always use; the processing of every major event not only helps people to learn for future action, but it can often bring out creative strategy for immediate use.

What is the organizer's stance during these three events: pre-, during, and post-meeting?

a) She must be analytical, never presuming to have all the answers, and always open to ideas. A model for the people.
b) She must constantly believe (and live out that belief) that the people will come to the right decisions, perhaps not right away – or maybe not without conflict or assistance – but eventually.

4. Ensuring the Best Possible Attendance

It is common to hear experienced, hard-working volunteer members complaining about apathy demonstrated by other members of their community (McAuley, 2007). Poor attendance at meetings is one of the major concerns and frustrations one hears about in community organizing. Factually this is true. It is indeed a real problem which often gets in the way of community problem-solving. However, when considering this problem, it is important to keep in mind some other facts such as:

a) Community members are also family members. This can have particular relevance to women. We need to be mindful of how the well-known double workday can become a triple workday with volunteer responsibilities.

b) They are also workers, outside and inside the home – and it is often women who are working a "double shift" (McGrath, George, Lee, Moffatt, 1999). People have conflicting demands on their time. For all but the most dedicated, community responsibilities are going to rank number three on any three item list. This does not mean that it is hopeless to expect people to come to meetings. It is a matter of appreciating the fact of competing and sometimes unpredictable demands in an individual's personal and work life. It means helping the leadership do a little organizing in the light of those demands.

Note: Unorganized or disorganized communities are not generally used to meetings (Speeter, 1978). The structure and formality may be new for many people, somewhat outside of their experience. Therefore, try to make sure that the social needs as well as the business needs of the community group are attended to, e.g. perhaps coffee, and donuts or small-talk time. Also, different cultural groups conduct meetings in various ways. We need to be sensitive to differences and be prepared to learn from them as well as manage them. Further, some communities, Aboriginal folks and others for example, tend to expect to share food with each other at meetings; it's part of the action.

c) Give people as much notice as possible. This is especially important for first or irregular meetings.

d) Go to, and advertise where, people live or play or hang out. This is particularly important for ensuring and encouraging turn out among diverse groups. Some may not venture outside of their comfort zone areas (or indeed may be discouraged from doing so).

Example: In attempting to ensure good turn-outs for a project focusing on diverse and marginalized youth, organizers made sure to get out to schools, of course, but also to malls, recreation centres and churches in the area. They even went around to the parking lots of some of the bigger housing projects and found youth hanging out. They were able to engage them more easily on "turf "where the young people felt more at home and in control.

e) Put it in writing. Leaflets and posters are helpful. Sometimes a local community newspaper will do inexpensive advertisements. Remember that communities are made up of sub-groups (often folks representing diversity). Have the range of languages covered.

Example: A Hamilton organizer was working in a project with three major language groups: Filipino, Vietnamese and English. He had to make sure to get quality translations for all leaflets and handouts.

Example: The Ethno Seniors Advocacy project in Toronto had over six ethno-cultural groups represented. This meant that not only did the funding have to take into consideration the need for translators, but that the organizer had to be aware of differing cultural taboos and practices. The meetings were always well attended, thanks to the organizer's stance of being a respectful learner.

f) In this context it is very useful to begin a newsletter as soon as possible. The regular delivery (door-to-door or through email lists) is an excellent way to keep people informed about events, concerns or developments and generally let them know that the folks in the organization who have taken leadership positions are keeping the lines of communication open. They don't have to be fancy, although attention should be paid to a neat and appealing appearance.

Example: The War Resisters organization in Toronto was set up to support the young people fleeing the United States Army because of the illegal war on Iraq. It does many things: finds emergency and long-term housing, enlists legal help, organizes lobbying campaigns to alter the discriminatory behaviour of the Canadian federal government, holds information meetings, and stages demonstrations against the war. They are great at keeping the members of the organization apprised of developments on each case, as well as overall developments. For all intents and purposes, they have a sophisticated E-newsletter strategy that maintains the strength and cohesion of the organization.

Lots of organizations, by enlisting volunteer labour, create web pages which in some ways can mirror the notion of a newsletter. Encourage people to visit the page regularly to keep up to date on what is going on.

Of course it's crucial that the page be maintained regularly so that no old information is left around to confuse folks.

g) Remind them. Remember, paper is never enough. A visit, phone call and/or leaflet blitz within twenty-four hours of the event is a good idea. Develop telephone or trees. The community worker may be part of this, but of course should not do it all.

h) It may be important for the organizer and leadership to do some visiting, encouraging individuals to talk up the issue and the event, letting people know how important it is. Individuals may need to know in a direct, personal way that their involvement will be valued (McAuley, 2007). There are other payoffs in doing this activity:

- It provides a firmer idea of who is, and who is not, coming;
- It lessens the likelihood of the leadership experiencing last-minute disappointment;
- It provides a sense of how the issue or issues are shaping up.

5. Preparation for Meetings

Meetings are rarely simply for information sharing. Almost always there is some kind of decision to be made. Thus, the participants in the meeting need to have sufficient information so they can make realistic decisions.

a) *Information: What kind?* Start with ourselves and put us into a participant's shoes. With that perspective, value our own judgement and encourage the groups we are working with to do the same. Chances are if we want to know something, others will too.

b) *Information: Where is it or who has it?* In effect, information may be everywhere (remember, it is an important power element.) The problem is that it has not been brought together. That is one of the reasons we're building an organization and having the meeting: to bring people and information together and to engage in a decision-making process so that some problem can be solved.

When we are thinking of where to obtain information, be creative. Information is not only facts – it is perspective, attitude, opinion; even rumour is sometimes important, either to confirm or deny it. Thus we have to look everywhere, in and outside the community. For example, if we are working with a number of tenants to organize a meeting to do something about a neglectful landlord, a broad array of information will be helpful:

- relevant legislation and regulations which can be found at municipal or provincial offices;
- the normal scale of rents in the neighbourhood are region;
- the experiences of the tenants with the landlord;
- experiences that other communities have had with other landlords;
- tenants' experiences with each other.

Example: The Hamilton worker mentioned two pages earlier found that there was little contact, but lots of negative stereotyping and distrust among the three language/culture groups in his project. This had serious implications for how meetings could be organized and how he approached each group.

Example: The Toronto worker mentioned earlier spent a good deal of her initial time encouraging and allowing time for the people involved to learn about each other and their various cultural practices. There was some negative stereotyping to overcome, but for the most part the group members needed time to develop ways of communicating and learning about each other and the way each saw the issues. This was particularly helpful and resulted in a very solid "group culture" of mutual respect and solidarity.

It is rather like doing the community survey again. Ideally, everyone needs to be contacted; only, the issue is much more focused and imminent. Try to make a point of contacting people in person (community organizing involves a lot of leg work.) Continuous and exclusive use of "paper talk" (such as flyers and posters) can eventually be "off-putting." Knock on doors or at least phone. Tell them why you want their data or opinion or experience – people sometimes tend to downgrade the importance of their own ideas because they are not clearly formed. Sometimes they need time and encouragement.

Even if a person does not have much to say now, she will likely appreciate being asked, and this can pay dividends.

- **It may spark or rekindle interest in the issue. Thus, people may make it a priority to get to the meeting.**
- **When another issue comes up that "grabs" them, they may then see the group as interested and caring and bring their concern to the organizer.**

Finally, *what do we do with information?* It is one thing to get data; it is another thing to make the best use of it. Sometimes it is sufficient to have information ready for use at a meeting. At other times it is important to get some clear and concise written material out to participants prior to the meeting. (Again, language may be an issue.)

Getting information out beforehand has a number of payoffs:

- **It increases familiarity with the issues and thus the meetings can get into "high gear" sooner**
- **It may clarify or increase the participants' sense of purpose**
- **It may give some participants a chance to think over, alter, or clarify their position**
- **It gives participants a chance to spot and question incorrect data prior to the meeting**

- It gives people a chance to lose it or forget it; so be sure to have extra copies if possible

Note: To avoid information overload, help the group to be as clear and concise as possible.

6. People Preparation

As we said before, at the beginning of an organization's life the participants may be unfamiliar with formal meetings, and may need some assistance in getting ready for them.

- Be sure people have a clear perception of why it is that they are getting together.
- Be sure the group has arranged for a discussion leader or chairperson. This person should be identified prior to the meeting. The person may need to get psyched up (or calmed down) or she might want to seek you out for support.

Example: The Single Mothers Against Poverty group in Hamilton used a rotating "chair" as they began. The members were very inexperienced, and the organizer used to spend a couple of hours with each person before each meeting. It didn't totally alleviate anxiety, but it was reduced when the women felt that they had some "training" and were not completely on their own.

It is also important to be aware that differing cultural groups will have different ways of typically structuring meetings. Some may be very happy with informal gatherings while others need some or a lot of formality. Some may value a hierarchical form while others value ways of meeting that emphasize equality. The organizer must be aware of her orientations and be prepared to solicit ideas from the people with whom she is working.

Example: In working with an Aboriginal community in New Brunswick, I found that wherever possible it was important to have participants sit in a circle. As well it was really useful that whenever we had a large meeting to make sure that we allocated time for people to meet in smaller "circle groups." Lots of the people felt uneasy speaking up in a larger assembly. We would then have the groups report on the discussion or raise "group" questions. It was also important to have food present. (This seems to be a pattern I have found while working with most groups of whatever culture).

7. Note or Minute Taking

There will likely be a need for a secretary – someone to record what happens and what decisions are made. (Watch out for inadvertent sex-role stereotyping here.) In any event, if the person has little experience it is wise to assist him with the following:

Pre-Meeting Responsibilities
• Be familiar with the agenda
• Be familiar with the notes /minutes for the last meeting and any confusions that may exist
• Be clear about how much to record. You don't need word-for-word notes. Focus on:
  - Decisions
  - Significant information on a topic
  - Major disagreements
  - Any "new" or important information

Responsibilities During the Meeting
• Listen carefully
• Be mindful of the needs of those whose mother tongue is not English
• Get the important stuff such as:
  - Decisions
  - Major disagreements
  - Any "new" or important information

Remember that in cases where folks are from diverse groups or backgrounds, notes may need to be translated. Have that resource (hopefully a volunteer) available.

Note: One of the attributes a group is looking for here is assertiveness. The person chosen to do the recording must be able to say to the meeting "Can I have that again?" "Can you say that a bit more clearly?"

Example: Note-taking is important. A student organizer, in a housing co-op, recruited a woman to take the minutes of a meeting. He didn't check with her beforehand as to whether she had any experience in recording minutes (it's not an easy job.) When the woman circulated the minutes prior to the next meeting they were pretty well unintelligible. The worker had to approach her and help her do some new ones in a hurry. Naturally, her feelings were hurt and other committee members were irritated at being represented so poorly. The worker had to do a good deal of work to get things straight and smooth ruffled feathers. He realized that if he had talked to and assisted the woman in the first place, he would have saved a lot of work and fuss.

It is important that meetings don't get dominated by a small group. For example, we know that *generally* women have been socialized to be less assertive than men (Gallagher, 1977); that people with higher education tend to be more vocal than those with less (Repo, 1977); and that some immigrant groups will have difficulty with English. If our group is going to be truly democratic it is going to have to break through these obstacles and facilitate broader involvement.

- **Get to the more timid folks and let them know their ideas and opinions are important.**
- **Remind the leadership that some members need patience and perhaps help in clarifying their presentations.**
- **Suggest to the more articulate and vociferous participants (diplomatically of course) that they restrain their own participation somewhat so that the more timid voices can be heard. This can also be important if we have folks whose first language is not English.**
- **A special caucus might be organized to give groups, like women or immigrants, a chance to share and think things through before a more general meeting.**

Example: The Hamilton organizer mentioned above had to organize three meetings for the three different groups to get at some of the stereotyping and distrust. These small meetings were useful in helping people articulate issues that were specific to them. For example, one of the groups tended to focus on cars and vandalism as issues in the community, while another group had practically no drivers among them and was more concerned about personal safety issues. Eventually the two issues had to be understood as part of the same dynamic.

Note: One way of structuring a positive environment in a group where there are tensions is to suggest that the group develop its own "Safety Rules" (Lee & Balkwill, 1996). Here members develop a list of rules for their own conduct at meetings such as: "no laughing at naive questions" or "no shouting down a person with whom you don't agree." Different groups will have different lists depending on their own experience. It is empowering to have influence over the process you are going to have to use.

8. Site Preparation: Instrumental Considerations

The real job of an organizer is first, to get to the hall early, make sure the doors are open, the lights turned on, the coffee ready and that there are enough chairs for everyone. The second thing is to stay behind and make sure the room is cleaned up, the chairs are put away, the lights are turned out and the doors are locked.
- Worker for the Company of Young Canadians

There is great wisdom in the above observation. People who involve themselves in community enterprises are coming from jobs at home or in business or trades etc. and thus need to use their energy to focus on the issues. Doing some simple instrumental stuff for them can be really helpful. In getting and setting up a meeting place there are some important things to be aware of:

- How many people are expected? A big room with a whole bunch of chairs can be a downer if the meeting draws few people. Alternatively, a too small place can be frustrating. Particularly if it is a fairly long agenda, we may lose people if they have to stand.

- Is it easy to get to? As well, does everyone know where it is? A place that requires navigation through dark streets might discourage women from attending. Is it accessible for people with disabilities?

- How is the room for ventilation? We don't want participants nodding off from lack of oxygen.

- Is the lighting sufficient? This is important if people are going to be doing any reading or writing.

- Is there sufficient room to break into small discussion groups if required?

- Does it have meaning to the people to be involved, i.e., will the participants feel comfortable and welcome? Sometimes a school or church will appear to have an ideal meeting room but may have a poor reputation among the people thus making them reticent to attend.

- Do we have the equipment needed: flip chart paper or newsprint, marking pens, a black board and chalk, a sound system?

- Can the space be set up to adequately reflect the needs of diverse group? For example if translators are needed, is there room for them?

9. Agenda Preparation

- Items should include: the issues that are going to be covered; and who is going to report on actions between meetings; also the agenda should include (under "New Business") issues that have come up since the last meeting.

- People: Make sure everyone who is going to make a report is aware and ready.

- Have an idea how long the meeting is going to be and how long each item is going to take, even though you cannot be sure. This helps people determine how long they can expect to be there and to plan accordingly.

- If possible get the agenda points out to people; if you have a good email list of those involved this task is simple. If you have to, use regular mail or get volunteers to hand deliver it.

- If there are diverse group participants whose first language is not English make sure that the agenda is available in their language.

10. Post-Meeting Responsibilities

Manage the debriefing for those involved in planning, an executive or committee members, etc.

- How did things go? If well then make sure pats on the back are given.
- Any surprises?
- Could things have gone better, why and how?

Start planning for the next meeting.

Elections

Sooner or later the group with which you are working is going to have to structure itself into some sort of formal democratic organization. Thus, in the great majority of cases, elections are required. This can be a tricky business for a number of reasons:

1. The most well-known people may not necessarily be the best folks to have in positions of formal leadership responsibility. They may be popular, but may not have the personal or organizational skills necessary for a new people's organization.

2. There may be people around who have a good deal of experience – in unions or housing co-ops for instance – but that experience may not have been very positive. Remember our discussion of the lack of availability of democratic models. The experienced person may indeed bring a very top-down, elitist view of a community organization or participation.

Example: An environmental group in southern Ontario was in deep trouble – its finances were in terrible shape; there was very little participation; and a vicious battle was being waged between two factions. The recently elected executive sought the services of a community organizer to try to sort things out. In the course of talking with people it became clear that a lot of the difficulty went back about 3 years to the first elected president. He had been very experienced in the movement, but had used this to dominate and browbeat members. He was secretive, effectively fostered conflicts, and discouraged participation. When he left a new group took over – one of the factions –who modeled their behaviour on his actions. They had some important unlearning to do.

3. Elections can begin a process of subtly splitting the community into in-group and out-group, winners and losers. This can be particularly difficult where there are racial or ethnic differences. Think of the pain and disruption that some feminist organizations have had to go through because they had not attended to issues of women of color. Thus, the process of who "runs" and how the election is handled is crucial. It is important to assist the silent majority (or minority) to be heard and any dominant types to listen.

4. Elections can suggest to people that the elected folks – the board, the executive – are now the ones that will do all the work and make all decisions. This, of course, can ruin any ethic of participation. As we have seen, genuine participation is a crucial objective of community development. On the other hand, if handled well, elections can begin, or rejuvenate, a democratic and empowering process. Then, if issues are clear, people have a good opportunity to express their views, and positive consensus can be forged; election of leaders will be framed in a positive way.

Organizing Priorities

Within this phase, priorities will become important and perhaps problematic – particularly as money is scarce, and issues emerge as complex and interrelated. Often citizens have to be assisted in organizing their priorities. We need to be clear that when we assist people to develop a needed program in the community, we are not necessarily doing "community development." Community programming can contribute to the development of community but it is not the same thing. Program development involves creation of a concrete benefit that the community needs, but to focus on it exclusively would be to miss the point of developing the community. Thus, a question that we should always be aware of is: "How does this fit with other efforts that are taking place to build a stronger people?"

McKnight (1995) makes the point that the development of programs in communities has sometimes undercut other aspects of community life, such as spontaneous support of one another. Therefore, we need to ask questions such as the following:

- Are we developing leadership as we create and manage the program?
- Does the organization of the program fit the culture of the community?
- Does the community feel ownership of the program?
- Is it the most necessary program, or are there others that are more in need of scarce energy and resources?

It is important that priorities be related to purposes or objectives (Dale, 1978). There are also other considerations:

1. It may be that there is an easy objective which will give people confidence to go on to more difficult ones. This may involve something very possible, what Alinky calls a "cinch victory" over a particular adversary or difficulty (like reaching a membership quota or gaining a meeting with an important bureaucrat or elected official).

2. On the other hand, the situation may dictate the choice of a difficult objective: for example, some funding may have to be sought for training before any other part of the program can be instituted. This type of objective should be avoided at first if at all possible, in that it can be a long, technical process which may be "iffy," has few immediate payoffs, and will involve few people.

3. Sometimes a number of goals or objectives are so interrelated that it is either easier, or even mandatory, to go after a number of them at once. Advantages of various courses of action can and should be pointed out, but not in such a way or at such a pace that the community people feel left behind or stupid. If the people in the community can do the analysis themselves with only small assistance from the organizer, the exercise can be even more productive (i.e., the members are developing their

own skills, confidence and sense of responsibility for their actions.) Popular education techniques, like Root Cause Analysis or Dotmocracy, can be useful in identifying and ranking priorities (Lee & Balkwill, 1996).

Analyzing Objectives

1. Each objective should be outlined in terms of the necessary strategies and tactics, and the likely resources (first in general and later in particular) needed to carry on a successful program.

2. As well, any objective must be examined in terms of other objectives: how do they influence each other? This will, in large part, determine whether some objectives can be combined in relation to strategy, or whether they have to be separated and addressed one by one.

3. Committees must be set up to investigate and plan the number of resources necessary for the attainment of particular objectives. This again will foster the development of analytical skills, allow for more participation, and as folks get experience in participating in and chairing committees, a proliferation of leadership roles – all of these lie at the heart of effective organizing.

Maintaining the Organization

I am against the reification of organizations. They are not things. They are people.
- Matthew Clark (Toronto Disarmament Network)

1. When must we keep people together?

- When large numbers are needed.
- When the organization needs a wide representation. (Remember the question that is almost always asked by the media and opposition, "Who do you represent?").
- When we want to make sure that the various voices (diversity again) are represented.

Example: In the Toronto MYLIFE (Malvern Youth Leadership, Inclusion, Facilitation and Enabling) project, a great deal of effort was put into making sure that all the ethno-cultural groups in Malvern were represented, and were quite proud of our efforts. At a large public meeting that was held about mid-way through the first phase however, we were confronted by a group of Lesbian and Gay youth who pointed out how this group had been totally, if unintentionally ignored. Fortunately it was not too late. The Gay and Lesbian youth at the meeting who had confronted us assisted in the recruitment of a number of folks. As well they provided consultation about how to meet their needs for safety, which is unfortunately a major concern.

- When key people are needed:
  - because they possess particular skills;
  - because they have credibility within the community;
  - because they represent a diverse perspective; and/or,
  - because of the credibility they have within the opposing group or institution or with media.

2. When can the organization afford to lose people?

- When some are trouble makers:
  - those who are working at cross purposes to the majority;
  - those who are rumour mongers and major gossipers;
  - those who are too impatient and cannot accept the necessary discipline of working collectively; or
  - someone who is on an "ego trip."
- To polarize a situation by serving notice that certain positions or classes, as represented by particular individuals, are not welcome. (Often these are found among the list above). Alinsky (1971) claims that polarization is of major importance in mobilizing people for action.
- For efficiency: when there are too many people for the tasks at hand.

3. How to keep groups going?

- Keep in mind that "ups and downs" in energy and relevance of issues are normal; don't panic during the downs, but be sure to attend to them. Don't get euphoric during the ups. Keep working at the basics as well as taking advantage of opportunities.

- Keep the key leaders identified and fuelled through the ups and downs.
- Keep an up-to-date list of names of members. Besides leaders there are, at least, three levels of membership. (See Figure 10-1: Range of Member Commitment).
  - *Mailing list types* - people who are generally not involved, but who would like to be kept informed. (We might be able to mobilize them later.)
  - *Active members* - people who will come out to meetings, deliver flyers on occasion, will sign petitions, etc.
  - *The committed members* - people who will have meetings at their houses, donate money, participate in fund raising, sit on committees, etc.

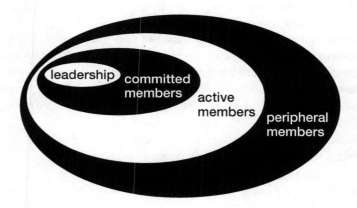

Figure 10-1: Range of Member Commitment

- Provide workshops, leadership, tactics and communication training, for example.
- Assist members to be always on the lookout for issues that can become the focus for group action – issues that have emotional appeal or are real and imminent, for example.

Example: An organizer, in talking about an energetic campaign being waged by the Parents of Peel organization, pointed out that members had been concerned about a number of issues but that none really seemed to be galvanizing support. "Things had been pretty quiet for a while. We were working on things but not with any great energy. Suddenly, we happened on the issue of mold in portable classrooms the mold seemed to be causing some real health problems. This galvanized a lot of interest. We didn't know it was there at first; we were just looking at various issues and this one – the health of the kids – hit a public nerve; and not just with parents, but with environmentalists and teachers too. Sometimes you just have to keep poking at various issues.

- Avoid the trap of being a narrow, one-issue organization; that may solve one problem but does little to mobilize people for the development of power in order to influence their environment in the long run.
- Make sure meetings are productive and as much fun as possible. Head off "busy work" where old issues are picked over.
- Keep trying for small victories or achievements, and keep the members informed.
- Ensure that enthusiastic leaders are not taking on too much for their strength or abilities, or pushing volunteers too hard. Watch for "burnout," for example, a suddenly developed short temper; habitual complaints about members; defeatist attitude: "yes we can try that, but I don't think it has much of a chance"; forgotten appointments, etc. (Cruikshank, 1989).
- Help the leadership maintain openness to citizens: flexibility.
- Have a fun event like a party or dance.

Planning

Planning is the process of developing structures, programs and actions for the attainment of a particular objective or objectives, through the development and the allocation of scarce resources: e.g., people, money.

The people who are to carry out the plan must be involved to the maximum. (Remember the participation objective.) The better a plan is understood, the better it will be implemented. The more someone has participated in the planning of something, the more that person will want to see it implemented, and have a stake in its success.

At this point, the expertise of the organizer is still of importance, but she has to stress clearly that it is the members' plan and thus up to them to carry out. It is their concrete interests that are involved here. It can be a tricky business, attempting to impart important consultation or direction while at the same time staying "behind the scenes," not taking from the people the responsibility of the planning task (Speeter, 1978). The victory – or what the American organizer, Heather Booth, calls "the struggle" – must be with and by the people (1974: 4).

Most of the planning will be done in committees, which are the most important vehicle for participation, and brought back to the larger "official group" for examination, criticism and ratification.

If elections are necessary (in a standing committee, for example), they can be frequent; even every six to eight months is not totally out of the question at the beginning of work, or if there has been a fair turnover in membership. This gives a number of people the opportunity to be involved, and to try out leadership roles.

Sessions should not occur too far apart, or be held sporadically. It is crucial to maintain enthusiasm and a sense of coherence and purpose through what can be a long, drawn-out, exacting process.

Training

More often than not, training is going to be necessary at more than one point in the group's life. It may be necessary to learn, for example:

- better communication in small groups
- intercultural training that may be useful for groups with a range of diverse populations
- program planning which might include priority or problem-solving skills, some models of planning, or approaches to problem solving, and budgeting
- decision-making styles that are often crucial in assisting the organization to achieve and maintain a democratic stance. It looks so much easier on the surface to have one or a few persons make decisions (remember our pyramidal models). Some reflection and some practice may be necessary in order to see the value of consensus and democratic styles of decision making. It might be a good idea, in this instance, to try a rotating chair model.

While keeping in mind that phases are rarely discrete, whatever is necessary should occur between planning and implementation phases of any particular strategy. The organizer usually has some training skills, but if she does not, some attempts should be made to bring in some-one. This will often require money. Training is a critical aspect of com-munity organizing. Since it may cost money it is often down-played or sometimes ignored. A well-planned strategy can easily fail if the people who are to carry it off are insufficiently grounded in the basics of what they have to do.

Example: The Affordable Housing Action Association was build-ing a tenant's organizing campaign in Mississauga, Ontario. They brought in George Lakey (the well-known U.S. trainer and writer) to lead a workshop on Direct Action strategies. Not only did he impart new knowledge, but his ability to connect the local struggle to some of his experiences with other groups provided the AHAA people with inspiration and energy. Training can provide more to a group than information.[1]

Funding

An organization may decide that it needs money for some particular program or task. Ideally it is preferable for a group of people to accom-plish what they can with volunteer labour because:

1. If some folks are getting paid while others are not, envy and dissen-sion can result; the organization might lose some people or waste energy on personal infighting.

Example: What had been a very effective anti-poverty group, after about a year and a half, obtained sufficient funding to hire a couple of the members as staff. The salary was to last only a year and was set at minimum wage. Nevertheless, one of the key members, who had applied unsuccessfully for one of the positions, became jealous. She used her position on the board to make life miserable for the two women who were now working for the organization. Eventually her

---

[1] For more on building and maintaining people's organizations see Lakey et al. (1995), *Grassroots and Non-profit Leadership;* and/or Gastil (1993) *Democracy in Small Groups.* Lee and Balkwill's (1996) *Participatory Planning for Action* offers a number of popular education exercises that are very useful in identifying action targets and planning strategy.

behaviour became so dysfunctional that other board members had to ask her to resign.

2. Voluntarism (the practice of relying on voluntary action rather than compulsion) will clearly provide the sense that the group has struggled for something and won.

3. There is always the danger that a "culture of funding" may result; meaning, that only through funded programs can things get done. Further, the search for funding may come to monopolize the activity and energy of the organization, i.e., the organization's life may come to be the primary goal rather than the issue(s) it was set up to deal with (Pivan and Cloward, 1978: xxii.)

Now, having made our case against the search for funding, it is clear that often it is crucial; training has been mentioned, essential travel may demand money, an office with telephones, computers, printers, fax machines, and other concurrent administrative costs may have to be established. And realistically, people are putting a good deal of their time into the organization and it may good sense to recognize that contribution by getting some funding to have them remunerated. Indeed, for some diverse communities, it is helpful to have some of their numbers be salaried. It suggests how much their efforts are valued. As well, it may provide some folks with some valuable "Canadian" experience which can be useful in obtaining employment in the future.

When going after funding it can be helpful to:

1. Indicate the amount of volunteer time the organization has, particularly in reference to the task for which dollars are being sought. Some funders require proof that we are already doing things – e.g., settlement integration of immigrant – before they will offer funding. Thus, we will need to have some form of record-keeping structure/process to justify need. They will want to see that we had people volunteering in the area. It is a good leverage on a potential funder. Also, this can give people a psychological lift when they see how much, and how important, their time has been.

2. Make a point of being clear on the priorities of the potential funders. It is demoralizing for people to spend a lot of time filling out the required forms, only to be told that our organization or request doesn't fall within the criteria. Often we can get annual reports or outlines that will be helpful.

3. Be careful not to tailor the request only to the funder's criteria. It is dangerous to set objectives which someone from outside of the community sees as important. On the other hand, we may be able to frame the language of a proposal that will sound good to a funder and maintain the objectives of the group's project. Be creative.

4. Ensure that our group understands funding process and forms. Incomplete information annoys funders. Often this is the only con- nection bureaucrats will have with an organization, so be attentive.

5. Ensure that the funding criteria are absolutely clear. Get, or give, a letter outlining your understanding of what has been given to us ver- bally. This can save us frustration, and keep your group from being accused of fiddling with the books. Watch for the problem of: "We don't fund X, but if you can get X funded we will fund Y and Z.".

6. Any people receiving funding should clearly possess the skills to do the job. When money is obtained there is always the tempta- tion to use it to reward loyal and hard-working people. This can be problematic if it appears that "insiders" are scratching each other's backs. It is important to not only be a just and equitable organiza- tion, but to appear to be so.

Example: The Single Mothers Against Poverty Group developed a creative way to handle some of the problems of funding when they received a summer employment grant. Instead of "hiring staff", they wrote up a list of tasks that needed to be done and put a dollar value to each one: typing a letter $X.OO; attending a community meeting, $X.OO; etc. In this way all members got a chance to be reimbursed a little for jobs that they were doing. No one got rich, but no one got jealous either.

7. Realize that funding staff and project officers, particularly from big funders, such as government foundations or the United Way, are often used to dealing with large, formal bureaucracies. They may have little experience with community-based organizations, and may need education as to the differences and advantages of such organizations.

Example: A grassroots project in Uganda of women dealing with AIDS issues faced the dilemma of a funder who demanded an evaluation process before releasing dollars for a second phase of the project. There were two problems: First, the women realized that they needed to spend energy on a needs assessment that would involve the members of their project. (This off-shore evaluation process, while perhaps useful for the funder, had a negative impact on their members: it would divert limited energy away from mobilization of local communities.) Second, the evaluation process had been developed in North America, and the women found that it did not connect well with their experience and culture. For some time the women and project officer wrangled over the issue. Finally, the problem was resolved when the members went ahead and did their own needs assessment and sent the results into the head office in Canada. The funder accepted it as an interim report, but suggested that the evaluation would have to be done sooner or later. A good deal of energy and time had been spent on a funder rather than community issues.

8. Remember that funders, particularly government, prefer to fund services over advocacy or organizing. At the very least, they will want us to delineate and prioritize each of these activities as different functions. Unfortunately the organizing life of community- based groups does not run along such clear, separate lines. Chaos is often the rule, and it is difficult to predict whether advocacy or organizing will be the focus at any given time. Thus, a worker who is funded to do program development may find herself in a situation where she may be involved in advocacy action – situations like this won't wait until there is a free day in program development.

Example: When (in 1995) the right-wing Conservative government was elected in the province of Ontario, one of the first things they did was to tell project officers not to fund any proposals that had the terms "community development" or "advocacy" in them. Their view was, apparently, that they did not wish to assist voices that would raise objections to their agenda of making war on the poor and marginalized. Proposals had to be presented in a very cautious manner. Even so, many useful programs lost their funding, and money and resources disappeared from many communities and important causes.

Some other considerations on funding:

Corporate Funding

If there is a particular project in mind that might lend itself to corporate sponsorship – hiring a fundraiser or buying a van to transport children, seniors or disabled people, for example – it may be worth looking directly to the private companies. If so:

1. Try to get funding for more than a year. It is not unlikely that with the vagaries of the economy, subsequent requests will be met with less than an enthusiastic response.
2. Try to put three or four requests together so that:
   • If one doesn't come through it isn't too damaging.
   • The company understands that it isn't being expected to "carry the load" by itself.
3. Check out the kind of project that the company is supporting. Don't waste time on places that have no interest in the kinds of things your groups are doing.
4. Send the proposal to the chief executive officer (call to find out who it is). However, don't expect to deal with the CEO.
5. Call and find out exactly what they want in a proposal. Don't waste time by giving them extraneous information, or waste their time and ours making them ask for stuff you have left out of your submission.
6. If the group can, be registered as a charitable organization —companies want that tax break. (You cannot do this in Canada if your organization has a so-called "political" purpose, which the government tends to interpret in very broad terms.)
7. If successful, be sure to:
   • Call and thank them.
   • Send them a report on how the money was used.

8. It can be helpful to get to them early on, or late in their fiscal year, when they have lots of money or some left over.

Note: Do not get connected with a company that has caused or is causing problems for the community. Be sure that the community is consulted if some company offers resources. There can be exceptions to this rule. In fighting the James Bay Hydro project, the Cree received company transportation help a few times. However, it was always made clear that there were no favours in return (McGregor, 1989).

Foundations

1. Again, be sure to get to them early enough in their fiscal year so we don't miss out; and take a crack at them late in the year to check if they have any money left over.
2. If turned down, try to find out "why" so that a better approach may be taken next time by your group.
3. It is often preferable to try for a three-year strategy. We may be better off than with a one-shot deal.
4. Be prepared to educate the funder. For example, the foundation may not understand that an organization cannot pay for a van out of its general operating budget if one has United Way funding. Another example is that funders are often not aware that the Department of Indian Affairs in Canada does not fund off-reserve organizations.

Service Clubs

1. Usually there are limited funds available ($200.00 - $1,500.00).
2. Keep in mind that these clubs are usually inundated by requests.
3. Requests often work best if the service club can take on the group as a project.
4. Local contacts can be important. It can be helpful if a member of their group can be involved with your group in some way.

Trade Union Movement

1. Best requests are around particular social issues (e.g., racism, equal pay or day care).
2. Sometimes they give money (or "in kind" assistance).

Example: A teacher's organization in southern Ontario provided money to a group that was attempting to organize parents around the issue of the quality of education resources and steep government cut backs. This allowed the group to acquire a part-time organizer and really expand its activities.

3. Sometimes they give consultation.

Example: A small union that was on strike received a loan of a labour negotiator. He was very helpful at both negotiating and teaching. With the skills learned from him, they were able to be more effective in future negotiating situations.

Direct Mail (or Direct Contact) Campaigns

1. Usually this is aimed at our own constituency. Usually these are people who support, or are in some way connected to, the issue.
2. We can only expect small amounts from each person.
3. A great many requests are needed, as the response rate is usually about 1-3 per cent. This can be boosted to 5-6 per cent with careful targeting (quite a sophisticated process). It can also help to carefully craft the "begging letter." In this regard it is useful to:
   • Keep the message short, clear and to the point. Long letters are simply not read.
   • Connect our message to the interests of our potential donors. How does our cause affect them?
   • As much as possible, use the language of your potential donors. That is, don't use jargon or revolutionary rhetoric or talk down to them. They need to feel a kinship with the people that are asking for the assistance.
4. With technology becoming more affordable, computerized mailing lists (regular,and now and increasingly, through email) are very helpful. Sometimes groups will share their lists with us if we can do something for them; free advertising if our group has a newsletter, for example.
5. After three weeks, do not expect any more responses.
6. Supermarkets will sometimes be prepared to put request material with the grocery bags. The same is true of laundromats and churches.
7. Other groups, which are similarly disposed to ours, might be doing mailings onto which we can piggy-back.

8. It can take some time but it can be very helpful to develop a support or "Friends Of..." group that will do some fundraising for you. These would be people who do not have much interest in grassroots organizing, but who see the utility of our organization and are prepared to organize an event, or lend their names to a fundraising campaign.

Dealing with Internal Opposition

A question that can be very important in this phase (and at other times as well) is: Is there in the general community, at least, a passive willingness for change in relation to the major problems or some particular problem? At least there must be no powerful person or group in the community who will actively resist action toward change. There may well be some, possibly a majority, who are indifferent but basically they can be left (not ignored) for the time being, until it is in their interest to become involved. There will be members, though, who will resist change. As Paulo Freire says, they resist change because they either fear power; they have a conservative notion of how the community should look and operate; they have an interest (ties to power elites) in maintaining the status quo; or they do not trust other members sufficiently to share power within their own community (big egos). There may also be people who are members of diverse communities who for historical or cultural reasons see issues in a different light than the mainstream or for language reasons are not as fully informed as mainstream folks. It is important that these people be informed and genuinely consulted. This can take some work, but is crucial to developing a reasonable level of unity at a time when action is necessary. Finally, as discussed in the first part of the book, we need to remember that a community that has been oppressed for a considerable period may legitimately have been left with scars. Whether it is colonization or systemic racism or other forms of oppression, the social and psychological wellbeing of the community are effected (Fanon, 1963; Erikson, 1994, Freeman & Lee, 2007; Lee, Moffatt, McGrath & George, 2007). Elites are good at the "divide and conquer" strategy which will often have left the community with feelings of inferiority and/or distrust among groups.

Example: In work I was doing with a First Nations community in the early 2000s, one of the first things that had to be brought into the open was a widespread lack of belief in the capacity of the community. There was a tendency to look to outside professionals, psychologists and psychiatrists for example, to deal with issues of youth suicide and the ensuing grief. On the other hand, my strategy was to build trust and belief through a series of workshops with members for every sector of the community. It took some time, but everyone agreed that it was worth the effort both to highlight the issue and to begin to allow members to build community courage out of their own personal courage.

The Federal and Provincial governments in Canada, for example, have been adept at using intergroup distrust to buy off different groups in Aboriginal communities to interfere with community cohesion which might result in folks coming together to bring some serious power to an issue.

Example: In my own practice I was once offered a community development position with a provincial department that dealt with various First Nations Reserves. As we discussed my exact responsibilities, the assistant director of the program offered, "You know your main job is to keep things from getting to a boiling point." When I asked what he meant, he gave an example: "Well, if a Chief or Band Council is making some serious trouble over an issue that might bring us into a long drawn out negotiating process, or that might cost a lot of money; or if the issue might cause a lot of publicity, your job will be to find out how we can buy them off, or some of them. Hey, I remember offering one Chief funding for some road building; lots of work there for his family or friends. The problem went away." I ended up telling him that I would be declining the position.

This kind of manipulation is not confined to Aboriginal communities so it is important to be aware of this pattern and the underlying feelings of fear, lack of confidence and intra-community distrust that will be the result of discrimination and oppression, which we discussed earlier; whether it is in terms of race, class, gender, etc. We will have to deal with them. We will have probably already picked up information on any potential or existing divisive issues in our private research. We (and the members) will have to develop some strategies for getting them to change, for neutralizing them, and/or for going around them in some way.

There are a number of principles to keep in mind when developing a strategy to do any of the above:

1. **The strategy must not divide the community or must divide it as little as possible.** (Remember, we may have to lose someone, and that may mean alienating their friends.) The people must gain strength from the exercise. It is not uncommon for communities to have a history of internal civil wars. Past history can breed some bad habits – quick reactions, rumour mongering, character assassination for example – and that can make it difficult for the members to come together in a positive atmosphere. (Remember our discussion of "frustration instigated behaviour.") It is important, in so far as it is humanly possible, to stress the commonalities among members, and help them see and accept opportunities to come together.

Example: A housing co-op was attempting to get the city to do something about drivers speeding through its grounds as a shortcut to a major road. There was real danger for kids. The community was unfortunately split on tactics. The executive wanted to move slowly. Some concerned parents wanted to take direct action (perhaps a barricade across the co-op entrance). The executive appeared to be fearful of angering the city bureaucrats and were stalling. Members of the parent group became so frustrated that they appeared at a board meeting and began to publicly berate the Chairman, accusing him of not caring about kids and of being a power monger. From that point on the issue became personalized. Two sides formed around the personalities involved, and many issues became subsumed by, "whose side are you on?" While the issue with the city was eventually solved, a year later the co-op was still dealing with the conflict. It is useful, in this context, to reflect back on one of the key role demands on an organizer: that of mediator. When possible, we need to be prepared to take on the responsibility of getting people to at least negotiate (a key skill) with each other. It will not always be successful, but it is our responsibility to consider and attempt it before events travel too far down an "us/them" divide.

2. The strategy and objective will be partially **determined by the understanding we and our group have about the reasons for resistance.**[2] For example, if a person has strong ties with the opposition, it is likely that tactics will be aimed at neutralizing or overcoming rather than changing. If a person is unclear about group vision or objectives, some sort of clarifying or teaching will have to be done.

3. **Do not be in too much of a hurry to totally resolve the situation** unless the person has sufficient clout to immediately stop positive action. Time can achieve many things, with a little assistance. Sometimes a slow groundswell of activity within a community can eventually bring the opposition around to becoming first-line advocates for militancy and change. Sometimes the opposition simply gets left behind by events and the people.

4. As Alinsky says, whatever one decides to do about the problem, **the tactic must be within the experience of the people.** Also, we must **move at the community's pace.**

5. In that vein, **always try to negotiate first.**

6. **It must be nonviolent.** This is important; in the heat of the moment, someone may want to "take a shot" at the person or persons who are standing in the way of the community's wishes. This would not only raise ethical problems; it can backfire and cause others to back away from our organization (seeing it as undisciplined or prone to violence).

7. If confrontation is necessary, whatever one does, it is important to **place and keep the person or people resisting on the defensive.** However carefully the people must be handled, we need to keep their negative position clear (explaining their position and accounting for its shortcomings). They must be kept off balance so that they cannot spend time attacking our group's position. In short, we have to keep the argument within our perspective.

---

[2] Early in Chapter II we will look at a way of analyzing the terrain of support and opposition in relation to action. The principles there are fairly applicable here as well.

8. If things really get confrontational, it is also important to heighten the awareness of the community as to the differences between that person and the rest of the community, i.e. **polarize the situation.** This doesn't mean that we have to make her look like "the bad guy" (though it may); it is, however, important for the community to see their interests as differing from hers. In short, the person's credibility on this issue – not on all issues – must be undermined.

9. Always **do our best to keep links of communication open and clear.** We want to be amenable to any positive move as well as ready to combat any negative tactics.

Reflection

There are lots of problems to face and deal with, and people can become either totally transfixed with organizational maintenance, or equally bored by the minutiae. These are challenges that must be dealt with creatively and sensitively. In a sense, a community organization must be able to re-invent itself as it responds to the unique and complex forces and situations it faces. It is worth the work. Organization development is a crucial objective and phase for community workers and it is the base from which coherent action will spring.

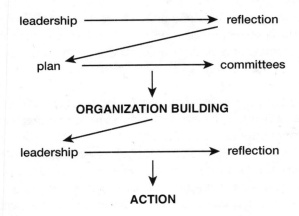

Figure 10-2: Organizational Development Phase Summary

Chapter 11

POPULAR ACTION

Never doubt that a small group of thoughtful, committed individuals can change the world – it is the only thing that ever has.

- Margaret Mead

The only way that anything serious will ever get done is by community movements.

- Henry Mintzberg

Treating action as a separate topic is somewhat artificial. Clearly, the organizer and the folks that make up the organization have been active for some time. Indeed, some of what is to follow – which tends to be focused on external community support and resistance – could be utilized in intra-community support building. However, as indicated in the last chapter, we will reach a point where the externally focused action (usually a campaign of some sort, but sometimes something more limited) is or should be more direct, as well as more clearly in the hands of the people. This is what the whole exercise has been about in the first place: people taking responsibility, or putting their new-found skills and confidence into action.

> Democracy is a way to balance money with people. And for that to work, people have got to act together, because it's through collective power that people can challenge the economic power of private wealth. So the goal is the power to alter policy, to alter circumstances, to change the world around you. – Marshal Ganz

The nature of community development – the attempt to reorder power and alter the pattern of resource allocation – tells us, that as well as mobilizing like-minded friends, community groups will find themselves facing serious resistance on any number of occasions. Elites are simply not going to do things that they see as detrimental to the maintenance of their privileged positions. As well, as movement activists remind us, it is not simply the "other side" that we have to influence, it is public opinion (Moyer, 2001). Social issues are complex, and the terrain in which we are working will have an array of groups that take various positions about the issue we are attempting to deal with; we need to be able to analyze the landscape. The following section provides a framework to guide strategy.

Also, in the previous chapter we mentioned that organization development was "an act of hope." Action is a further step on this road. We cannot act coherently and effectively without hope of success. As well, successful action underpins the growth of hope in our future.

In the following pages we will get into a variety of specific issues involved in action, but to start we will discuss briefly the idea of a campaign which is typically the instrument used by community and social movement groups for bringing about change.

Issues in Campaign Organizing

First of all, we define a campaign in very simple terms: *as a coherent series of actions designed and undertaken to bring about a particular result.*

Campaign organizing is not simply a series of discrete activities and events. While the ideas that follow are put forward in this linear way, it is important to acknowledge and be clear that organizing is a transactive endeavour. That is, actions, people, and events (many of them quite unpredictable) exist and occur in relation to each other. While we can and must plan, we cannot expect to be "in control." Rather, we must try to be as intentional as possible and as creative as we cause and react to specific, concrete situations.

I. Campaigns

Campaigns can be organized at various levels of complexity. They can focus on single issues or ones that involve various related issues. The environmental movement, for example can be seen focusing on a local bit of environmental degradation or on how they interact to produce accelerated climate change. Campaigns may engage a single protagonist, like a landlord or an array of protagonists or a very complex business or government entity.

1. *Local or Single-issue Campaigns.* These are very focused and specific efforts aimed at bringing about or blocking change in a region – for example, attempting to close down or limit a polluting industry in a particular area, or efforts aimed at getting a landlord to maintain a building properly. This would probably take relatively small organization and a limited series of events.

2. *Local, Mass-based Campaign.* Here the venue is local though probably larger than a single urban neighbourhood or involving a more complex institution than a single company, perhaps an array of business or a government institution. It would also involve more than one organization (hence the term "mass") but they would come together under an organization created by them and accountable to them. An example here would be a group of neighbourhood organizations coming together to form a single campaign organization. A second example would be a group of interested citizens coming together to advocate for improved policing. Another would be advocacy groups pushing for improved rights of seniors or women or a specific diverse minority.

3. *A Social Movement Campaign.* In this instance the aim is to bring about a change or preservation that benefits people in a wide range of geographical locations (folks concerned about climate change for example or anti-war/peace issues) and/or interest contexts (Aboriginal people, students, or women for example). It requires the development of sophisticated analysis of issues, a significant time frame, and the creation/acquisition of significant resources. An example of this kind of effort would be the coalition that came together to fight for improved services for folks dealing with AIDS.

II. Purpose, Process and Structure

Campaigns will have three interrelated aspects or dimensions. The first two are referred to by Rothman as task and process. As task can be confused with action, or something that we do, we will substitute the terms goals and objectives. The third is how the various parts of the campaign organization are to be configured.

1. *Goals and objectives* are simply the things that we want to achieve by our actions.

   Goals are the very general outcomes that we want to see and are related to our values. As such, they don't have to be expressed in very concrete language. For example, we might speak of improved health situations for Aboriginal Canadians, the reduction in racist attitudes and actions by local police, or increased employment opportunities for diverse people such as immigrants and racialized minorities. Also, goals are related to our values and principles and express the approach that our group has to organizing. Therefore, if we are seeking social justice outcomes we would wish to reflect them in the manner in which we organize ourselves – in anti-racist, egalitarian ways, for example.

   Objectives on the other hand are concrete outcomes; ones that we specify we want our campaign to achieve. Examples of these would be, specific increases in funding for Aboriginal health-care organizations, or that police undergo specific cultural training, or hire a specific number of racialized minority recruits.

2. *Process* involves the manner in which we are going to go about achieving our goals and objectives. They have to do with the analysis we have of the issue and context; and thus, the strategies we consider and the tactics that flow from our strategic choices.

The engine of movement is not protest and boycott but strategy and discipline, the when and how we protest and boycott.
- John Jackson and Manuel Pator,
Facing Race Conference Sept 21, 2010.

Strategy: the overall approach to solving a problem. For example, if a community group is attempting to combat discriminatory behaviour by police or other officials they might develop an anti-racism public-education strategy. That is, they would attempt to educate the larger public to the issue and the injustice with the expectation that the more people who understand, the more likely public policy can be affected. On the other hand, they may believe that a more confrontational approach may be required in the expectation that the police and officials will react in a positive way to direct demands for accountability. Or they may choose a political lobbying campaign in the hopes that they will be able to get politicians to rein in the officials and police. In each case different resources and tactics (see below) would be required.

There are a number of issues that need to be dealt with as far as strategy and tactics are concerned.

A. Development of a Strategy Framework: Here the trick is to find the positive opportunities relating the nature of our constituency, our type of organization, the types of actions considered, and the target opposition. Some factors to consider are whether it is:

(i) a general issue, of child poverty or environmental degradation for example;
(ii) an issue of redress for some form of discrimination, of race of ability or gender for example;
(iii) a personalized issue with a clear "villain," for example, a slum landlord or obstructive bureaucrat or politician or predacious business executive.

B. We need to analyze which of these (or other) approaches will be most useful in meeting our ends or exerting pressure and educating the public. So we need to consider:

(i) How do we best cut *the issue?* What demands and slogans will be most effective in helping people see the issue in the correct light?
(ii) An important question here is: do we focus on a specific event, the passage of a particular piece of legislation; or on

some principle like "Affordable Housing for All," for example; or on a pragmatic narrow focus, such as support for a specific housing project?

(iii) Whatever the demand it should be expressed in terms that are as clear and simple as possible. It should not express analysis or understanding that is beyond the experience of the membership, constituency, or the majority of the public. It should stress the utility of our position.

Therefore we need to think about whether it is best:

- to place the issue on the opposition's terms of reference (when it is weak). Alinsky calls this making them play by their own rules or;
- to place the contest in our terms of reference (when we have a strong one).

(iv) Try to figure out the "winnability" of potential actions. Are there times we might wish to act, even if the situation is not winnable? We might, for example, simply wish to raise the profile of an issue or of our group or organization.

(v) Relate our presenting issues to root causes like class inequality or colonial policy.

- Develop questions, discussions and actions that focus "blame" on the system, person or institution rather than on the "victim."
- Consider tactics that will show how power holders utilize their power in order to generate ideas that justify their positions.

(vi) Consider what kinds of resources – human, financial or physical – are required to mount a successful campaign.

- Where can they be found?
- Who in the organization is the best person(s) to seek and acquire them?
- Are specific strategies required for particular resources?

(vii) Consider whether there are any natural allies that can be of support; for example, a Native campaign for improved health services may wish to look at feminist groups who have similar concerns about women's health care needs.

Tactics: The specific set of actions that we use to accomplish our objectives within the overall context of a strategy (see above). Thus, in a public education approach, we might develop pamphlets with our position to distribute in various places, or we might call a series of public meetings where our issues would be articulated. If we were to choose a strategy of confrontation we might call for demonstrations at public offices. If we choose political lobbying we will look to find people with the best contacts with politicians and engage them in putting pressure on these officials.

3. *Structure.* A critical part of any campaign is how well it is organized and the key to this is the actual organization structure which allows for the focusing of its effort over time (Lee, 1999). Occasional strides are made in social justice by spontaneous disruptions or uprisings. For the most part however, gains are only made when there are organized groups ready to take advantage of events or protests in the interests of the folks that they represent, and through direct pressure or the mobilization of public opinion. Thus, a campaign requires a coherent structure that allows for a variety of tasks to be undertaken and coordinated – research, fund raising, networking, public relations, etc.

The structure of a campaign is the actual make up, the organizational structure of the efforts, which will bring the campaign to life. A community or social movement organization may and probably will be the entity that undertakes a campaign. But the actual structure of the campaign will in most cases not be the same thing. The community organization or social movement may be moving on a wider array of issues than the one(s) with which the campaign is focused. Thus, it will be a specific structure that is set up within the parent organization, with a responsibility of undertaking particular actions for the attainment of specific goals and objectives.

Example: A senior's advocacy organization had a general goal to improve the lives of diverse racialized seniors in a city. It had a specific goal however that related to the improvement of the quality and access for recreation services. It undertook a campaign to do this and a campaign committee was set.

A campaign committee might look something like the model set out in the simple diagram below. The organization has three purposes:

- **Develop a strategy (see above) to achieve the goals and objectives of the campaign.**
- **Choose the tactics (see above) that flow from the strategy and are appropriate to the situation and context.**
- **Implement the tactics chosen.**

Figure 11-1: Campaign Organization Structure

In this approach we assume five committees: research, public communication, fund raising (if necessary), action planning, and negotiation. The coordination function in even this simple structure is crucial. Thus a key player here is the coordinator who will communicate with the parent organization (we have made an assumption that there is one), keeping its members informed so they are able to vet any important strategic or tactical decisions made by the committee. He (or they, in the event that the issues are so complex and two people are designated as co-coordinators) will also undertake the responsibility of coordinating communication as represented by the dashed circle connecting the committees. The coordinator may or may not be a paid organizer. Whoever takes on this role however will be doing a great deal of important work – a fact that should be recognized.

Committee Responsibilities

A research committee will need to gather necessary information to provide facts on the issue being pursued. For example, if we are attempting to change a city regulation we need to know what it is, the basis on which it was enacted, and who has the power to change it.

A public information committee will be responsible for getting the story of the campaign out to media, and to actors that may be key to the issue but not directly involved such as senior politicians or other groups with an interest in the issue. So they need to cultivate contacts and learn how to write press releases, scripts for presenting the group's position, and other pieces of communication.

Fund raising may or may not be required. While a community organization may have funds for day-to-day work, it's very likely it will not have the money to mount and sustain a campaign. That money will have to be found and the responsibility of the **fund raising committee** then will be to find ways to bring it in. For example, members might design a program of reaching out to "friends" of the organization (people and other organizations that would be sympathetic to the cause); or it might attempt to stage an event – a concert perhaps or an invited speaker – that would generate some cash.

An action committee is the group that will coordinate the actions that are planned to disrupt (like a union strike or a boycott for example), and to direct public attention (for example, distribute flyers or stage a protest). This is an exceedingly serious job. The folks involved must be prepared to work hard and listen to the people they are attempting to motivate and coordinate in carrying out an action.

A negotiation committee is going to come into play if the campaign needs to engage directly with a decision making body.

Each committee will obviously focus on its own area of work, but someone from each committee will be chosen to be on the campaign committee itself.

Now we are going to go into more detail on some of the issues introduced above.

Understanding and Addressing Levels of Support and Opposition

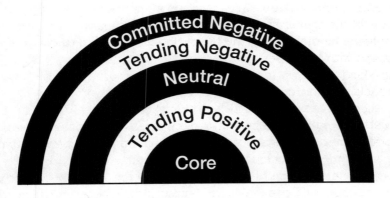

Figure 11-2: Spectrum of Support and Opposition

If we are facing resistance, there are typically two broad groups that we tend to identify: those for us, and those against us. If the issue is very

important we may think of them as "the good guys" and "the bad guys."
As far as rhetoric goes, it is rather nice to maintain these divisions. Life,
however, is rarely so simple; and if we are going to have any chance at
gaining our points, it is important that we develop a more sophisticated notion of the ground upon which our struggles are played out. The
analysis in the model presented here is one aspect of strategy development. What we want to do is to analyze the various tendencies that
occur when there are two opposing points of view. As we can see in
Figure II-2 (Spectrum of Levels and Opposition), we can loosely divide
the field into five groups: those who are committed to the cause; those
sympathetic; those neutral; those tending to be unsympathetic to our
cause, or sympathetic to the cause of the opposition; and finally, those
committed to opposing our cause. In developing a strategy for dealing
with opposition, all positions will have to be considered and a number
of issues will need attention.

Since popular groups rarely have unlimited resources, it is important that we use the resources that we do have for the greatest
impact. Thus, it is important when dealing with opposition that we
understand clearly with whom we are dealing, why and how these
people relate to our group's objectives. Following such an analysis,
it will be clearer to us how to act – with or on them. With this in
mind, let us examine the categories from a few important perspectives: the type of people in each group; their reasons for supporting,
resisting or hesitating; the resources that each group has available
to influence others; and the tactics we may be able to use to deal
with each group.

Core Group

This group certainly would include community leadership and core activists. There may be others who – for reasons of self-interest or solidarity – will enthusiastically work with our group in what we want to do
or achieve.

Example: New Orleans activist Louise Martin became involved in
a struggle to block the creation of a massive warehouse store in an
African-American community near her family's home. She was concerned both as a "neighbour" of that community (solidarity) and as
one concerned about the negative impact the development would

have for the people who lived in the famous "Garden District" of the city (self-interest).

These folks will constitute a major part of the resources available for carrying through our strategy: they come to all the meetings; and they may have social relationships outside of community business (though this is not necessary). They tend to contribute ideas and time, and possibly resources (like money, specific expertise or contacts with elites).

For these folks in the Core Group it is important that:

* we understand their motivations;
* they have good communication among themselves;
* they know what to do;
* they be kept well informed;
* they have good support (they are doing a big job).

Swing Group Tending Positive

These are people who, the strategy team knows, are supportive in general, though the extent of that support may be unclear. They generally see their interests and values bound up with those of the core group, or the population that the core group represents but are hesitating for some reason. So we need to be clear on:

What underpins their positive motivation?

* How are they connected to the issue?
* Are they personally affected? Sometimes there is a person-to-person relationship that tends to draw someone toward supporting our position. Is there a personal loyalty to a committed member or members?
* A third possibility is that a person or group generally is ideologically sympathetic to the position of your group.

Why are they hesitating?

* Do they have some kind of connection to the other side? Personal loyalties can swing both ways, and a person or group may hesitate because they happen to respect people who nevertheless are against us.

- Are they concerned with some aspect of our campaign? Is our rhetoric needlessly putting some people off?

Example: In the 1995 winter occupation of the Revenue Canada Offices, by First Nation groups protesting treaty violations, some supporters (Native and White) were alarmed when one of the women elders read out a statement which included an implication that the protesters might use violence. This was unacceptable to most of us and we immediately sought clarification that this was an error. (It was.)

- Do they have an incorrect, or unclear, idea of what the issue is about? Not uncommon, as many disputes involve complex aspects which the media tend to oversimplify or misrepresent.

Whatever the issue, they are not acting. We need to keep them supportive and perhaps move them into a more active relationship. So, we need to:

- Understand their motivations and concerns;
- Develop information and arguments for them based on those motivations and concerns;
- Provide them with opportunities for action;
- Negotiate with them (what do they need in order to become more helpful);
- Keep in communication with them and support them.

Neutral Group

These people are usually the most numerous. They are the folks who say, "I can't be bothered" or "Well, both sides have their points" or "Everyone has their own opinion." Some are uninformed and don't see the need to alter this situation. Many times they are folks who fear the conflict inherent to the issue, and they either try to avoid it or not recognize it: "I just don't know what all the fuss is about." They may, on the other hand, be genuinely unclear on the issues; or have some relationships with people on both sides that they worry about upsetting. Or, they may belong to sub groups (a cultural or ethnic minority for example) where the majority have extremely strongly felt views and where to go against the majority is seen as being traitorous. For example, a peace organizer in the Jewish community told me that he felt a number of folks did not always want to support the actions of the State of Israel against Palestinians in the occupied territories. "But it's very hard for them to speak out you see. They feel they would be ostracized by the rest of the community. So they keep their heads down and say as little as possible." With this group we need to:

- Try to understand their concerns about the core position and the opposition position;
- Try to understand their particular social position;
- Provide information and support where possible;
- Help them to find common ground with our position, and be prepared to negotiate and expand that common ground;

Example: A Toronto community group was fighting a "block busting" landlord who was turning good, low-income apartment housing into "dumps." He was trying to force his present tenants to leave so he could develop the buildings as high-rent condos. The small group desperately needed the help of the local ratepayer organization to put pressure on city council, and the by-law enforcement department, to take action. Most of the ratepayer executives were neutral: they didn't want to take sides because the people at risk were tenants, not home owners. The activists had no luck in talking them into getting involved, though the organizer was able to get the ratepayer's president to go through the building to see the conditions people were being forced to live in—holes in the walls and ceiling, no hot water, etc. When the little delegation got there, the owner turned up and attempted to block the entrance. He and the president got into quite a heated argument and some pushing and shoving took place. This incident convinced the president that the group deserved support against this nasty person and he was instrumental in getting the ratepayers to take action in assisting the tenants.

- If we cannot move them to sympathy make sure that we don't do anything to force them toward the other side.
- Keep the lines of communication open. We may find ways to bring them on board; and we also want to be aware if the opposition is attempting to connect with them.

Example: A group was organizing to support the establishment of a badly needed Aboriginal youth shelter in a middle-class neighbourhood. Public meetings had been held and things were moving ahead relatively well. A staff member who had been organizing public meetings had established friendly relations with a number of the neighbours who, while lukewarm to the project, were not actively opposing it. One of these folks called him one day very agitated. A very active opposition resident had been calling around making very unsettling assertions – that the shelter would house youth that police described as violent, for example. The worker was able to use his contacts. He started calling around to the "neutral folks" to counter the negative and untruthful campaign.

Swing Group Tending Negative

These are people who generally see their interests and principles bound to the opposition. As well, they may have important relationships there. They also, of course, may be quite misinformed about the issues. They may be interested in taking action against your project but are not looking for a fight. Our emphasis with this group is to try moving them to a more neutral position. Thus it is important to:

- Try to understand their motivations and concerns;
- Develop arguments which negate concerns and enhance motivations;
- Look for issues and personalities that can move them away from the opposition and toward the core;
- Be prepared to negotiate with them if the possibility arises;
- Avoid provoking them if possible.

Committed Opposition

These are our opposition. They have interests in opposing the position of the community with which we are working. They will be working hard, attempting to defeat our group. They will have their own networks which they will use to develop a strategy— part of which will be to do the very things we are recommending in this section. The basic approach here is, at least in the short range to isolate, not convince them. With these people it is important to:

- Not underestimate them; but not become totally focused on their negativity either;
- Understand where they get their power;
- Develop clarity as to their objectives, and keep our analysis of their strategy sharp;
- Plan counter strategies and tactics;
- Keep lines of communication open so that we can negotiate with them if possible.

There are three aspects to action we have to keep in mind here, and each has to do with gaining or maintaining public support.

a) Alerting the public to the issue or problem.
b) Convincing a majority, or a significant minority, that it is an issue worthy of support.
c) Offering a convincing alternative for the resolution of the issue.

It is the public to whom we must, for the most part, make our case, not the committed opposition which usually is not very open to rational argument.

Organizational Linkages

We spoke in the last chapter about developing an organization as an aspect of building our capacity for action. Sometimes it becomes important to connect our organization with others to increase that action potential. Our group may need to link with other organizations, either within the community or outside of it. There are two main reasons why this connection can be useful:

1. We may need to gain resources that our group cannot hope to acquire;

Example: Chetwynd, the Toronto-based community organization project that worked with assisted-housing communities, focused on helping residents to strengthen local networks, and to identify community issues on which they wish to work. There were ongoing attempts to connect with both existing community organizations (such as a residents' association) and public-service organizations. The project had fairly limited resources; so, through linkages, they felt they could increase the resources that could be made available to the community, while helping to improve the quality of relationships between the community and service providers.

2. We may discover a like-minded organization which is fighting for issues that have relevance to our group's struggles (e.g. Community planning organizations sometimes join with Labour groups to advocate on behalf of the poor and marginalized).

Types of Linkages

1. Liaisons - Sometimes different organizations identify a couple of their own people to help keep each other informed of the events and plans developed by each group. In this case it is simply a matter of maintaining a good communication line with the other group. We do not meld our organizations or processes, but try to coordinate certain activities and information.

Another form of liaising involves having people from one organization sit on the board of another. Again, it is not uncommon to find representatives of Labour groups sitting on boards of community planning organizations.

2. Coalitions - In this case we are joining formally with another group, or groups, and agreeing to take joint action on specific issues. We are creating an "umbrella" organization, one which will speak and act for us on the identified issues and to which we agree to contribute resources. We may integrate some activities, and often become part of a group to decide strategies and tactics. We do not, however, give up our own specific identity; and we will continue to work, by ourselves, on issues of our unique concern. There are several examples of this kind of linkage between First Nations, peace, and environmental movements; as well as with anti-poverty groups. A coalition allows us to focus resources and effort on the larger issues with which many groups also identify.

Example: When an Ontario Native group started to resist the Canadian Federal government on its attempt to break treaty rights regarding taxation, a number of groups came together to contribute to the effort of the "Revenue Rez" occupation in Toronto. One organization leader became the spokesperson for the whole group, though all groups were involved in decisions concerning how to develop the protest and how to get the message out to the general public.

3. ***Mass-based Organizations (MBOs)*** - These are a type of coalition popularized by Alinsky in the 1950s and 1960s. In this case, small local organizations come together and form a new "super organization" under one elected leadership. This organization is mandated to deal with the agreed upon issues; and the leadership develops strategy and acts for the organization. The member organizations continue to carry out their own activities on issues not covered by the mass-based organizations. Examples of MBOs can be seen in the work of Saul Alinsky with the Woodlawn Organization in Chicago (Horwitt 1989, Alinsky 1970).

4. ***Amalgamation*** - In this case, we decide that two or more groups must come together and give up their identities as separate groups. This can come about in a situation where all groups involved are so focused on the same issue that it makes no sense to maintain separate organizations. It may also occur where one or more groups have lost steam and cannot continue with any sense of effectiveness.

In entering into anyone of these organizational relationships, we need to be clear about what we are gaining as well as what we are giving up. We need to understand clearly the organizational culture and values of the other folks, so that we do not get into unnecessary philosophical or strategic wrangles. We also need to be clear and open about our own culture and values so that the other group(s) will be in a similarly informed position.

There are a few questions we can ask when examining which, if any, organizational linkage is appropriate for our group:

1. What is the vision of the organization with which we are negotiating a linkage?
2. How clear is the other organization on what we are about?
3. What resources are involved – from us, or for us?

4. How important is our autonomy?
5. Is this a long term situation, of a one-off activity?
6. Who is going to be responsible for the activity of bringing the linkage into being?

The answers to these questions can assist us in figuring out the path to, or away from, forming a particular organizational linkage.

Public Events and Demonstrations

We are defining demonstration, broadly, as any public event that will bring positive attention to the issues we are raising. At some point, in most organizing situations, there may be a need for some sort of public display. This is particularly true in contest situations, but may be important for any organizing endeavour. Rallies, marches, street dances, concerts, community fairs, or fun runs are examples of demonstrations.

1. Why Demonstrate?

a) *For publicity.* The group may merely want to call attention to its existence, namely, what its problems are, or what it is trying to do for the community. On the other hand, it may wish to call attention to what someone, or some institution, is doing to the community.

b) *For internal morale.* The group may need to show community members that they can be mobilized, can pull something off successfully. This may range from putting on a street fair, to calling a press conference, to putting on a mass protest.

Example: In the 1990s the Big Cove First Nation in New Brunswick had experienced a terrible suicide epidemic. In nine weeks, eight young men had taken their lives. The population (about 1800) was in shock. While there were many problems facing the people – racism, unemployment, and a cycle of abuse for example – leaders understood they had to demonstrate that the community could do something constructive for itself. They chose to mount a "Mourning and Healing Week" (Lee, 1993). They organized ceremonies, brought in Elders and healers from around North America, and outlawed alcohol from the reserve for the duration of the event. Many community members recognized the importance of coming together, publicly sharing their grief, and building determination to face their problems. Importantly, the epidemic of suicides ceased.

c) *To reinforce its ability to represent.* By showing the person or institution trying to extract something that it does indeed represent a high number of people, and/or that it can garner media attention.

Example: A small community organization in Metro Toronto has a "community fair" every spring. There are a variety of events: face painting, concerts, clowns and a huge garage sale where neighbourhood folks buy tables at a very reasonable cost and sell used goods. It is well publicized, and people come from all over the area. This event raises money which the community group uses the rest of the year, mostly for children's programs. It is interesting that this event invariably draws the local mayor and councillors, who always make a point that they "support" the community. Interestingly, this organization is seen as one of the more influential in the municipality, and one of the few that is routinely kept well informed by politicians as to what is going on at city hall.

d) *To disrupt the operation of the opposition.* This reason is most commonly found in relation to a union picketing during a strike, and when there has been no success in moving management at the bargaining table. Sometimes it is used to get management to come to the bargaining table. However, it is used by other groups as well: for example Greenpeace actions against sealing and nuclear tests; the Native blockades and occupations for treaty rights; and the United Farm Workers grape boycott pickets.

Example: The Friends of the Lubicon, a support group for the Lubicon Cree Nation's struggle in Alberta, has taken on the multinational resource company Daishowa. That company has been threatening the ancestral lands of the Lubicon with logging. The "Friends" have mounted a long campaign which has included the development of a boycott of businesses (secondary targets) that use Daishowa products (like Pizza Pizza). This pizza company had to be picketed and leafleted for months before it finally agreed to join the boycott of Daishowa products (paper bags in this case).[1]

e) All of the above. More often than not there will be multiple reasons for putting on a demonstration. One good example is the "unofficial" women's conference on the Canadian constitution in 1981; after the official one had been cancelled by the government. It was effective in gaining publicity for women's issues, embarrassing the government (particularly the Secretary of State), and showing everyone just what women could achieve.

Example: The Mohawk standoff at Kanehsatake in 1990 drew a great deal of attention to Canadian First Nations' grievances. It also demonstrated what they could accomplish in withstanding the power of the state. Further, when the Sûreté du Québec and then the Canadian military moved in so violently, it unmasked the oppressive nature of national policy against Native People.[2]

2. Principles

a) Nonviolence. This is definitely a first principle. If we are ultimately searching seriously for a world where all life is sacred, we have to take note of the dismal failures of movements where violence has been espoused. The use of violence clearly sanctions violence in the opposition, no matter what lofty aims are advocated. In the words of Walter Wink (Christian scripture scholar and nonviolence advocate): "Violence simply is not radical enough, since it generally changes only the actors but not the way power is exercised" (Desroches 1996). The medium is the message. There is a tremendous pressure and provocation to use physical violence against our fellow human beings but it must be resisted so that we do not

---

1   By 1996 Diashowa had experienced so much damage from the strategy that it attempted to smash it by applying for a court injunction against the actions of the Friends. While a court provided the injunction in 1998, a higher court denied the petition on the obvious grounds that the company was attempting to suppress free speech.

2   See Richard Wagamese (1996) *That Terrible Summer;* and the film by Alanais Obonsowin, "Kanehsatake 270 Years of Resistance" for excellent documentation.

merely end up, as Freire would say, mirroring the oppressor. While they are few in number, there are some compelling people after whom we can model our behaviour: Cesar Chavez, Gandhi, Martin Luther King Jr., and (generally) the Suffragettes.[3]

Nonviolence can be difficult in situations where people have been trying for a long period to have serious problems redressed (remember the principle of frustration instigated behaviour). As we've indicated earlier, oppression leaves people with social and psychological scarring that may render them with less energy to modulate behaviour in times of crisis and tension. Thus we may have to spend time helping people to understand the necessity and power of non-violent direct action. In organizing with Aboriginal people in some of the numerous and necessary confrontations with various levels of government, youth have sometimes become frustrated, lost patience, and responded to provocations with violence. We can understand the frustration but Elders have been concerned that some of the leadership did not prepare the young people with sufficient care. A physical attack by anyone among an oppressed group will almost always be turned into a media circus. The issue will become drowned in a sea of "concern" about violence (not the violence of the state or the system of oppression unfortunately). And it puts leadership in a difficult position. They will not want to condone a violent act, but also will not want to abandon folks who they are attempting to represent. Therefore, there is not only a moral principle here but a very practical one of public support and internal solidarity. It is complex but must be acknowledged and dealt with in a rigorous and caring way.

Another issue here is the importance of training for non-violent demonstrations where we know that the response of authorities will be a strong and perhaps violent one. From my own experience I know how intimidating it can be to see a long line of police, fully armoured, banging their shields slowly, but relentlessly while advancing toward us. Training is important to help us remain cool and to know how to respond in a peaceful manner – but one that

---

[3]   Many of struggles entered into by these people necessitated the use of civil disobedience. (See "An Historical Perspective" in Introduction.)

maintains safety. An activist (McRae, 2008: 1) relates her experience at the Quebec rally against the FTAA in 2004:

> As my group marched, chanted, sang, made noise and immersed our-
> selves in solidarity, we, or myself specifically, did not see any indication
> of violence on behalf of the protesters. I saw a bit of graffiti, a couple
> of "smashed" items, but did not see it occur with my own eyes. At the
> point that I was tear gassed, I and some of my group were standing
> still, not close to the constructed fence where the meetings were taking
> place, but probably a quarter of a kilometre away. There were protesters
> sitting, and we were all singing. A line of riot police moved in, as they
> were attempting to "change guard" with another group of officers. My
> only escape in this instance was a narrow staircase, and yet, a canister
> of tear-gas was thrown and landed on my friend's backpack directly in
> front of me. The gas flowed up into my face, choking me and making
> it difficult to catch my breath as I ran for the staircase. The burning,
> of course, was practically unbearable. Meanwhile another group of my
> colleagues were witnessing perhaps the most excessive use of tear gas
> that was, we would later find, indicative of the event. I later watched on
> video as three seated people holding their hands in peace signs were
> repeatedly assaulted with the gas, though they were not close to the
> fence, and clearly not a security risk. Indeed, it was obvious that exces-
> sive force was used[4]

It was crucial that she and her colleagues had had the training to deal with what was an extremely terrifying situation.

---

[4] It is important to note that McRae understood how difficult the situation was for the police involved and that they were being given direction from officers— those who they probably understood had a strategic view of the whole scene. It may be that the officers on the ground thought themselves in immediate danger. This of course does not, as a whole, absolve the police action of its responsibility for the violence. McRae also raised the issue about the culture of policing and how it limits the view and actions of individual officers. "I understood the oppressive contributions made by police actions on our collectivity. So I do not propose to say that the police were innocent bystanders to the event. As individuals, one would hope that they considered the injustice that was served in this event and others like it. Disappointingly, the opportunities for police to question such actions are slim and to express concern about injustice, simply not fostered in the culture known to them as law enforcers" (McRae, 2008: 2).

b) Stay outside the opposition's experience. This principle, popularized so well by Saul Alinsky (1970) can be (and increasingly is) a tall order, as everyone's experience is broadened through the media. However, keeping the other side off balance has important payoffs:

- It allows them feel their vulnerability, something that may be foreign to their experience
- This may then lead them to respond in ways with which they are unfamiliar, and that is advantageous to our people.

Example: Even old tactics that haven't been seen for a while can have good effects. The use of sit-ins, by students in universities across North America in the late 60s and early 70s, was successful in part because initially the university administrations would overreact, call in police, and refuse to meet with the demonstrators. It is interesting to note that in 1995 the same scenario was played out by Aboriginal people who took over the Federal Revenue offices in Toronto to protest treaty violations. The occupation lasted 30 days and generated some good publicity.

c) Within the experience of the community. This is another principle that is strongly recommended by Alinsky (1970). It is a corollary of the above (b), and is rather like the old social work principle, "move at the client's pace." No matter how tempting it is to pull off something that will really grab media attention or really stun the other side, it must also be something which will not violate the taste, ethics or sensibilities of the community members.

Example: In 1969 the Just Society (an organization fighting for the rights of Ontario welfare recipients) had a television confrontation with the government Minister John Yaremko. The confronters, single support mothers, decided to represent themselves as strong, determined women who would not be pushed around. They had solid facts and made forceful statements. Unfortunately, a couple of the women got excited, and started to shout and swear at the minister. Yremko just sat there looking like an innocent cherub under siege by maniacs. People in general, and welfare recipients in particular, were not used to this kind of behaviour and not ready to see authority figures treated quite so disrespectfully. It might be different now, after a number of years and scandals have passed, but given the mores of the time, government ministers could not be sworn at in public. The women, in attempting to strengthen their image and prove how unafraid they were, succeeded in turning off their own constituents as well as the Liberals (whose support they wished to maintain).

d) *Discipline.* A public display should always be disciplined. People should be clear on what to do, where to do it, and how it is to be done. This does not mean that spontaneity is out, or that people should not enjoy themselves. Nevertheless, the spontaneity and fun have to occur within some sort of coherent framework. The most loose and enjoyable demonstrations are often the ones that have been planned with the most care. A demonstration cannot simply be a bunch of people informally getting together to celebrate or demand something; it must have a focus, an agenda. Speakers should be given time slots (who will follow whom), and time frames (how long they should speak). It is especially important to make sure speakers stay on the relevant topic.

e) *Novelty.* Campaigns for significant change are rarely short. The higher the stakes, the more difficult it is to convince a community that it can do something, or an opposition that it must do something. Thus, it is important that, whatever kinds of public display the group puts on, they should not be allowed to grow stale. Innovation is important over the long haul so that people don't feel like they are in a rut. Similarly, if the group is going against a tough adversary, tactics used with great frequency come to be expected and easily countered. Obviously, in a strike, picketing is going to have to be an everyday affair; however, who pickets where, the organizing of "monster" rallies, and diversions on the picket line can somewhat alter the rhythm.

Example: During the "Revenue Rez" 30 day occupation of the Federal Revenue offices in Toronto in the mid-1990s, organizers put on a series of events: drumming, a celebration, even a weekend pow wow. These culture-based activities gave participants a strong sense of community. As well, it countered images of "angry, aggressive Natives" and generated some great publicity

f) Relevant Opposition. In any public display against an intransigent institution or person, it is important to be clear on the connection between your action, the objective you have, and the opposition itself. Piven and Cloward make the point that successful protest can only take place if the protesters have some relationship with the protest: "work in his factories, buy his products, go to his school or live in his apartments" (1978: 21). The focus of any action should be the person or body who can make change happen, not merely the handiest target (Dale, 1978).

Example: Social workers and teachers in Ontario who have struck against their employers are often told by these agencies that it is not the agency's fault, and they should be dealing with government – the body that develops funding and policy. The correct response has always been: "Yes, but we work for you. Negotiate fairly with us and we'll help you develop strategies to deal with government." Social workers and teachers rarely have direct access to government. Their leverage is only with their employers (See Piven and Cloward's *Poor Peoples Movements*, Chapter 1).

g) Secondary Targets. Having noted the above example, it is often possible to find secondary targets who, if lobbied or threatened with action, might put some pressure on the primary target. Native groups concerned with pollution have been reasonably successful at this, particularly in getting churches to lobby companies in which they have stock. Secondary targets then can be relevant potential target groups, providing they have some leverage on the primary target.

Example: A group of ex-psychiatric patients, fighting to get decent housing and financial support, staged a "boarding home lunch." They served the mayor of Toronto and other officials the same food that was provided in the "facilities" – watered-down soup, cheap white bread, etc. This was a short, small demonstration, but one that got a lot of attention.

h) *Role Play.* Some, perhaps all, of the people may never have done anything this "public." They may have to be both trained and "psyched up," so that they can handle the excitement, the pressure, and the demand of the action. Also, this gets people into the habit of using other members' input. People can be asked to think up questions and share them with the group, and then have the group think up ways of dealing with them. Remember, the demonstration belongs to everyone. Everyone owns it. You don't want anyone feeling used by the organization.

Demonstration Tactics

1. Planning

As mentioned above, planning is important to the success of an action. There are a variety of areas that should be considered:

a) Is there transportation needed to get people to and from the site?
b) Is it at a time when most people can attend?
c) Is the site familiar? Is it a large or small place?
d) What numbers are appropriate?
   • enough to get attention and impress the media, and/or opposition?
   • not so many that it will be difficult for organizers to keep it going the way our people want it?
e) How long is it going to last?
   • How long can our people "hang in"?
   • Do some members need child-care assistance?
   • Are members clear on the time demands?
   • Is there an estimate of how long the opposition can hold out?
f) Who is in charge?
   • Are there going to be marshals directing the members?
   • How many marshals are necessary?
g) Is everyone clear on the strategy and on what is expected of them?
h) Is there a protocol for handling rowdies and hecklers? (see number 8 in this list)

i) Are all the speakers lined up?
- How many?
- People belonging to the community organization? Sympathetic others? Is it clear what they will say?
- Is it clear how long they will take? Watch out for the well-intentioned long-winded person, or the guy on the ego trip.

j) Can we accommodate all the people who might wish to take part? For example, is there wheelchair access and/or translators for those with hearing and speech disabilities, etc.?

2. A People's Event

The organizer should not be seen as a major force in the event. If somebody is to have her picture taken, or is asked for a quote, it should be a community member who:

- Is representative of the group;
- Is not the local egomaniac that will be seen as merely grabbing notoriety for herself.

Example: It is not hard for an organizer to get caught in this. A community worker in Northern Ontario related how, at one of his group's first demonstrations against a school closing, he had been asked all the questions by the media present – the local paper and radio station. "It felt great being a media star at the time. I cringe now when I think how I took the spotlight away from the citizens who had a lot more at stake than I did."

3. The Correct Focus

It is important to be clear as to who has the information or the decision-making authority in relation to the particular action contemplated. There is nothing more frustrating for a group than to have mobilized itself to march up to city hall or the legislature and be told that the relevant person is up or down one level. Obviously this can be a strategy that various levels of government play all the time: obfuscation of the issue, and buck-passing. Thus, it is important for the organization to have done its homework really well – make the opposition live up to its own rules as Alinsky advises – and be at the correct party's door with the correct demand.

4. Protocol for Engagement

Again, it is very disconcerting to march to some official's office or house only to find he's at a conference in out of town. Sometimes the opposition tries one ploy of setting up a meeting where grievances will be aired or negotiations are to start. At the last minute – often as the meeting is to about to get underway – it is announced that the Minister or Director cannot be there, but that he has delegated so-and-so to sit in for him, and that so-and-so will give him all the details later. A good general rule is that the organization should leave immediately, conveying the message that we will talk to the Minister or Director, or no one. While it is frustrating not to be able to "have your say" it is preferable to staying and wasting our time with some "flak catcher" who cannot (we can bet) give us anything but, "I'll be sure the ... sees your request and I am sure he will give it appropriate consideration." In effect we want to say: "We are important enough to deal with the top person and you are going to have to learn to treat us that way."

5. A Word on the Event

There are a number of purposes for putting out sufficient word about our event:

a. Some people may want to join the demonstration. We may wish to see them join, either to swell the numbers present, or to show the level and breadth of our support to the general community.

b. There may be some important people who are straddling the fence on the issue for which the organization is fighting. It may be wise to keep these people informed on the objectives and scope of the action, rather than risk them getting a distorted view from either the media or the opposition. There is always, of course, a risk that some of the strategy may get "leaked," and this possibility must be weighed against the possibilities indicated above.

c. There may be sympathetic people who wish to work behind the scenes on the issue, and for whom it is wise not to be at the scene of the event. This way they are not forced to take a "public position.".

Example: During a strike at an Ontario Children's Aid Society, there was one agency board member who, after some soul-searching, decided that management was manipulating the situation to prolong the strike and break the union. Her strategy became one of raising embarrassing questions with the Director and the agency bargaining team, and occasionally to leak board discussions to the union. Obviously, this person was invaluable to the workers and great care was taken to keep her informed of the time and place of any major demonstrations, so that she could avoid potentially embarrassing situations and maintain her credibility with her co-board members.

6. Invitations to "talk"

Occasionally, the people (or institution), against whom the demonstration is taking place will offer to talk things over with the demonstrators. It is a good idea to be prepared for this because, whether the intent is sincere, or merely a ploy to cool down the event, it is an opportunity to escalate the pressure and to demonstrate the competence of the organization.

Sometimes the other side will invite a small number of leaders to go inside for a talk. It is important that the people decide:

a) *Do we accept the invitation?* This is a question for the members to decide. Don't worry about making the other side wait; take some time to let our folks talk things over and make the decision.

b) *How many people do we send?* It should not be everyone because the demonstration, or picketing, etc., must be maintained. On the other hand, it is important for the organization not to silently submit to the instructions of the opposition. The number chosen should reflect the needs and desires of the people, not those of the institution.

c) *Who does the talking?* The other side, operating on their bureaucratic model, may want the leaders of the organization. The people, on the other hand, want to be consistent with the democratic nature of their organization. Besides this, the leaders of this public display may not be the organization leaders, and neither group may be the best suited to lead a delegation in this situation. Thus, it is important to have some sort of contingency plan on how to make these kinds of decisions, so that confusion does not occur and the appropriate decision can be made in good time.

d) *Remember accountability.* If there is any chance that what may go on inside could lead to a decision that will affect the organization or the people demonstrating, the group that goes in must understand that they are accountable – that the decision is not final until the people say it is. It is a good idea to try to anticipate an offer so you don't get caught off-guard.

e) *To whom will the delegation talk?* It is important for the group to clarify "what" is to be part of the discussion. As indicated above, it is frustrating and a waste of time to talk to a "flak catcher" who has no authority. Make sure that our people are going to be talking to decision makers.

7. Use of Symbols

It is a good idea to use images that are symbolic of the principles or cause for which the community stands. Aboriginal groups are often very good at this but so are others.

Example: Marian Porter tells of how she with other disability activists in Cork Ireland wanted to draw attention to the many obstacles confronted by people with disabilities. A group with various disabilities – hearing, sight, etc. – pushed one of their wheelchair members all over the city. They videotaped themselves struggling with the wheelchair over curbs, and confronting inaccessible buildings. They presented the tape to a government Minister as support for their demand to have money spent on redressing the situation.

8. Hecklers and Rowdy Bozos

One of the things that strikes fear into the hearts of many group leaders and organizers is that a well-planned demonstration will be disrupted by people intent on turning things ugly, such as a brawl or a profanity-riddled shouting match, where the message gets lost in a hail of four-letter words. If the potential for such a situation becomes apparent, we can consider the following:

a) Try accommodating the heckler. Most hecklers thrive on situations where they are allowed to stand on the periphery of the crowd and yell inane comments and questions. It is important that the organization's speaker not get into a shouting or name calling match with them. It often can disconcert them to have a speaker offer them a few minutes "to have their say" or to ask their questions. They are not prepared for this – the strength of a heckler's position is his ability to play himself off what the speaker is saying – yet it is hard to refuse the offer. They have to come up and do the best they can or else they lose face. What they say is most often incoherent. Even if they are able to ask an embarrassing question, the speaker has gained time to think of how to deal with the issues the heckler has raised, as well as the sympathy of the audience. After being given the floor for a couple of minutes, it is difficult to go back to being a heckler. After all he's been given "his opportunity."

Note: If our people decide it is a good idea to heckle the opposition meeting, we must go armed with a prepared statement, or some facts and figures, in case the other side tries to pull this stratagem on us.

b) Be firm with the rowdy. Rowdies come in all shapes and sizes and with various motivations. They range from young fellows who have had too much to drink at the street dance, to a trained provocateur at a march on a picket line (Lakey, 1987) – witness the two undercover policemen carrying the banner at the April 1981 gay rights march in Toronto, and the ensuing violence. Both situations are tricky to deal with. Whatever one does, the general rule of thumb is to be prepared to handle the situation quickly.

- One method is to have a small group of marshals patrol the site of the event prepared to single out would-be trouble makers. This method works best for keeping tabs on single people, particularly if it is a community person who is drunk or cranked up on drugs. The objective is to reduce the attention he is causing, and convince him to calm down or leave quietly.

Example: There is a wonderful scene in the 1939 film *Grapes of Wrath* in which a company goon squad tries to infiltrate the celebrations of a group of migrant farm workers in an attempt to start a riot, and discredit the people and their camp. Before they can foment anything, however, the thugs are quietly surrounded by a group of marshals who had been organized by the camp residents. The marshals escort them, firmly but peacefully, away from the celebrations.

- If things look at all like they might get out of hand, ask (or even demand) that the police handle it. If it is any kind of large event - particularly if it is a picket or a march - you know the police will be around. Do not let the situation get so out of hand that they will feel compelled to close the event down.
- Police themselves can be a provocative element. At a March in support of Native rights during the week of the notorious G-20 talks in Toronto in 2010 a police officer attempted to provoke some of the marchers by yelling at people to move so he could let a car that had been parked illegally move. Some of the folks started to resist but very quickly a marshall appeared, intervened with the driver and the upset marchers and lowered the temperature. The officer looked disappointed and frustrated as the marchers moved on. The quick and calm actions of the marshal prevented a senseless confrontation and possibly the arrest of some of the participants.[5]

9. Permits and Permissions

Any event that is going to use a public place – streets, a school yard or parking – is going to need some sort of authorization, perhaps a permit and maybe the co-operation of the police. Be sure someone in the organization is assigned to handle that.

Using the Media

Keep in mind, no matter how much "right wing" politicians and business people accuse the press of being "left wing," the various print and electronic media are owned by people who are not in the least disad-

---

[5]   Many situations of course did not have this kind of positive result and in the two days that followed there were around 1000 arrests. Most of the people were eventually released without charge, or had charges dropped in subsequent weeks, of course. This is a typical police tactic: arresting activists simply to disrupt a march.

vantaged. Conrad Black's Hollinger International once owned almost 50 per cent of Canada's newspapers; Rupert Murdoch (the Australian multi-billionaire) owns huge pieces of both print and electronic media around the world. The economic journalist, Linda McQuaig, tells a story of when she was working for the *Globe and Mail* (Canada's national newspaper). She was asked to come into the managing editor's office to discuss a series she had been doing on the Canadian tax system. He warned her not to suggest that there was "some sort of class struggle out there." As Ms. McQuaig told her audience, "It was alright for there to be a class struggle, so long as we (the media) did not call attention to it" (McMaster University School of Social Work Field Forum, March 18, 1997).

There is no automatic belief in, or sympathy with, our cause; in fact it may be more reasonable to expect antipathy. Note the fact that, in 1998, David Black (owner of more than 60 newspapers in British Columbia) gave a directive to his journalists: that nothing in favour of the Nishga Treaty will be allowed in any of his newspapers' editorial sections – clearly an example of elites using the media to promote their own views and interests. Thus, it is unlikely we will ever get the kind of coverage we want. The welfare-rights groups of the late 1960s were generally portrayed by the media as a gang of left-wing fanatics. The first social work strikes of the 1970s got very little print coverage at all. Later ones did not fare much better. Members of both "The Right to Life" movement and "Abortion on Demand" groups complain that coverage is insufficiently sympathetic to their causes.

Example: In Melbourne, Australia in 1991, a group of men held a rally and march to focus on male responsibility for violence against women. The event attracted over 300 participants; not bad for a first attempt. The major coverage came from a right-wing columnist who ridiculed the purpose for, and the numbers of, the rally. For most of the rest of the media, it was treated as almost a non-event. By and large, then, it would be unwise to depend on getting positive media coverage to further our group's interests. However, there are a few basic guidelines that should be kept in mind when planning a media event:

a) *Be sure the various media know that an action is going to take place.* It is a good idea to have certain members develop contacts with particular media. However, even if this is accomplished, do not rely on that contact to be perfect and to always get our story right – the way we want it. The greatest benefit a contact can offer, especially on a newspaper, is his ability to let the organization know "the slant" the paper or station likes so that we can tailor our communication with that in mind. We can also get a sense, from a good and honest contact, of how interested the particular medium is in the particular issue or cause represented by our organization. Finally, we can get a sense of "why" our great monster rally received no TV coverage, or only got four lines on the bottom of page 92 in the morning paper just under the liver pill ad.

b) *Keep the message clear and simple.* The more complicated the points that we're trying to make with the public, the more likely the reporter or her editor will get something wrong. Be vigilant that our message does not get distorted by media which want a sensational story

Example: An American organizer related her frustration with media. "They did back flips for the attention of the media, but lost all control over the coverage when it came. On the rare occasions when reporters decided to do an 'East L.A.' story, they wrote up protestors and their targets Hollywood-style – as difficult warring 'personalities'. Or if they were especially sympathetic, they presented a sentimental victim scenario, utterly at odds with the IAF philosophy of competence and self-reliance" (Skerry, in Kerr 1993 c).

c) *Make a TV event a TV event.* If the group wishes particularly to get some TV coverage then tailor that action for TV. (Watch political parties during election time.) There are media events and there are mass rallies. The two often don't mix. A TV event should have something unique about it, such as a major announcement or some guerrilla theater; something that gives the station a reason for using it.

d) *Be prepared to be innovative and take advantage of immediate conditions and situations.*

Example: Shannon Beard, a Canadian disability-rights activist, tells the story of an initial information session held by the "Ontarians With

Disabilities Act (ODA) Committee" for Halton-Peel at the public library (stress on the "public"). This facility turned out to be most inaccessible for persons using wheelchairs, or with vision impairment. Though ramps were available for use, wheelchair users found them too narrow, and placed inappropriately. Very tight turns and a lack of space were a big problem. Persons with vision impairment had great difficulty, as the lighting was very dim, making reading material (and navigating one's way independently), very tricky. Ironically, this facility's barriers served to address the ODA Committee's very core issues: lack of accessibility. This development proved beneficial when talking to the media and promoting the committee's goals. At a different time, some ODA Committee members went to see an MPP in York region and found the office inaccessible by wheelchair. Despite chilly winter conditions, the meeting was held in the parking lot, with local newspapers standing close by. It was a great media catcher and a great statement to the community.

e) Designate a media liaison. Have someone in the organization delegated to handle the media. He must be calm, and be able to handle himself in confusing circumstances.

f) Be careful not to get public media coverage before we are ready for it. We want to utilize the media to get the message out, not simply to be used by them to sell papers or advertising time. One danger is that the media coverage may raise expectations, and suggest that the issue is popular when it isn't (yet). It may raise expectations that something is going to happen quickly, when we know rarely does any community development happen fast.

Also watch out! The press is pretty good at grabbing a member who is unprepared, and getting him to say something that sounds silly or inappropriate.

Example: At a deputation, at a Hamilton City Council meeting by a local Native group, a couple of reporters were all over members of the group, asking if the members felt the remarks by some councilors had been racist. Everyone in the group referred them to one of three spokeswomen who were calm, prepared, and able to keep the tenor of the event "cool." It would have been good copy for the paper if racist charges had been levelled, – and in fact one particular councillor had indeed angered the people with some paternalistic comments – but it had been planned by the organization, not as a media event, rather as a low-key education for councillors. There was no payoff for the group to start a controversy at that time.

g) Prepare for your press conferences.
- Send out a press package ten days before an event with: basic information; address; time; and any other information you think they should have;
- Repeat sending a press package the same the day of, and just prior to, the press conference;
- Have someone to: stop/start the conference; and to introduce those involved (make sure we know what they are going to say;
- Target the particular press that we want. We will not want to bother with a station or paper that is likely to do a hatchet job on our organization or the issue;
- Be there half an hour early, because the press will be there about then;
- Have the press package with us, of up-to-date information that we want them to have. They will find it easier to report accurately, if they have this to use.

Technological Media[6]

One way of getting information out on our group – its events, or about issues in which we are interested and involved – is to use computer technology (O'Malley, 1998). This is an increasingly popular method of information exchange, keeping ourselves informed, keeping in touch, and for actual organizing. This can be a complex subject and one which we will only touch on briefly, but there are some clear reasons "why" we should consider the use of cyberspace.

---

[6]   For a good discussion of the use of high-tech communication, see Kady O'Malley (1998), *"Grassroots in Cyberspace"* or Rykert and James (1998), *Working Together On-Line.*

So what are the possibilities that internet technology provides to community organizing?

The internet has provided a method for community groups and organizations to communicate internally, with each other and with the wider community including participants of their programs and users of their services, community members, other local businesses, institutions, and groups and organizations external to their community. Emails, email lists, and websites are popular internet technologies that the many community organizations use to communicate with their constituents and stakeholders. In particular, LISTSERV is an email list that does not require management by a human. Individuals provide their email addresses to become part of an electronic mailing list and the messages are sent automatically to everyone on the list at the same time, but individual addresses are not displayed. Through LISTSERV, organizations can more easily share information and have discussions among large numbers of people.

Similarly, Google Mail allows users to send out emails to large groups without LISTSERV software using Google Groups. This orientation to organizing was famously in evidence in the recent campaign for the presidency of the U.S.A. by Barack Obama. It was perhaps pioneered by the campaign of Howard Dean who took a run at the Democratic nomination for president in 2004 (Trippi, 2004). Both campaigns utilized the internet to inform and mobilize constituents and potential supporters by "crowdsourcing". This is a method where supporters are encouraged to connect with each other over the internet and create message boards, LISTSERVs to inform each other as to the important events and issues in a campaign. In effect it is extremely democratic in that those who become involved are encouraged to become active in organizing in local areas. Thus, this is a very interesting notion for campaigns that are far flung and where-face-to-face communication is difficult or even impossible.

There are limits of course. One organization suggests that email has limited efficiency in some ways since people are relying on it to share information that could be more effectively communicated in other ways:

Email is used extensively to distribute information – but it can be problematic because it is often used to send large documents to all staff and takes a lot of room on the organization's system. For example, often large Portable Document Formats (PDF) may be sent to everyone and result in crashing the system and using up space when what really needs to happen is an email which includes a link and directions of how to get the information.[7]

Outside of email, websites provide one of the most popular ways to connecting with constituents online. Community organizations can have a basic website which outlines the history, mandate and vision, programs and services, map/directions and some include information about work that they've done and projects they are involved with. For example, the Toronto Neighbourhood Centre's network website provides links to several member agencies.[8] More recently, a number of community-based agencies are using social networking tools such as YouTube, Facebook and MySpace to connect with their younger constituents who are already using these methods as a primary means of communication, and to teach their older constituents how to use these methods as a way to access news about their country or city of origin, as well as a way to communicate with family members who live other countries and cities.

Example: One Toronto-based organization has created a web-based version of tools from their seniors' program. It uses theatre to raise awareness and address concerns about issues that participants face. In addition to providing a background to the program, the website includes online demonstrations of plays with a photo gallery, a manual, an opportunity for feedback, and a forum to ask questions or to volunteer. This website is also a resource for groups who are interested in replicating this program: www.seniorstheatre.org/manual_program.html.

The internet can provide community organizations with a quick way to reach very large numbers of people relatively quickly and efficiently

---

[7]　Interview with Rick Eagan, Community Development Coordinator, St. Christopher House, July II, 2008.

[8]　Links to Neighbourhood Centre websites, Toronto Members. http://neighbourhoodcentres.ca/links.htm. Retrieved July 30, 2008.

without the time, effort, and expense required by usual methods of mass communication such as meetings, press releases, door-to-door campaigning, telephone trees and mail outs.[9] A single email can be sent to hundreds or thousands of people on a listserv in an instant, and a social networking profile is continuously connected to hundreds of different people who participate in networking sites. In addition to simply connecting people, online networking sites create an opportunity for people to engage, buy into, dialogue and respond to issues. There are many examples of times when email lists and social networking tools were used to initiate discourse, educate, and influence potential constituents about an issue.

Some community organizations have used internet technologies in more innovative ways to engage their constituents in their work. For example, organizations have included tools on their website to allow community members to connect with others in new ways through exchange of writing, pictures, and other types of information.

There are also some problems, associated with the use of cyberspace, that need to be recognized and considered:

1. Some folks are a bit put-off by, or fearful of, complex technology for a variety of reasons;

2. Some folks will simply not have access to the technology either because of geography, or a lack of infrastructure (e.g. a rural village in Africa or Latin America may not have electricity, let alone computers or software);

3. Some groups (here in North America and abroad) may not have the financial resources to purchase the basic technology required; or they may not even have limited training to develop the skills needed to participate in such high-tech communication. In some sense, an uncritical espousal of high-tech information sharing can increase the distance between haves and have-nots. Some of this can be overcome by organizing those "with access" to support those "with-

---

9 Tech Rocks. *Why Internet Organizing Benefits your Organization*. http://livemodern.com/why_final.pdf, Retrieved June 13, 2008.

out ready access" but this takes time, and we need to be clear on the payoffs for our group.

None of these limitations should be read as reasons to not consider and utilize Information Technology (IT). It is simply like any tool, it needs to be used with thought; how it fits with the needs, abilities, expectations of the people with whom we work and the issues which they face. Information Technology is here to stay; it is not a substitute for basic organizing but rather an important adjunct.

A Word about Civil Disobedience

Our discussion of demonstrations did not at any time focus on civil disobedience. This might seem strange, given the militant tone of much of this book and the urgency of many of the problems with which disadvantaged and marginalized people are faced. The reason is not because such a discussion is unimportant. Indeed it is an important topic for an organizer, and requires consideration when the forces of a particularly odious status quo prove themselves to be totally unmoved by reasonable argument and legitimate protest. Mohandas Gandhi and his movements in South Africa and in India were forced to resort to civil disobedience. We note also some examples of civil disobedience in the civil rights activities, and Vietnam War protests of the 1960s and 70s. Today we see examples in the activities of Aboriginal People (attempting to bring resistant governments to the bargaining table over land claims and pollution issues) and in the actions of social justice groups, like the Ontario Coalition Against Poverty, confronting the neo-conservative agenda of the Ontario government and its aftermath. People who, after agonizing over an issue and deciding that as a last resort they must engage in an activity that risks arrest on a civil (not a criminal) offence, must think through the implications both for themselves as individuals and for their organization (Amer, 1980: 115). Some unions have been fined thousands of dollars for defying court orders.

So, if civil disobedience is so important, why not deal with it at length? There are two reasons. First, as indicated above, civil disobedience is a serious and complex strategy undertaken as a last resort. Be clear, it means that some law or laws must be broken and the risk of arrest and imprisonment is real for participants. A decision to engage in an endeavour of this kind requires sophisticated reflection and discussion. Defying a law – a civil one, even for very compelling reasons – is not something that is generally socially accepted in our society. When such a decision is made, it is necessary to spend time in planning and training. The law and its sanctions must be understood and training must be provided to ensure that none of the participants get injured, and discipline is maintained. (Police can become frustrated, angry, and even frightened when faced with a large number of committed people). This book is primarily oriented to student organizers or those relatively new to the field. It is not anticipated that these workers will be required to be involved in issues that call for the last resort of civil disobedience, at least not as organizers. As well, since most of the members of our society are not comfortable with the notion of "law breaking," and tend to equate it with violence, it is relatively unlikely that civil disobedience will occur as an option to very many groups. Secondly, there are some books available that treat the subject with sensitivity and creativity. *Yes We Can* (Amer, 1980: 15-20) and *Allow the Water* (Desroches, 1996) offer a Canadian perspective, and some interesting case examples. The three volume series *The Politics of Non-Violent Action* (Sharpe, 1973), and Lakey's (1987) *Powerful Peacemaking* offer excellent material from an American perspective. As well there are organizations that offer workshops on non-violent action. For example, the Centre for Applied Non-Violent Action and Strategies (http://www.canvasopedia.org/); the Irish Network for Nonviolent Action Training and Education (http://www.innatenonviolence.org/), Training For Change (http://www.trainingforchange.org/content/view/131/53/index.html) and the Alliance for Non-Violent Action (http://www.connexions. org/Groups/Subscribers/cxg5450.htm). The AIDS action group, ACT UP Civil Disobedience Training (http://www.actupny.org/documents/ CDdocuments/Affinity.html) offers some great on-line tips. There are many others.

Negotiation

In a contest situation, we expect that sooner or later (hopefully sooner) the opposition is going to accept the invitation to sit and discuss the issues. Our folks are going to be asked to make their case, and are going to be offered less than they demand. This is what happens when groups begin to negotiate. Each side will begin with their "realistic ideal" position and over time will agree upon a realistic possible solution to the issue. The trick in negotiating is to have the final agreement closer to the people's "realistic ideal" than that of the opposition. It can be a long process, sometimes exciting but often tiring; and, as in every aspect of a community's striving to gain a measure of control over its own destiny, it takes diligent work and careful planning. Remember also that, ultimately, a deal is about redefining a continuing relationship in which the people will share power and resources.

1. Principles Guiding Negotiation

Never begin negotiating without:

a) *A clear and firm idea of what we need.* If we go in waffling, the other side will have every opening to waffle too. We are trying to change the other side; thus we have to be clear on what the situation is, and how we want it changed.

b) *Helping the members be clear on the values, principles and analysis, of what we are doing.* There will come a time for compromise, and these are the moments that will guide members in what we must have, what we can do without, and what can be altered.

c) *A reasonably strong organizational base.* Remember, power – the ability to make something happen or not happen – depends on money, and/or information, and/or numbers of people. It is the latter that our organization has, as well as an issue. But having an issue that people are excited about is clearly not sufficient. Organization brings in people, and hopefully information; and thus, sometimes expertise. This gives the people more power, without which negotiation will never really take place.

d) *Being clear on the context within which our group is negotiating.* This includes our own experience: be aware of our own personal style of using power and dealing with conflict. Obviously, we are not in a negotiating position because everything is smooth, everyone is in agreement and we can do what we want. Negotiation presupposes – even if at very low levels sometimes – conflict and power. Therefore, we need to be clear about our own personal tendencies, so that we can set that in the context of the principles that are at stake and the realities we face.

Example: On a personal note, my experience is that of a social worker and adult educator. I have worked as a union organizer, child welfare worker; with Aboriginal groups, neighbourhood organizations, and housing co-operatives. I grew up in a tough neighbourhood in Toronto, where we Irish Catholic kids fought over turf against Orange Protestants[10] and most kids didn't finish high school, and where I was unique in having a two-parent family. This experience has given me a particular slant on organizing, power, and the use of conflict. My initial tendency is to look for the bad guys and the good guys, to be somewhat abrasive and aggressive, and I need to be aware of that and moderate it. Abrasiveness and aggressiveness have their place but they have to be appropriate to the conditions and the needs and abilities of the people involved.

Some other questions to consider:

- What are the experiences of the people involved? (Be aware of areas where we may be weak in knowledge and experience, and work to strengthen them or minimize their impact.)
- What does the opposition want? What are the opposition's strengths, and how do we deal with them?
- What is the history of the relationship with the opposition, and how might this effect the process?

e) *Be clear on our own bottom line*. That is, what we absolutely have to have. Again, be sure our people have thought this through.

---

[10] Indeed Catholics were barred for jobs with the City, whose administration was dominated by the Orange Lodge, and they couldn't work in some of the major businesses such as the Eaton's Department Store. This changed in the mid-1950s as immigrants – the majority of them Catholic – moved into the city and began to take part in political life. Finally in 1954 the population elected its first Jewish mayor who had run on a platform, "A Mayor for All the People."

2. Tactics

a) Role play. Never do any important negotiating without doing some role playing. Try to think of, and act out, the other side's feelings, tactics and responses. Practice our responses to these. Reduce surprise as much as possible.

b) Begin with a realistic but ideal position. Do not start with our compromise position. Initially, our group will "have to have" things we may be prepared to give up, but the other side should not see too soon what they are.

c) Don't send a leader to negotiate alone. Use a delegation—a negotiation team. This gives the group an opportunity to broaden leadership and involvement. The team should be representative. There are three kinds of people for delegations:

- **those with a following;**
- **those who work hard; and,**
- **those who are able to take discipline.**

d) Practice discipline. While we should use a delegation, watch out for the other side's attempt to pick us off one by one, or trying to alter the focus of discussion such as: "Nice dress you have on there."; "Why is she so angry?"; "We don't have to be impolite." They will probably try to undercut our leadership, particularly if we are new at the game and they know it. Even though we can "smart-mouth" their people back, it can ruin our sense of order. Our leader should be the one to do the majority of the talking (see below).

- One person should be in charge of the delegation to avoid confusion. This is the "spokesperson" or chief negotiator, not necessarily the leader of the organization. All comments should come from the spokesperson, unless our group has some planned operation; in that case the spokesperson should give the signal.
- Use the spokesperson to run things through and keep things on track. If a member of our delegation has something to say, he

should ask the spokesperson to ask it. Then the spokesperson can do what he wants with it. If their "chief" tries to deal with anyone else in our delegation, direct him back to our spokesperson. Usually that kind of discipline is unexpected by, and thus disconcerting to, the other side. We may want to use this tactic to keep control of an enthusiastic hot-head in our ranks, but at the same time train him in negotiation.

- If the spokesperson gets led off the agreed-upon track, or begins to go for a compromise too early or something much less than is reasonable, ask for a caucus of our group. Ask their chief to take his delegation and leave the room. If he will not leave then say: "We'll go outside." Regardless of whether they cooperate, this tactic is usually disconcerting to the other side (outside their experience). It is always up to the chairperson to actually call, or to O.K., or delay the caucus if necessary. Don't caucus unnecessarily or repeatedly. That can make us look silly or unprepared. If there is a disagreement during the group's caucus, then we may have to use a disciplined majority vote (for speed in this kind of situation). The rules for "caucusing" must then be clear for everyone. (How to signal, always go through the leader, etc.) If someone breaks the rules she must be disciplined, **but** not in view of the other side. People **must** be prepared to call a caucus when they see the leader losing her way. At the same time, we have to be responsible and disciplined. As indicated above, we can't be yelling caucus every five minutes. The best rule is to get things as straight as we can before going into the meeting. It may be the organizer's role to move through the delegation encouraging or calming.

e) Be clear about our own power. Don't get into situations in which we have to produce but can't. This can hurt our group's credibility and morale.

f) Define the rules of the negotiating meeting. Keep pushing for our rules and be sure everyone is clear on them – where sessions are held; when it is most convenient for us and our people; whether the deliberations will be confidential; what items are on the table. (Numbers: we may want to bring more people than we agree to, unless the other side is on to this tactic, then bring less. Keep them off balance, if necessary).

Example: An instructive example of this tactic was related by a community worker in Northern Ontario. The area school board had decreed that in the interests of financial expediency, the local community school should be closed. This was a serious problem for the Aboriginal and White families of the area, as it meant that their children would have to be bussed many miles. After a lot of pressure they managed to get the Board to negotiate. A key session was held at the community school itself. When the Board delegation arrived they found practically the whole community assembled. An Aboriginal leader had been elected chairperson because of his ability to deal with large gatherings, and sat at a table at the front of the hall. The Board people were allocated seats throughout the auditorium. It was a matter of "we talk you listen," with the power positions completely reversed. By the end of the meeting the closing decision had been completely reversed. While the tactic was not the only factor in the outcome, it did provide the community with an edge in confidence, and allowed them to push their position with as much force as possible.

g) *Be careful about seating arrangements.* Don't let one of the team members become isolated. Be sure our people are in a position to easily communicate with each other.

h) *Plan a mass action.* (If appropriate, see Demonstrations.) Some people can go inside and negotiate, and the rest stay outside to educate the public on the issues under negotiation. While we grab the publicity (or merely allow members to sing, dance, and enjoy themselves) this makes the other side uncomfortable. The negotiating people inside must know who is outside. The mass action must be well choreographed. Plan ahead of time who is to go in, and who is to stay out. The people inside should be responsible to those on the outside— remember accountability. The negotiating team should report at the end of the proceedings, or in the middle if negotiating goes on very long. This action keeps the other side off balance while helping to solidify our group. Also, it is good modeling as an open, **evolving** people's organization.

i) Control the experts. If experts (lawyers, accountants, architects) are used, they should "know their place" i.e., under the control of the popular leadership. If, in an actual negotiating session the organization has an expert to use, make sure the leader is still in control of our team. The experts work for the people. Do not let them jockey for position with those from the other side in a struggle that has nothing to do with why we are there. It is actually better to have the leadership extremely well-schooled in the pertinent expertise, though sometimes it is also good to have a surprise (or mysterious) expert to keep the other side off balance. The important thing is teamwork and having a captain who will pilot the action through.

Example: A group of child welfare workers, who were trying to negotiate their first contract, used a "mystery consultant." I was introduced simply as a "consultant" but nothing more. In actual fact I was helping the union do some organizing, and merely came along to observe. It turned out that my presence knocked the management lawyer's concentration for a loop. For the first two long sessions the lawyer would stare at me. Finally, near the end of the second session, I asked for a caucus (because I thought the social workers' position was getting a bit confused). When the bargaining team came back in, the agency's lawyer stood up triumphantly and yelled, "Ah ha, I knew it all the time, you're their labour relations expert." The group burst out laughing. Nobody said anything, but you could feel the team's confidence rise as they perceived the other side was confused and off-balance.

j) Look for common principles and practical common ground. Our group may have a number of issues it wants resolved. Some will be easier than others because they do not challenge the power of the other side. It is helpful to look for commonalities because: it gives everyone on both sides a sense of accomplishment; it sets a constructive tone; and, if issues are left to the end of a tough continuous set of negotiations they may turn into hard issues. Help the other side see where its self-interest is enhanced by our position, or at least where it is not banned.

k) Do sufficient research on the other side (this may cost money to hire someone for the work.) Understand where their "bottom line" really is. It is important for us to be able to recognize when there is some real movement, or compromise, on their part. It is no use trying to push them further than they can legitimately go, or further than our people need. On the other hand, we don't want to be fooled into accepting a supposedly magnanimous offer, when the other side can afford to give more.

l) Use third parties. If things get tough, don't be afraid to slow down the process. (We may want to see if we can get other people involved as mediators formally, informally or even secretly). Remember our "neutral" group from earlier in the chapter. This may be a good place to look for a mediator.

Example: A group of Aboriginal people were involved in a struggle with the administration of a Native Centre. They felt (not without reason) that the Director had not been managing the Centre in the interests of the whole community. The Director had supporters— mostly on the Board of Directors. After months of bitter negotiations about what should be done, the two sides were so far apart that they could not even meet. The citizen group called on a non-Native professor at the local university. He was sympathetic to them, but not directly involved. Because he was seen to carry little political baggage he was to get the parties back to the table.

m) Get the other side to put its points in writing. If there is some agreement, get them to specify the actions to be taken, any steps involved, and the timelines.

n) If we decide to compromise, be sure to make it clear to the other side that we have given up some of our position. We don't do this in an attempt to be holier than thou or sanctimonious. We are doing two things:

- Modeling unselfish behaviour which can lower the temperature of a heated situation;
- Gaining or maintaining a moral high ground.

By the way, if the "other" does some compromising of significance, we have to be prepared to acknowledge that and consider what this means to our position. (Be aware, however, of the "yellow carnation[II] the tactic of one side making some sort of offer which is pretty looking but does not bear on the fundamental issues we are dealing with.)

o) *Be prepared that in some cases there may be irreconcilable differences.* This is rare. Nevertheless, it is not useful to keep negotiating – no matter how much we want to come to an agreement – if we are being jerked around. Sometimes, for our sanity or reputation, we have to walk away from negotiation and either seek more adversarial strategies or abandon the issue.

A Word about the Effort of Community Members

McMaster University student, Sarah McAuley (2007) wrote her MSW thesis about a campaign against a polluting company. In interviewing the participants one of the issues she found that they highlighted was how much work campaigns required and how much energy it took for the folks to be involved. One of people told her how, *"it can take over your life, and that was what we felt like when we first started along and for the first part of the campaign I guess it's overwhelming because it's such a huge information gathering and learning curve."* (McAuley, 2007: 55) This person really draws our attention to the fact that it is not simply a matter of coming to a few meetings or even taking part in a picket. People are rarely born activists. They come to it because of the need to do something and they have to learn the ropes. And invariably some of those involved will have to take on more responsibility than others. One woman told Sarah:

[II] The symbol of being offered a yellow carnation comes from a story told by a California organizer. The group he was working with was campaigning against a bank that refused to lend to people living in a particular area of the city. Issues of racism and classism were strongly suspected. During the initial negotiation session a bank officer said that the bank could not change its policy but would offer to give everyone who opened a bank account there a yellow carnation (most of the organization was made up of women). It was rightly seen as a sign of not only deep classism but sexism that was part of the bank's modus operandi.

It's always so short changed, like the minutes, the communication, the making the appointments, just, you know, keeping track of contact information and mailing and that sort of thing. It's great to have volunteers to do a lot of those chores but the thing is that you have to have someone putting it all together first. ... I think that too often people don't understand that there is a lot of coordinating that goes on ahead of time in order for them to do their volunteer work (McAuley, 2007: 55-56).

Thus one of the important things the organizer has to do is to help activists be aware of the demands of the various levels of involvement and be understanding and supportive (remember that role from our earlier discussion) of how hard the members are working. Of course another task this might demand of the organizer is that s/he assist participants to realize the importance of sharing the load. McAuley (2007) found that in some instances resentment built up among group members when they felt really tired and they felt that others weren't doing enough. One of her respondents put it forcefully:

People look at a group and think, well I don't know what they think, but that someone's getting paid to run it and they're gonna show up to a meeting and tell people what to do. And maybe you need to state it at the beginning of every meeting, we're all volunteers and we need all the help we can get, cause that would wear you down (McAuley, 2007: 57).

So again, it may be useful for the organizer to help the people involved see the likelihood that sometimes the help won't be as strong as they would like (in the previous chapter we talked about the multiple demands on members); or that some work was simply not interesting (though necessary) and folks would not readily volunteer.

Some members felt as though people were willing to come to community meetings and make suggestions for what could be done, however they did not offer to help with it. Some work that is more difficult, or less exciting, is often left for a small group of leaders who are willing to put in the work. This left the participants tired and overwhelmed (McAuley: 2007: 56).

On the other hand members may themselves come to see solutions. McAuley recounts what the group she researched did:

> It is important to note that members of the group did not simply "stew" over the problem. ... A couple of the participants agreed that that the solution to this problem would be to find out what people are good at, what they like, and what they are comfortable with, and having them work on those tasks. In fact the group came to the conclusion that if people don't enjoy what they are doing they won't participate, leaving the brunt of the work to a small group of people. As one participant said: "You gotta match, and you do that, by doing what [the organizer] did, it's just having people choose what they do and attracting enough people to the group that there are enough people to cover all of the bases by not overwhelming them ,and making it fun" (McAuley, 2007: 57).

There are a number of issues that can arise because of the amount of work required to pull off an effective campaign. The important thing however is to be aware of the demands it places on community members (not how much it may be in their own interests), be ready to assist them and to facilitate their own creativity in coming up with solutions.

Reflection

Popular action is the key to positive change. It involves citizens doing what they believe needs to be done, on issues that they have chosen and understood as important to their lives. It is not always about winning – not that this is not important. In popular action we are not only trying to achieve concrete results; we are also learning from our reflections on our actions, learning about ourselves, our adversaries, and the issues themselves. Popular action is not only limited to strategies and tactics, though of course they are important in taking strong, positive action. It is worth repeating Freire here: activity without reflection is simply activism. Part of what we want to achieve is an increase in the people's (and our own) understanding of the world in which we act.

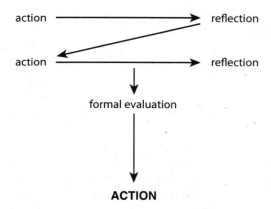

Figure 11-3: Popular Action Phase Summary

Chapter 12

EVALUATION

The unexamined life is not worth living.
- Socrates

Evaluation is important to community organizing (Fraser, 2005; Joseph Rowntree Foundation, 2000). We undertake it as part of more systematic critical reflection upon programs and projects we are involved in, and as a way of thinking about doing things better in the future. Moreover, monitoring and evaluation are not just technical processes, they are "fundamentally social, political and value-oriented activities" (Kenny, 2002: 1). This orientation frames the material in this chapter. It's important for a couple of reasons. Typically, evaluation is understood as part of implementing accountability to funders (Pictoff, 2004). This is no small matter. It is reasonable that a funder that provides resources to a project or campaign expects that the folks who have used those resources have used them for what was agreed. However, this should not be the sole way we think about this important aspect of community organizing. It is rare that a sponsor can specify objectives that are sufficiently concrete and measurable. As Pictoff (2004: 28) notes: "...But building human capital does not lend itself to scientific methods, it's about human dynamics, and trying to take a measure of such relationships is much more difficult than simply looking at organizations to determine what's working and what's not."

As well, when the funder is a secondary or outside entity, it is not in a strategic (or moral) position to develop objectives that are sure to be relevant to community members. We have spoken already (see Chapter 7) of the process of transferring accountability for what the organizer does from the funder to the community itself. So, as well as relating to the goals and objectives of the sponsor, the community's goals, objectives and strategies must be taken into consideration. For example, does the community now have better resources, better participation, and skilled, sensitive leadership? Is there an improved ability to engage in the wider society to get their agendas on the table? Is there evidence that members are more confident? Is there improved community cohesion?

While these are good questions in general, they are just that – general. For example, they don't really direct us to think about whether the objectives are realistic, or how widespread within the community is the power that has been achieved, or how anything was accomplished. A comprehensive evaluation will ask both descriptive questions (such as "what happened?") and analytical ones (such as "how did things happen?" and "why did they happen the way they did?" or "how were people involved and why?")

As well as the "informing" questions that need to be asked for a thorough evaluation, there are some principles that are useful to keep in mind throughout this process.

Principles Guiding Evaluations

1. *Early and explicit inclusion of evaluation process.* As stated earlier, evaluation is most helpful and most possible if it has been built into the organizing process at the outset. This does not mean that we've had to arrange for a set of "before and after questionnaires" and a computer program. It does mean that the "fact" of evaluation, and reality that the funder will indeed want a report, should be made clear as soon as possible. It should also be clear "why" the evaluation is to be done, and what implications it has:

   - End or scaling down of the project or community worker time?
   - Refunding?
   - A new role for the worker?
   - A new direction for the project?
   - Anything else?

2. *Community awareness and involvement in the evaluation.* The people in the community must be aware that it's occurring. Further, they should be involved in a central way (Checkoway, Dobbie, Richards-Schuster, 2005). After all, this evaluation is bound to have some effect on them; and, given our stance that the community should be able to affect their environment and their lives, this should be somewhat under their control.

- The process of developing the evaluation generally should be an open one, with the opportunity to give input available to as many members as possible. (Remember the community analysis.) Thus, it is important to be clear about who gets to frame the questions, and why.
- Similarly, it is important to make sure there is widespread opportunity for people to have their opinions heard. There is also the issue of form and language. The report must be useful to the membership – not simply a bureaucratic or academic exercise that will gather dust on someone's shelf.
- The findings should be available to everyone. One of the frustrating things that funders sometime do is evaluate programs or agencies and then sit on the results.

Example: A team of community workers was contracted to provide an evaluation of a small, but very active, Northern Ontario community. Both the organization and the evaluation were funded by a government ministry. The evaluation showed that the organization was well known and well thought of in the community. The report was sent in to the ministry, but after a couple of months it had not been released to the community or made public in any way. This seemed strange as the ministry officials had been very adamant that it be done. After a lot of insistence by the organization and the consultants, the report was finally released at a meeting among the organization, ministry officials and the consultants. The officials were highly critical of the report, and claimed the findings were not useful. Later, however, at a private meeting with the consultant, the official said that he hoped that there were no hard feelings. He noted that the report really wasn't that flawed, and said, "The problem is simply that you wrote the wrong report. We wanted ammunition to end funding for this project. We didn't want good news. We thought you'd understand."

3. *Very few surprises.* Because the process is "built in," and as it is a "public" one, the members the community should be prepared for both the questions and findings. Of course, there will be nuances, but there should not be anything that comes out of left field.

4. *Clarity about who gets to frame the question and who does not.* This is very important. Whose perspectives are going to be presented?

Questions Concerning the "Content" of Evaluation[1]

The questions that are developed are going to be more specific and oriented to concrete community situations (remember our objectives in Chapter 5) than these below, but these are the types of questions that can be asked.

1. The Community

a) Did the community develop some degree of influence relative to its needs, its environment or its problems?

b) How is success to be measured in its relationship with the broader community? Is it seen more positively? Does it have more influence?
   - By the degree to which identified problems have been solved?
   - By the presence or absence of necessary, new, or improved resources in – or available to – the community (members)?
   - By the degree of participation of members in the community?
     - Is the participation meaningful? Does it have an effect?
     - Is it around minor issues or major ones? Why?
     - Is the participation varied? (i.e. are some types of issues or events more "popular" than others; or are some areas of the community more active than others?)
   - By the change in degree or nature of conflict within the community? Is there more conflict or less conflict within the com-

---

[1] Ideally these questions can be established and data collected throughout the process too. Typically, however, projects rarely get the kind of funding to undertake this level of rigor. That doesn't mean that it's not a good idea to try to get funding for it at the outset.

munity? Just as important, is conflict dealt with in a healthy constructive manner?
- By the change in communication patterns within the community? How would people see the quality of communication among themselves, and between themselves and the community organization?
- By the number and quality (effectiveness and accessibility) of grassroots organizations?
- By the change in the breadth of leadership within the community? Has there been a proliferation of leadership roles?
- By the extent to which the leadership has been effective? And how?
- By the knowledge and skill level of members?
- In the extent to which the community has developed a better analysis (or picture) of itself and the conditions its members face?
- By an increase in pride of membership, in the way people see themselves, their knowledge, culture, and traditions?

2. Programs and activities

a) Which strategies have been successful and which have not? How is this success to be measured:
- By the numbers involved?
- By the degree of consumer satisfaction?
- Through the measurement of some sort of behavioural change? (Such as less vandalism or drug use or more visiting among members).

b) Were the programs and activities consistent with the goals and objectives of the community? This is not a pejorative question. If inconsistencies are present it may merely mean that the original goal and objectives were not "right", or that the process that developed them was lacking in some way.

c) Were there unforeseen results – positive or negative – from any of the programs or activities?

d) Were there any changes in objectives at any time?
- When did they occur?
- Under what circumstances?
- What process of change was used?

e) Are present directions clear? Do people know what they, as a community, wish to accomplish; or are they waiting around for someone to give them the word?

3. Opposition

a) Who turned out to be the opposition?
   - within the community
   - external to the community
b) Under what conditions did opposition arise?
c) Relative to what issues was there opposition?
d) How effective was the opposition?
e) How effective was the community in countering it?
f) Were we able to swing people from opposition to neutrality, or even further?

4. Allies (outside of the community members)

a) What individuals or institutions turned out to be helpful?
b) Under what conditions did allies surface?
c) Relative to what issues were allies available?
d) How effective were the allies?
e) Did we maintain the support of our original supporters?

5. The Organizer

Clearly many of the questions outlined above reflect on the organizer. In some ways the organizer can take some credit or blame in that he has initiated and facilitated many of the processes that have shaped the present circumstance of the community. However, some specific questions that get at organizer effectiveness are:

a) Can the activities run without him? Why or why not?
b) Has an unapproachable elite been formed within the community?
c) Have internal divisions been cleared or exacerbated?
d) Are internal divisions being handled in a better way?
e) Do members see him realistically (e.g. as a facilitator or initiator) or unrealistically (e.g. a saviour or a devil)? Are members able to see the part, or role, that the organizer has played in their growing sense of themselves, and growing sense of responsibility and power over their own lives?

Reflection

Sometimes it is more appropriate for a community to undertake a review of its activities rather than an evaluation. The differences between the two are important. An evaluation suggests that the project will be investigated and judged according to some set of "objective" criteria. Emphasis is placed primarily on outcomes. A review, on the other hand, seeks to understand the work that the group is doing in a critical manner; namely the issues members are dealing with, and the context within which they exist. This reflects the fact that people grow and change. Often, in community work, it is difficult to arrive at so-called objective (unchanging) criteria on which to make judgments. The context is highly complex and the work is fluid, responding to local and surrounding changes. A review can be critical, useful in posing and answering questions, but it can also be useful in mobilizing thought and support for progressive change among those who participate. McGrath (1998) reminds us: "Critical investigation helps people to look at social problems in the light of what they wish to achieve as self-reliant and self-determining social beings."

All this is not to suggest that evaluations are not necessary and useful – indeed they are often required – but rather that it is wise to strive for the spirit of a review. Its breadth and fluidity offer us a way to focus outcomes, context, and process as dynamic, interrelated parts of a puzzle – one that is never quite solved, but becomes more interesting and intelligible the more we examine the pieces in various combinations.

Chapter 13

THE END

We shall not cease from exploration.
And the end of all our exploring, will be to
arrive where we started.
And know the place for the first time.
- T. S. Elliot (from The Four Quartets)

Sooner or later the organizer is going to be pulling up stakes and leaving the community. Ideally this should happen when she has "worked her way out of a job" and the community no longer needs her. However, there are many reasons for separation from the community when there is still work to be done.

Reasons for Leaving a Job Early

1 .Worker Fatigue

We become tired from meeting the demands of a very challenging job. We may need to take time off, or may need a fresh experience.

Worker fatigue or burnout is an all too common occurrence in all forms of social helping or solidarity work. Lakey et al. (1995), Shields (1994), Cruikshank (1989) and Burghardt (1982) have all pointed to how hard and frustrating the work is; and how it can affect us in negative ways. They suggest various ways of managing and/or overcoming it. Three simple approaches are outlined below:

- Be reflective – Take time to think about how we are reacting to people and situations.
  - How much of it is the situation? Sometimes it is just plain chaotic and crazy.
  - How much of it are the people with whom we are working? They too get tired, or caught up in their own unresolved issues.
- Get or stay connected – Don't try to be a "Lone Ranger." We need to find people we can trust, and with whom we can build supportive relationships. Others can also help us reflect.
- Take a break – If we are not operating effectively we may need to rest a bit. While the pace may be hectic, we can only put off taking care of ourselves for a limited time.

2. Need for New or Different Skills

Difficult though this is to face for most of us, we are not masters of all trades. A developing community may have continuing need for an organizer, but one with different skills than the ones we possess. This can be difficult for both the organizer and the community to deal with; after all, organizing is a personal as well as a political endeavour. Particular relationships will become highly valued and will cause some pain to break off. However, staying beyond one's time can be injurious to both the community and the organizer.

3. The Funding Dries Up

There are times when, through no fault of anyone in the community, a project loses its funding. This can happen when, for example, government is elected or a new administration enters the picture. It can be relatively sudden; and even when it is not, the pain of seeing long-term work go for nothing can be disheartening. In this case, it is important for people to come together to understand that it is not the fault of the community, and to celebrate some of the good things that have taken place along the way. As well, it is important to allow participants to voice their feelings of anger, frustration or betrayal. This was in much evidence when the Conservative government of Steven Harper suddenly scrapped programs that would assist women and for organizations that assisted marginalized/disadvantaged people from mounting court challenges when their rights had been violated. This also needs to be a time for support and analysis – a time to be shared among activists.

Example: In Ontario, when the right-wing conservative government took office, it all but scrapped its Housing Advocacy Program. Many good projects were cancelled, among them the Affordable Housing Action Association of Mississauga. At one of the last meetings, a number of people spoke of the disappointment and feelings of defeat. However, a couple of participants, stated that while they had worked hard, and had hoped for long-term success, they had seen enough of life to realize that the group had been engaged in something that would require a long battle against some powerful elites, and one where many losses could occur. They pointed to some of the small successes that the group had, maintaining that they were disappointed but not defeated – they would continue looking for opportunities to involve themselves in good projects. People started to build on this, and the gloom began to lift. This helped the group see itself in a more positive (but not unrealistic) light, and helped to maintain a level of hope for the future. It helped turn what could have been a defeated, disempowered group of people into one that saw itself as part of a long-term struggle.

4. The Organizer Becomes a Target

As has been noted all throughout this book, community work is hard. It's hard for the workers, and for the people with whom we work. Previous discussions that noted they may have undergone lengthy, serious, and damaging situations which makes it difficult for them to act in the most logical or long-term manner. (Remember the notion of frustration instigated behaviour). Almost all community workers can relate stories of really good people, workers and activists, who ran into trouble as a result of internal community or organizational politics.

Every so often a community worker does make a serious mistake. One situation that can force a person out occurs when serious division arises in the community between two equally strong factions. The organizer may feel she has to take one side or the other— perhaps because she feels one side is totally wrong, or is being very destructive. In this kind of situation the organizer herself can sometimes become the issue (i.e. a target for the internal hostility). It can become like a civil war and, as we know, these are the most vicious and dirty of all conflicts. Again, it can be a hard thing to face; but if she feels that she is becoming the issue, or is becoming personally consumed by it, then it is time that she seriously considers leaving. Clearly this is a very difficult issue and she should seek some outside consultation before she makes up her mind to do anything drastic.

Example: A white community worker was involved in some volunteer work in a Native community. A small but powerful group (including another white person) attempted to seize control of an important Native agency in the city. Part of their strategy was to accuse the worker of "manipulating" the agency and people. After consultation with some community members, it was decided that the worker should withdraw from the conflict and the community. In his absence the issues were relatively easy to clarify, and the 'power grab' became obvious. With time the community was able to resolve the issues creatively. The other white person who had chosen to stay in the conflict had to leave the community and the volunteer worker was invited to return. His credibility was stronger, and the community had gained confidence by handling a difficult situation itself.

5. The Organizer Gets Another Job

It is quite possible that a good organizer may receive a number of job offers in the course of working with her community. An offer may be made that she "cannot refuse." On the other hand, we need to be careful that we don't move from a job too soon. A good community worker will become well known, and attractive job offers may come after only a short time with a community. The opportunities of the new position must be weighed against any possible damage to one's reputation or to the community. It is not a sign of failure for the community to need a worker to follow us.

Note: It is important to realize that, while we may need to move on, that community may still require assistance. Don't get caught in the myth that unless we have worked our way out of a job we are failures. Given the difficulties that communities face, that may be unrealistic in the time we have had together. As one thoughtful community worker once said, "Most of the communities we work with have so much against them that it may take years and years of hard work before they won't need a worker to follow us anymore."

Taking Our Leave

1. Negative Possibilities

Whatever the reason for the termination, it is a crucial event for the organizer and her community. It is not uncommon for people to feel abandoned, hurt, or even angry, no matter how long they have known about the departure. There may be some fear that "we can't make it without you." Even though the members may be able to stand on their own feet, and may have been doing so for a while it is still frightening to do things without the familiar backup of the community organizer.

a) Community members may act negatively toward the organizer. People can make an organizer "pay" for abandonment. This may take the form of:

- guilt trips;
- displaced anger – sometimes an organizer who is leaving can become the target of anger that is really aimed at other organizations or community members. The organizer can be blamed for work being incomplete;
- unreasonable rejection of the organizer's ideas; and/or,
- unrealistic last-minute demands.

Example: An organizer in a housing co-operative had two weeks to go before she left her position. At that point, one of the members of the Board of Directors suggested that she mount and complete a survey of the 125 or so member families in the project. Needless to say the organizer had only sufficient time to explain why she could not take on that big a job in that short a time.

b) The organizer may act negatively toward the community. It is possible too for the organizer to feel guilty and vulnerable. If she is not clear on her feelings she can inadvertently do some destructive things like:

- leaving with very short notice, and leaving the people with the feeling that they have been abandoned;
- making unrealistic last-minute demands on members;

Example: A community worker with a subsidized housing group attempted to get his members to purchase some leadership training from some consultants about three weeks before he was to leave. When he felt that they were not moving so that the contract would be in place before he left, he got angry and berated the president of the association in front of the executive and the consultants. The president was embarrassed and just as confused as the consultants. They had to spend some time dealing with the damage done to the president's confidence. The worker had been concerned that he left no loose ends. However, his anxiety got in the way of good sense, and he actually hurt his own purpose.

- volunteering to do a bunch of tasks for which he or she has little or no time;
- projecting an "I don't care" image;
- suggesting or taking on new projects that mean something to him, but for which the community organization is not ready etc; the possibilities are many.

2. Positive Possibilities

Having laid out the potential for difficulty, we should stress that it need not be a doom, defeat and despair situation. The reverse can in fact be the case. People can see the departure as an indication that important work has been accomplished. The departure of one organizer can be a catalyst for the community to look at itself, its objectives, and its tactics; this can either be within the framework of evaluation (review chapters 7 and/or 9) or outside of it, if necessity dictates. Finally, it can be a time for the organizer to receive a few positive personal strokes.

3. To Ensure the Best Results

a) The majority of our relationships are, in some ways, transitory. At some time, every relationship but the most brief involves feelings, and often their passing involves victories as well as losses. We should be able to talk about each, i.e. it is important that we model the appropriate handling of termination and acknowledge feelings (ours and theirs).

b) Make sure the community has sufficient lead time— two weeks is not enough, six months may be too long. This is not to suggest you should keep things secret. However, if something appears to be too far in the future people may just ignore it; so the organizer has to be prepared to remind people ten to twelve weeks in advance.

c) Be prepared for negative feelings and actions. They may not be too overt; you may have to do a little verbalizing for folks to get their feelings into the open, or so they will free themselves to talk about them.

d) Don't wait too long for people to raise the question of your departure. This may be the first time you have had to initiate something for some time. There is nothing wrong with initiating discussion now if the people aren't up to doing it themselves.

e) Be clear about why you are leaving. Of course, it may be obvious; but if it is not, be declarative. Any attempt to soft peddle or avoid tough issues may lead to rumours and distrust; this can drain community energy from necessary tasks and objectives.

f) Be clear about how we feel about leaving. This helps your members do the same; good modelling is as important at the end as at the beginning.

Example: A worker in a small Northern Ontario community related that, after overcoming some fears of how an announcement would be treated, he found people more than ever before open and direct with him. They even began to joke with him, "over-verbalizing" not only their own feelings, but his own. His leaving, or rather the way in which he handled it, probably liberated some feelings and energy to deal with important issues facing the entire community.

g) Be sure to tie up any loose ends as much as humanly possible. Whether someone is following us or the members are on their own, it is neither fair nor good practice to have others finishing things that we could have handled.

h) Affirm realistically that people can do what they need to do. We may need to point out how much they have achieved.
i) Clarify our future role:
   • **don't undercut the next worker;**

- don't set up false expectations;
- don't dismiss the feelings of members. They are real and need attending to.

j) If a new community worker is to be following us, get it clear as to if and how we will be involved in the replacement process. Will we be involved through:
  - being on the hiring committee;
  - developing a job description; or
  - ad hoc consultation?

Don't Forget to Celebrate

However we have come to the end of the journey, we owe it to ourselves to have a bit of a celebration. We may not (likely have not) won everything that we wanted. On the other hand, unless things have gone seriously awry, something has been gained. We need to look at our accomplishments with the people we have been working with, and celebrate them. Moyer (1990) and Burghardt (1982) have pointed out that community workers sometimes miss the opportunities to celebrate the big as well as the small successes. As we end our association with our group, we should not let the opportunity pass by.

Reflection

Leaving a community may be every bit as difficult as connecting with it, though the dynamics are clearly quite different. In any event, both entry and exit demand creativity and courage. In both instances there is an understandable temptation to "do it quickly," or to "run away." In both instances the pay-off comes in being careful, complete, direct, and clear in: our communication; our purposes; and caring for the people we've worked with. As in the beginning, we had to give the citizens the opportunity to use us, and in the end they need to have the opportunity to let us go.

AFTERWORD

Community Work: An Unfinished Practice

In the first sections of the book we briefly took a look at a number of activists, organizers and leaders who had been successful in bringing people together, and assisting them to alter significant aspects of their lives and those of their brothers and sisters. We also examined the social, political and economic inequalities that so many people face; in effect, the reasons that they need to organize themselves. We then suggested the specific goals and objectives of the actual work of community organization. Finally we suggested some of the key roles and skills that are called for in community practice. For the rest of the journey we discussed the issues and tasks that practitioners face in attempting to help people reach those objectives, the pragmatics of the work. As we end, it seems worthwhile to describe some territory that reflects some of the contradictions or unfinished aspects of community organization.

Early on we made a plea to consider the phases of community work as interweaving and not discrete bits of business. While we might be emphasizing one group of tasks over others at a particular time, the development of community power requires attention to all of them. While objectives and phases are different categories of business, they are not separate in action. Though there is no real road map to guide us precisely in the right direction, it is the challenge for each community worker to think about aspects of tasks and objectives as deeply coherent.

A second important piece of territory is that broader context of our work. We noted the pervasiveness and the importance, particularly of class issues. These are clearly more marked and urgent as globalization and capital become stronger. Often we respond (need to respond) defensively, attempting to hang on to what security disadvantaged communities have gained in the past. Of course this is important. On the other hand, however, we also need to take a more proactive stance. In this vein it might be useful to pose a couple of rather broad questions. They are by no means the only queries that can and should be asked about context. Rather they are examples that suggest linkages among broad issues of experience, values and policy, and the specific questions of community development practice.

First, why haven't the values of capitalism worked? Since the fall of totalitarian Communism in Eastern Europe and the ascendancy of a more market-oriented China, there has been a great tendency to ask questions of why socialism did not work (or simply to dismiss it as a quixotic blunder). Leaving aside the question as to whether genuine socialism has ever been attempted, let alone existed, we should perhaps be focusing people on the real failures of the values of industrial and post-industrial capitalism – competition, depersonalization, rigid bureaucratization, elitism. Many of the values of community work – collective action, egalitarianism, cooperation – are linked to those of socialism. In focusing on why socialism has failed, we are really asking why those values failed. A rather more useful strategy is (surely) to challenge the values of capitalism. Have we seen an eradication of poverty, sexism, homophobia, racism, ableism, etc.? Indeed the case can be made that capitalist values have contributed to the sum total of misery and pushed our physical environment to the limit and perhaps beyond.

As well as alienating individuals from their work and corporate bureaucracy (continually downsized or globalized and fitted out with the latest in technology) all over the world have failed miserably in the goal they most cherish – making money efficiently. The failure of so much of the industrial banking sectors in North America and Europe, as well as the increasing evidence of the degradation of our environment and the attendant danger to animal life, and human life – often the poorest world citizens – is surely testimony to how counterproductive the values of capitalism are. We have every right to ask whether this capitalist onslaught is at all suitable for a modern society. We clearly need to search for different models of production and consumption, ones that place the quality of life – rather than profit and efficiency – at the centre of the discussion.

We cannot consider the question of the efficacy of capitalist values separate from the manner in which technology and media (forces that are deeply intertwined) have served to impel us toward atomization – the feeling that we are only individuals caring only for ourselves or at best our families. At this writing the movement calling itself the Tea Party, is at full fury in the U.S.A. The anger evident at the centre of this phenomenon is that tax rates are out of control and that government is increasingly intrusive in every aspect of life. In Canada, the government of Stephen Harper has been attempting, with some success, to import this feeling of discontent with our public institutions. We are being urged to go back to some mythical period where we were somehow free to pursue our economic and social interests unimpeded by concerns with the sensitivities and conditions of others. Why are we being urged to "go back" to a society that was based on individual (cut-throat) competition? Is not the potential result, if not motive, of these messages to tear at the social fabric that helps each of us to perceive and understand our dependence and responsibility to our brothers and sisters, to move us away from a shared compassion? In whose interests is it that we are being sold a vision of society that fits with the deplorable conditions of the 19th century's "Gilded Age" with its robber barons?

These questions are important. They are posed not as part of some academic exercise. They have practical implications for us and for the people we help to organize. Community development is deeply concerned with social institutions and organizations. They in turn, reflect the underlying social, economic and political attitudes of society. They are the mediating structures that shape the relationships that express our empowerment or disempowerment. It is in this sense – of holding a critical stance toward the dominant ideas and institutional arrangements – that our practice should never be finished. Of course, community workers need to continually hone intervention skills – communication, analysis, strategy, etc. We must also be constantly prepared to reflect critically on where and how our society is being influenced; and how we are influencing others to either accept or challenge the status quo.

A bit of unfinished business relates to an irony in community practice. Though community organization is a collective endeavour, the person hired to do the "organizing" is more often than not an outsider – a person not "of" the community. We are often not members of, or live in, the community in which we work. We are not leaders who can draw strength and energy from the feelings of the other community members. No matter how much we identify with a people's struggle, we are outsiders. This of course, as mentioned earlier, not only provides dilemmas but opportunities for finding ways to connect and learn. While there is no doubt that our liberation must be intimately bound to that of the people, and though we can share in their victories and defeats, in the final analysis those victories and defeats must remain uniquely theirs. We must not attempt to create some romantic notion that we have somehow become mystically the same as the oppressed. We must come to terms with that. As such, the community practice journey can at times be a lonely one. Some link burnout to this dynamic. It can be difficult to find someone with whom to share the unique experience of being an organizer. It is quite important then to look for someone with whom to share the specific experiences of organizing. In doing the ongoing research on community practice objectives and process, it has not been uncommon to hear someone say, "You know, I never get to really talk about stuff like this. I know I need to; it clears my mind. But it's hard to find people who know what I'm feeling or talking about." It is in our interest to make the effort to establish connections among ourselves; to challenge and support each other and to assist in the work of thinking critically, and hopefully, about the work of community organizing. Community work is something that, like society itself, is always growing and changing. We as practitioners must change and grow as well.

> Let no one be discouraged by the belief there is nothing one man or woman can do against the enormous array of the world's ills, against misery and ignorance, injustice and violence ... few will have the greatness to bend history itself; but each of us can work to change a small portion of events, and in the total of all those acts will be written the history of this generation.
>
> It is from the numberless diverse acts of courage and belief that human history is shaped. Each time a person stands up for an ideal, or strikes out against injustice, or acts to improve the lot of others [they] send a tiny ripple of hope, and crossing each other from a million different centres of energy and daring, these ripples build a current which can sweep down the mightiest walls of oppression and resistance.
>
> - Robert Kennedy (1920-1968)

BIBLIOGRAPHY

Abadian, S. 2000. From Wasteland to Homeland: Trauma and the Renewal of Indigenous Peoples and Their Communities, Unpublished doctoral dissertation. Cambridge, MA: Harvard University.

Aboriginal Healing Foundation. 2004. Historic Trauma and Aboriginal Healing, The Aboriginal Healing Foundation Research Series.

Abrams, C. et al. 1994. *A Manual for Social Development Practice (2nd ed.).* Colombo: National Institute of Social Development.

Adams, I. 1970. *The Poverty Wall.* Toronto: McClelland and Stewart Ltd.

Adamson, N, Briskin, L & McPhail, M. 1988. *Feminist Organizing for Change.* Toronto: Oxford University Press.

Albert, J. 1992. *If we don't do it who will?* Vol. 23. Canadian Social Work Review. pp. 665-684.

Alexander, J. C. 2004. Toward a theory of cultural trauma, *Collective trauma and collective identity* (pp. 1-30). Berkeley: University of California Press.

Alinsky, S. 1971. *Rules for Radicals.* New York: Random House.

Amer, E. 1980. *Yes We Can.* Ottawa: Synergistics Consulting Limited.

Amnesty International Bulletin. The breaking of minds and bodies: The long journey home, December 1989/January 1990. Vol.XVII: no.1 (10-13).

Anderson, 1997. *Bayard Rustin: troubles I've seen: a biography.* New York: Harper Collins.

Angell, G.B. and Dunlop, J.M. 2001. Social Welfare and North American First Nations: A Socialist Political Economy Perspective. The Canadian Journal Of Native Studies. XXXI, No.2 (333-353).

Antone, R. Miller, D. & Myers, B. 1986. *The Power Within People.* Deseronto, Ontario: Peace Tree Technologies.

Arnstein, S. 1969. Eight rungs on the ladder of citizen participation. *Journal of the American Institute of Planners.* 35:4 (216-224.)

Atkinson, D. and Elliott, L. 1998. Anxious? Insecure? You'll get used to it, *Guardian Weekly.* June 21, (1-4).

Baines, D., 2007 (Ed). *Doing anti-oppressive practice: building transformative politicized social work.* Halifax: Fernwood Publishing

Ball, R.A. 1973. The analgesic sub-culture of the southern Appalachians. In LA. Spergle (ed.), *Community Organization: Studies in Constraints.* Beverly Hills: Sage.

Bandura, A. 1978. The self system in reciprocal determinism, *American Psychologist.* April:344-358.

Barack, L. 2008. The squeeze on the middle class, Sympatico MSN. Finance. http://finance.sympatico.msn.ca/savingsdebt/insight/article.aspx?cp-documentid=5944699

Barker, R.L. 1991. *Social Work Dictionary (2nd. ed.).* Silver Springs, MD: NASW Press.

Barndt, D. and Freire, C. 1989. *Naming the Moment (monograph).* Toronto: Jesuit Centre for Faith and Justice.

Barnesley, J. and D. Ellis. 1992. *Research for Change.* Vancouver: The Women's Research Centre.

Berton, P. 1980. *The Invasion of Canada.* Toronto: McClelland and Stewart.

Biddle, Wm. and Biddle, L. 1965. *The Community Development Process.* New York: Rinehart and Winston.

Biklen, D.P. 1983. *Community Organizing Theory and Practice.* Englewood Cliffs, New Jersey: Prentice-Hall Inc.

Bishop, A. 1994. *Becoming an Ally: Breaking the Cycle of Oppression.* Halifax: Fernwood Publishing.

Bloomberger, W. Jr. 1969. Community organization, In R.M. Kramer and H. Specht (eds.), *Readings in Community Organization Practice.* pp.91-127. Englewood Cliffs, New Jersey: Prentice-Hall.

Boff, L. 1982. *St. Francis - A Model for Human Liberation.* New York: Crossroads Publishing Company.

Booth, H. 1974. *Handbook for Organizing Women.* Chicago: Midwest Academy.

Boothroyd, P. 1991. Community development: The missing link in welfare policy, In B. Kerwin (ed.), *Ideology, Development and Social Welfare: Canadian Perspectives.* Toronto: Canadian Scholars Press.

Bowles, S. and Gintis, H. 1976. *Schooling in Capitalist America.* New York: Columbia University Press.

Brave Heart, M. Y. H. 1999. Oyate Ptayela: rebuilding the Lakota nation through addressing historical trauma among Lakota parents, *Journal of Human Behavior in the Social Environment* 2(1/2): 109-126.

Bregha, F.J. 1971. Community development in Canada: Problems and strategies, In J. Draper (ed), *Citizen Participation in Canada.* pp. 72-83. Toronto: New Press.

Brennan, R. 2008. ACCESS DENIED. TheStar.com. April. 07. http://www.thestar.com/News/Canada/article/410909.

Breshlow, R.L. 1976. *Worlds of Pain.* New York: Basic Books Inc.

Breton, M. 1995. The potential for social action in groups. *Social Work with Groups, 18*(2/3), 5-13.

Brown, J.M. 1989. *Gandhi: Prisoner of Hope.* New Haven: Yale University Press.

Brueggemann, W.G. 2002. *The Practice of Macro Social Work,* (2nd ed.). Chicago: Nelson-Hall.

Burghardt, S. 1982. *The Other Side of Organizing: The Personal Dilemmas and Political Demands of Daily Practice.* (Chapter 3: Broadening the use of self: Steps toward tactical self-awareness). Massachusetts: Schenkman Publishing Company.

Burke, B. & Harrison, P. (1998). Anti-oppressive practice. In R. Adams, L. Dominelli, & M. Payne (eds.) *Social work themes and critical debates,* London: MacMillan. 229-238.

Burris, V. 2001. The Two Faces of Capital: Corporations and Individual Capitalists as Political Actors. *American Sociological Review,* Vol 66(June) 361-381

Burstow, B. (2003). Toward a radical understanding of trauma and trauma work, *Violence Against Women 9*(11): 1293-1317.

Cain, R. 1993. Community-based AIDS services: Formalization and de-politicization, *International Journal of Health Services.*

Cameron, D. 1994. Debt politics. *Canadian Forum.* Vol.LXXIV:no.835 (December, p.4).

Camp, D. 1998. Me, Conrad and Hacksaw Al. *Toronto Daily Star.* June 21:F3.

Campion-Smith, B. (2009) Turned-off Canadians tuning out, *Toronto Star.* June 21: A 10.

Carniol, B. 2005. *Case Critical (3rd Ed.).* Toronto: Between the Lines Press.

Carr, B. 2002. Globalization from below: labour internationalism under NAFTA, *International Social Science* Journal Volume 51 Issue 159: 49-59. (http://www3.interscience.wiley.com/journal/119064072/abstract?CRETRY=1&SRETRY=0).

Chambon, A., McGrath, S., Shapiro, B. Z., Mulugeta, A., & Dudziak, S. (2001). From interpersonal links to webs of relations: creating befriending relationships with survivors of torture and of war. *Journal of Social Work Research* 2(2): 157-171.

Charlesworth, S.J., Gilifillan, P. & Wilkinson, R.G. 2004. Living inferiority. *British Medical Bulletin*. 69: (49-60).

Checkoway, B. 1995. Six strategies of community change. *Community Development Journal*. Vol.30: no.1 2-19.

Checkoway, B., Dobbie, D., Richards-Schuster, K. 2005. Involving young people in community evaluation research. Community Youth Development Journal. Volume 4, No. 1 Spring 2003. http://www.cydjournal.org/2003Spring/checkoway.html

Chenoweth, L., & Stehlik, D. 2001. Building resilient communities: social work practice and rural Queensland. *Australian Social Work* 54(2): 47-54.

Chossudovsky, M. 2008. Global Financial Meltdown: Sweeping Deregulation of the US Banking System, *Global Research*. Centre for Global Research, November. http://www.globalresearch.ca/index. php?context=va&aid=10588

Choudry, A. &. Shragge, E. 2007. Constructing Immigrant Workers: Adaptation and Resistance, INRS: Toronto.

Cochrane K. 2008. Now the backlash, *The Guardian*.co.uk. (http:// www.guardian.co.uk/world/2008/jul/01/gender.women)

Colorado, P. and Collins, D. 1987. Western scientific colonialism and the re-emergence of Native science, *Practice: the Journal of Politics, Economics, Psychology, Sociology, and Culture*. Winter:.51-65.

Contenta, S. 2009. Falling Down, *Toronto Star*. June 16: IN 1&5.

Cruikshank, J. 1990. The outsider: An uneasy role in community development, *Canadian Social Work Review*. vol.7:no.2: 245259.

Cruikshank, J. 1989. Burnout: An issue among Canadian community development workers, *Community Development Journal*. Vol.24. no.1.40-54.

Curtis, J., Grabb, E., & Guppy, N. (Eds.) 2003. *Social inequality in Canada: patterns, problems and policies*, 4th Edition. Pearson Education Canada.

Dale, D. 1978. *How to Make Citizen Involvement work*. University of Massachusetts: Citizen Involvement Training Project.

Dale, D. and Mitiguy, N. 1978. *Planning for a Change*. University of Massachusetts: Citizen Involvement Project.

DeFina, R. A Different Ponzi Scheme, Commonwealth. February 27. 33-34.

del Moral, A. 2005. The revolution will not be funded, *LiP Magazine*. http://www.lipmagazine.org/articles/featdelmoral_nonprofit.htm.

Desroches, L. 1996. Allow the water, Toronto: editions DUNAMIS publishers.

Dobbin, M. 2007-2008. Forgoing billions in needless tax cuts weakens Canada, *The CCPA Monitor*: 29.

Dobbin, M 2003 *The Myth of the Good Corporate Citizen: Canada And Democracy In The Age Of Globalization*. Halifax: James Lorimer & Son.

Dobson, C. 2006. The citizen's handbook, a guide to building community. Vancouver Citizen's Committee. http://www.vcn.bc.ca/citizens-handbook/.

Dominelli, L. 1999. Community, citizenship and empowerment. *Sociology*, 33, (2), 441-446.

Dominelli, L. 1998. Anti-oppressive practice in context, In R. Adams, L. Dominelli, & M. Payne (eds.) *Social work themes and critical debates*. London: MacMillan: 3-19

Dominelli, L. 1996. Deprofessionalizing social work: anti-oppressive practice, competencies and postmodernism. *British Journal of Social Work*. 26(2):153-165.

Dumbrill, G.C. 2008. Anti-oppression perspectives and the real world. *Challenging Silences*. School of Social Work, McMaster University: 10.

Edmunds, R.D. 1984. *Tecumseh and the Quest for Indian Leadership*. Boston: Little Brown.

Ehrenreich, B. 1993. They call it democracy: The worst years of our lives, *This Magazine*. Vol.27:no.3 (pp.12-15).

Entourage. 1989. Insecure incomes (summary of a report of the G. Allan Roeher Institute). Vol.4:no.2, spring: 3-7.

Erickson, K. 1994. *A new species of trouble: the human experience of modern disasters*. NY: Norton.

Erlich, J.L. and Rivera, F.G. 1995. *Community organizing in a diverse society (2nd ed.)*. Toronto: Allyn and Bacon.

Fals-Borda, O. and Rahman, M.A. 1991. *Action and knowledge*. London: Intermediate Technology Publications.

Fanon, F. 1963. *The wretched of the earth*. New York: Grove Press.

Fiki, C. & Lee, B. 2005. Conflict management, local capacity governance, and inclusive human security in northeastern Nigeria: a case study. *Regional Development Dialogue* (United Nations Centre for Regional Development, Japan). Vol. 26, No. 1 Spring: 77-88.

Finks, P.D. 1984. *The radical vision of Saul Alinsky*. New York: Paulist Press.

Fishlock, J. & Lee, B. 2004. Constraints and Opportunities for Social Development and Private Sector Co-operation: the Case of Resource Extraction Projects. *Social Development Issues*. Volume 26, Number 1: 38-50.

Forcese, D. 1975. *The Canadian class structure*. Toronto: McGraw Hill Ryerson Ltd.

Francis, D.R. 2004. Salary squeeze threatens middle America, *Christian Science Monitor*. September 08. http://www.csmonitor.com/2004/0908/p03s01-usec.html.

Fraser, H. 2005. Four different approaches to community participation. *Community Development Journal*. Vol. 40, No. 3 July: 286-300.

Freeman, B. & Lee, B. 2007. Towards an Aboriginal model of community healing. *Aboriginal Social Work*. Volume 6, March. (97-120).

Freeman, L. 2006. *The development of social network analysis*. Vancouver: Empirical Press.

Freire, P. 2000. *Pedagogy of the oppressed*. New York: Seabury Press.

Freire, P. 1994. *Pedagogy of hope: reliving pedagogy of the oppressed*. New York: Continuum Publishing Company.

Friedman, T.L. 2008. *Hot, Flat, and Crowded: Why We Need a Green Revolution – and How It Can Renew America* Farrar, Straus and Giroux.

Fromm, E. -1966. *You shall be as Gods*. New York: Fawcett Premier.- 1964. *The heart of man*. New York: Harper and Row.
- 1961. *Marx's concept of man*. New York: Fredrick Ungar publishing Co.
- 1955. *The sane society*. New York: Fawcett Premier.

Gallagher, A. 1977. Women and community work. In M. Mayo (ed.), *Women In the Community*. (pp. 121-144). London: Routledge and Keegan Paul Ltd.

Gandhi, M.K. 1951. *Non-violent Resistance*. New York: Sihocken Books.

Gastil, J. 1993. *Democracy in Small Groups*. Philadelphia: New Society Publishers.

Ganz, Mashall (2005) in Enviros need to get social, says activist-turned-sociologist Marshall Ganz. Gregory Dicum. *GRIST.*, [accessed Dec. 2]. http://www.grist.org/article/dicum4/.

Gecan, M. 2004. *Going Public*. New York: Anchor Books.

George, U., Lee, B., McGrath, S. Moffatt, K. 2002. Community Practice in Diverse Communities in Toronto, Canada, in Cheng, Q. & Peng, J. (eds.) *Community Development in China and Canada*. Beijing: Ethnic Press.

George, U., Lee, B., McGrath, S., Moffatt, K. 2003. Exploring Citizenship in Contemporary Community Practice, *Journal of Community Practice, Organization, Planning and Change*. Vol. 12, No. 3: 71-86.

Germain, C. and Gitterman, A. 1980. *The life model of social work practice*. New York: Columbia University Press.

Gilroy, J. 1990. Social work and the women's movement. In B. Warf (ed.), *Social Work and Social Change in Canada*. Toronto: McClelland and Stewart.

Gladwell, M. 2010. The revolution will not be tweeted. *The New Yorker*. Oct. 4 http://www.newyorker.com/reporting/2010/10/04/101004fa_fact_gladwell.

Global Issues, 2008. Social, Political, Economic and Environmental Issues That Affect Us All. http://www.globalissues.org/article/26/poverty-facts-and-stats.

Goff, C. 2007. Anti-slavery pioneers, *New Internationalist*. March. 24-26.

Grant, T. (2008). *Globe and Mail*. May 1, L1.

Hall, E.T. and Hall, M.R. 1987. *Hidden Differences*. New York: Doubleday.

Hariman, R, Lucaites, J.L. 2007. *No caption needed: iconic photographs, public culture and liberal democracy*. University of Chicago Press.

Harris, J. (2003). *The social work business*. London: Routledge.

Health Canada. (2002a). *Community-Based Research Program: Unique and Effective*. http://www.hc-sc.gc.ca/hppb/hiv_aids/can_strat/research/ community.html.

Hedges, C. 2009. The case for democratic socialism: what is needed is open confrontation with the corporate state, *The CCCPA Monitor*. Volume 15, No. 10: 30-31.

Hedges, C. 2007. *American fascists: the Christian right and the war on America*. New York: Free Press

Hernandez, P. 2002. Resilience in families and communities: Latin American contributions from the psychology of liberation, *The Family Journal: Counseling and Therapy for Couples and Families* 10 (3): 334-343.

Herz, S. & Ebrahim, A. 2005. A Call for Participatory Decision Making: Discussion Paper on World Bank-Civil Society Engagement. Commissioned and Presented by the Civil Society Members of World Bank-Civil Society Joint Facilitation Committee (JFC) April 14.

hooks, b. 2003. *Teaching community. a pedagogy of hope*, New York: Routledge. 160 pages.

Hope, A. and Timmel, S. 1984. *Training for transformation*. (Vol. 13). Gweru, Zimbabwe: Mambo Press.

Hopton, J. 1997. Anti-discriminatory practice and anti-oppressive practice: a radical humanist psychology perspective, *Critical Social Policy*. 52(17). 47-61.

Horwitt, S.D. 1989. *Let them call me rebel*. New York: Alfred A. Knopf.

Howe, N. and Longman, P. 1992. The next new deal. *The Atlantic*. vol.26:no.4 (April, pp. 88-99).

Hustedde, R.J. & Ganowicz, J. 2002. The basics: what's essential about community development practice? *Journal of the Community Development Society*. Vol. 33 No. 1.1-19.

Hutchinson, A. & Lee, B. 2005. Exploring social inclusion in practice: Views from the field. *Canadian Social Work Review*, 22(2): 1-15.

Illich, I. 1972. *Deschooling Society*. New York: Harper and Row.

International Federation of Social Workers. 2008. Definition of social work. http://www.ifsw.org/en/p38000208.html.

International Fund for Agricultural Development, 2007. http://www.ifad. org/events/past/hunger/empower.html.

Jeffries, D. 1993. *Community Development and Aging: A Case Study of Conflict Resolution in a Seniors' Housing Co-op*. Gerontology Development Project: School of Social Work, McMaster University.

Johnson, L.C.& Yanka, S.J. 2007. *Social Work Practice: a generalist approach*. Allyn & Bacon.

Joreen. 1973. The tyranny of structuralessness. In A. Kordet et al. (eds.), *Radical Feminism*. New York: Quadrangle.

Joseph Rowntree Foundation, 2000. An evaluation of a community development worker project. http://www.jrf.org.uk/knowledge/findings/housing/620.asp.

Kahn, S. 1994. *How People Get Power.* Silver Springs, MD: NASW Press.

Kahn, S. 1982. *Organizing.* New York: McGraw-Hill.

Kahn R. & Kellner, D. 2004. New media and internet activism: from the 'Battle of Seattle' to blogging, New Media and Society, 6:1. 87-95;

Kempf, H. 2008. *How the Rich Are Destroying the Earth.* Chelsea Green Publishing.

Kenny, S. 2002. Evaluation and Community Development: Mantras, challenges and Dilemmas. Paper presented at the 2002 Australiasian Evaluation Society International Conference October/November – Wollongong Australia.

Kerr, S. 1993. A tale of two cities: review of Peter Skerry 1993, "Mexican Americans: The ambivalent minority," *The New York Review of Books.* Vol.XL:no.21 (3).

Kershaw, I. 2000. *Hitler: 1936-1945 Nemesis.* London: The Penguin Press.

Kieffer, C.H. 1984. "Citizen empowerment: A developmental perspective." In Rappaport, J. and R. Hess eds. *Studies in Empowerment Groups: Towards Understanding and Action.* New York: Haworth Press

Klein, N. 2007. Disaster capitalism, *Harper's Magazine.* October, (47-58).

Kramer, R.M. 1970. *Community development in Israel and the Netherlands.* (Research series No. 14). Berkley, California: University of California Institute of International Studies.

Kretzman, J.P. and McKnight, J.L. 1993. *Building communities from the inside out.* Chicago ACTA Publications.

Kuyak, J. 1991. *Fighting for hope.* Montreal: Black Rose books.

Laidlaw, A. F. 1961. *The campus and the community: The Global Impact of the Antigonish Movement.* Montreal: Harvest House.

Lakey, G. 1987. *Powerful Peacemaking.* Philadelphia: New Society Publishers.

Lakey, B. et al. 1995. *Grassroots and nonprofit leadership.* Philadelphia: New Society Publishers.

Langer, E.J. 1983. *The psychology of control.* Beverly Hills: Sage Publications.

Laxer, J. and A. Martin. 1976. *The big tough expensive job.* Montreal: Press Porcepic.

Learner, M. 1979. Surplus powerlessness. *Canadian Social Policy.* Jan./ Feb.:pp.18-27.

Lee, B. - 2008. Will the real community research please stand up? Canadian Social Work Review. Vol. 25, no. 1.

- 1992. Colonialism and community. *Community Development Journal.* Vol. 27 no. 3 (pp.211-219).

- 1988. *Purpose and Meaning in Community Development.* Doctoral Thesis, Ontario Institute for Studies in Education/University of Toronto.

Lee, B. and Balkwill, M. 1996. *Participatory Planning for Action.* Mississauga: CommonAct Press.

Lee, B. & Hutchinson, A. 2007 Facilitating the voices of marginalized racialized youth. New Directions in the Humanities Conference. Paris, July 18.

Lee, B., George, U., McGrath, S., Moffatt, K. 2002. Exploring the Role of the Insider in Community Work in Marginalized Communities. *Critical Social Work.* Vol. 2, No. 2, Fall. pp. 69-87. http://wwwCriticalSocialWork.com.

Lee, B., McGrath, S., George, U., and Moffat, K. 1996. Community practice education in Canadian schools of social work. *Canadian Social Work Review.* Vol. 13 :no.2. pp.221-235.

Lee, B., Moffatt, K., George, U. & McGrath S. (2007) "Community practice within traumatized communities," New Directions in the Humanities Conference. Paris, July 19.

Lee, B., Sammon, S., & Dumbrill, G.C. 2007. Glossary of terms for anti-oppressive policy and practice. (Monograph) Mississauga: CommonAct Press.

Lee, C. 1993. Big Cove suicides find relief in healing week. *Beedaudjimowin.* Vol. 13:no.2. October, pp.23,29,38.

Lee, M. 2008. Overall tax system no longer meets basic test of fairness, *The CCPA Monitor.* Volume 14, No. 8 (1, 6-8)

Levy, J. 1985. *Cesar Chavez: Autobiography of la Causa.* New York: W.W. Norton and Company Inc.

Lepischak, B. 2000. Supporting our Youth: building community for Queer youth in Toronto. Unpublished research paper. Graduate Programme in Social Work. Toronto, ON: York University.

Lotz, J. 1995. The beginning of community development. In B. Wharf and M. Clague (eds.), *Community Organizing: Canadian Experiences.* Toronto: Oxford University Press.

Macpherson, C.B. 1977. *The life and times of liberal democracy.* Toronto: Oxford University press.

MacRae, K. 2008. Reflection on Police Actions. Unpublished MSW paper, McMaster University.

Maier, N. 1961. *Frustration.* Ann Arbor: University of Michigan Press.

Maier, N. and P. Ellen. 1965. The integrative value of concepts. In R. Lawson (ed.), *Frustration Theory.* New York: MacMillan.

Mallinson, I. 1995. Moving from anti-racist practice to anti-oppressive practice. *Issues in Social Work Education.* 26: 297-331.

Market Oracle, The. 2008. Banking System in Meltdown, Fed Fights to Keep Dead Banks Alive, http://www.marketoracle.co.uk/Article6504.html

Marshall, T.H. 1950. *Class, citizenship and social development.* Cambridge: Cambridge University Press.

Martin, B. 1998. *Information Liberation.* London: Freedom Press.

Martinez. M. 2001. Civil Society, the Internet and the Zapatistas, Peace Review,13:3,. http://www.desal.org.mx/IMG/pdf/MEMartinezPeaceRev. pdf.

Matthiesson, P. 1992. *Indian Country.* New York: Viking Press.

Mayo, M. 1977. Community development for social change. In R. Bailey and M. Brake (eds.), *Radical Social Work.* pp. 129-143. London: Edward Arnold.

McAuley, S. 2007. Inside experience of community organizing: a case study. Unpublished MSW Thesis, School of Social Work, McMaster University).

McDermott, P. 1992. Employment equity and pay equity: And never the twain shall meet. *Canadian Women Studies.* Vol.12:no.3 (spring, pp.24-27).

Mackenzie, H. 2007. The Rich are getting even richer – and we're all helping, *The CPPA Monitor.* November, (42).

McFarlane, P. 1993. *Brotherhood to nationhood: George Manuel and the making of the modern Indian movement.* Toronto: Between the Lines Press.

McGrath, S. 1998. *The Politics of Truth: a case study of the Social Planning Council of Metropolitan Toronto:* 1957-1988. PhD. Thesis: University of Toronto.

McGrath, S., George, U., Lee, B., Moffatt, K. 1999. Community Capacity: The Emperor's New Clothes. *Canadian Review of Social Policy.* No. 4. (9-23).

McGrath, S, Lee, B George, U., Moffatt, K. 2007. Seeking social justice: community practice in diverse communities. Social Development Issues. 29(2), Summer. (77-91).

McGregor, R. 1990. *Chief.* New York: Viking Press.

McKnight, J. 1995. *The Careless Society: community and its counterfeits.* New York: BasicBooks.

McQuaig, L. 1998. *The Cult of Impotence.* Toronto: Penguin Books.

McQuaig, L., 2007. Inequality among fish and humans, *Toronto Star,* October 2, p. AA8.

McQuaig, L., 2008. Rich wage class war, not StatsCan, *Toronto Star,* May 6, p. AA8.

Memmi, A. 1991. The Colonizer and the Colonized. Boston: Beacon Press.

Miles, N., 2006. Cultural sensitivity in Third World development. In Lee, B. & Todd, S. (eds.) *A casebook of community practice: problems and strategies.* Mississauga: CommonAct Press, pp. 56-60.

Moffatt, K., George, U., McGrath, S. Lee, B.1999. Advancing citizenship: a study in social planning. *Community Development Journal.* Vol. 34, No. 4. 308-317.

Moffatt, K., George, U. Lee, B., McGrath, S. 2005. Community Practice Researchers as Reflective Learners. *British Journal of Social Work.,* Vol. 35, No 1 January: 89-104.

Moffatt, K. 2006. Dancing without a Floor: The Artists' Politic of Queer Club Space. *The Canadian Online Journal of Queer Studies.* (2)1. http://jqstudies.oise.utoronto.ca/journal/viewarticle.php?id=12.

Mowbray, M. 1985. The medicinal properties of localism. In R. Thorpe and J. Petruchenia (eds.), *Community Work or Social Change?* London: Routledge and Keegan Paul.

Moyer, B. with McAllister, J., Finley, M.L., & Soifer S. 2001. *Doing Democracy, the MAP model for organizing social movements.* Philadelphia: New Society Publishers.

Moyer, B. 1990. The Practical Strategist (Monograph). San Francisco: Social Movement Empowerment Projects.- 1987. The Movement Action Plan (Monograph). Philadelphia: Movement for a new Society.

Mullally, B. 1997. *Structural social work, ideology, theory and practice (2nd. Ed.)*. Toronto: Oxford University Press.

Murray, D. 2006. *neo-conservatism: why we need it*. New York: Encounter Books.

Napier, A.D. 2002. *The Age of Immunology, Conceiving a Future in an Alienating World*. University of Chicago Press.

Narayan, U. 1994. Working together across differences. In B.R. Compton and B. Galloway (eds.), *Social Work Processes (5th ed.)*. (pp.177-188). Pacific Grove, Calif.: Brooks/Cole Publishing Company.

National Round Table on Aboriginal Urban Issues. 1993. *Royal Commission on Aboriginal Peoples*. Ottawa: Minister of Supply and Services.

National Union of Public and General Employees 2008. The real Walkerton water culprits never went to court. http://www.nupge.ca/news_2004/n21de04a.htm.

New Internationalist, 2008. Plenty to shout about," April. (pp. 12-13).

New Yorker, The. 1989. The Talk of the Town, June 26:pp.25-29.

Obomsawin, A. 1993. *Kanehsatake: 270 Years of Resistance*. (Film). Ottawa: National Film Board of Canada.

O'Brien, C. A. 1994. The social organization of the treatment of lesbian, gay, and bisexual youth in group homes and youth shelters, *Canadian Review of Social Policy* 34: 37-57.

O'Malley, K. 1998. Grassroots in cyberspace. *Canadian Forum*. Vol. LXXVI: no.866 (Jan/Feb, pp.21- 22,27,29).

Omatsu. 1993. In K. Aguiter-San Juan (ed.), *The State of Asian America's Activism in the 1990's*. Boston: South End Press.

Parada H., Barnoff, L., Moffatt, K. & Homan, M.S. 2010. *Promoting community change. Making it happen in the real world*. Toronto: Nelson Education.

Paton, R. 1994. The need to reform information policies. *Canadian Speeches: Issues of the Day*. April:pp.20-24.

Paumgarten, N. 2007. The humbling of Eliot Spitzer, *The New Yorker*. December, 10., pp.72-85.

Perlas, N. 2003. *Shaping Globalization: Civil Society, Cultural Power and Threefolding*. Center for Alternative Development Initiatives. Philadelphia: New Society Publishers.

Pictoff, W. 2004. Investing in People: Building the Capacity of Community Development, Training and Social Enterprise Practitioners. Human and Institutional Capacity Building: A Rockefeller Foundation Series Issue Number 1.

Piven, F. and R.A. Cloward. 1977. *Poor Peoples Movements*. New York: Pantheon Books.

Playboy Magazine. 1972. Interview with Saul Alinsky. March: pp.59-178.

Polanyi, K 2001. *The Great Transformation: The Political and Economic Origins of Our Times*. Bostom: Beacon Press.

Ponting, J.R. 1986. Institution building in an Indian community: A case study of Kahnawake. *Arduous Journey: Canadian Indians and Decolonization*. Toronto: McClelland and Stewart: p.155.

Ravitz, M. 1982. Community Development: Challenge of the eighties. *Journal of the Community Development Society*. Vol. 13 :no.1 (pp.1-2).

Reinharz, S. 1992. *Feminist Methods in Social Research*. (Chapter 10: Feminist Action Research). New York: Oxford University Press.

Repo, M. 1977. The fallacy of "community control". In J. Cowley et al. (eds.), *Community or Class Struggle?* pp.47-64. London: Stage 1.

Revkin, A. 2005. The Burning Season, The Murder of Chico Mendes and The Fight for the Amazon Rain Forest. Island Press.

Reynolds, N. 2009. The real fat cats of the auto industry, *The Globe and Mail*, April 44. p. B2)

Rice, J. 1990. Volunteering to build a stronger community, *Perceptions*. Vol. 14:no.4 (autumn, pp.9-16).

Rice, J. and Prince, M.J. 2000 (2000). *Changing Politics of Canadian Social Policy*. University of Toronto Press

Rifkin, J. 1998. God in a lab coat. *Utne Reader.* May/June: pp.66, 106-108.

- 1995. *The End of Work*. New York: G.P. Putnam's Sons.

Ristock, J.L. and Penell J. 1996 *Community Research as Empowerment*. New York: Oxford University Press.

Rivera, F.G. and J. Erlich. 1995 *Community organizing in a divided society*. Boston: Allyn and Bacon.

Roberts, H. 1979. *Community Development Learning and Action*. Toronto: University of Toronto Press.

Romero, P. 1987. *E. Sylvia Pankhurst: Portrait of a Radical*. New Haven: Yale University Press.

Ross, D.P. Scott , K.J. and Smith, P.J.,. 2000. *Canadian Factbook on Poverty - 1994*. Ottawa: Canadian Council on Social Development.

Ross, M.G. 1972. *Community Organization* (2nd. Ed.). New York: Harper and Row.

Rothman, J. and Tropman, J. 1987. Three models of community organization and macro practice perspective: their mixing and phasing. In F.M. Cox et al. (eds.), *Strategies of Community Organization* (3rd ed.). Itasca, Illinois: F.E. Peacock Publishers.

Rubin, R.J. and Rubin, I. 1986. *Community Organization and Development*. Toronto: Merrill Publishing.

Russell, B. 1977 1918. *Roads to Freedom*. London: Unwin Paperbacks.

Rykert, L. and James, M. 1998. *Working Together Online*. Toronto: Metastrategies Inc.

Saleebey, D. 2006. *The strengths perspective in social work practice 4th Edition*. Allyn & Bacon.

Saul, J. Ralston. 1995. *The Unconscious Civilization*. Toronto: Anansi.

Schutt, R. (undated) . Notes on consensus decision making. http://www.vernalproject.org/papers/process/ConsensNotes.pdf.

Sennett, R. and Cobb, J. 1972. *The Hidden Injuries of Class*. New York: Vintage Books.

Shah, A. 2001 WTO protests in Seattle, 1999. Global Issues. http://www.globalissues.org/article/46/wto-protests-in-seattle-1999.

Sharpe, G. 1973. *The Politics of Non-violent Action (vol.* 1-3). Boston: Porter Sargent Publishers.

Shields, K. 1994. *In the Tiger's Mouth*. Philadelphia: New Society Publishers.

Shragge, E. 2003. *Activism and social change*. Peterborough: Broadview Press Ltd.

Sibley, A. 2008. "The cult of capitalism, Hayek, Novak & the limits of laissez-faire". *Commonweal*. (April) 18-21.

Sigelman, L., Roeder, P.W., Jewell, M.E., & Baer, M.A. 1985. Voting and nonvoting: A multi-election perspective. American Journal of Political Science, 29(4), 749–765

Skidmore, R.A. and Thackery, M.G. 1976. *Introduction to Social Work*. Englewood Cliffs, New Jersey: Prentice-Hall Inc.

Slouka, M. 2009. Dehumanized. Harper's, September; 32-51.

Specht, H. 1969. Disruptive tactics. In R.M. Kramer and H. Specht (eds.), *Readings in Community Organization Practice*. Pp.372-386. New Jersey: Prentice-Hall Inc.

Speck, R.U. and Attneave, C.L. 1973. *Family Networks.* New York: Pantheon.

Speeter, G. 1978. *Power: a Repossession Manual.* University of Massachusetts: Citizen Involvement Training Project.

Speth, J.G. 2009. *The Bridge at the Edge of the World: Capitalism, the Environment, and Crossing from Crisis to Sustainability* Yale University Press

Staples, L. 1984. *Roots to Power.* New York: Praeger Special Studies.

Stinson, A. 1979. North Frontenac community services: Case study of a rural community service. In B. Warf (ed.), *Community Work in Canada.* Pp.87-1128. Toronto: McClelland and Stewart Limited.

Sone, D. 2008. Transnational policy communities and their networks *Policy Studies Journal,* 36:1, 19-38.

Strean, H.S. 1979. Role theory. In F. Turner (ed.), *Social Work Treatment (2nd ed.).* New York: Free Press.

Suzuki, D. 1995. Why the U.S. is a dismal model for us, *Toronto Daily Star.* Dec.2:C5.

Swift, J. and B. Tomlinson. 1991. *Conflicts of Interest and the Third World.* Toronto: Between the Lines Press.

Tarrow, S. 1994. *Power in movement: collective action, social movements and politics,* Cambridge University Press.

Thomas, D.N. 1983. Participation in politics and the community. In D.N. Thomas (ed.), *The Making of Community Work.* London: George Allen and Unwin.

Thompson, N. 1997. *Anti-discriminatory practice.* Basingstoke: Macmillan.

Touraine A. 2002. The importance of social movements. Social Movement Studies, *Volume 1, Number 1, 1 April.* 89-95(7).

Tracy, J. 1997. *Direct action radical pacifism from the union eight to the Chicago seven.* Chicago: University of Chicago Press.

Tremain, R. 1973. *The Fight for Freedom for Women.* New York: Ballantine Books.

Trippi, J. 2004. *The revolution will not be televised.* New York: Regan Books.

Ulbig, S.G. 2008. Voice is not enough. Public Opinion Quarterly 2008 72(3):523-539; doi:10.1093/poq/nfn030.

Wadsworth, Y. 1984. *Do it Yourself Research.* Melbourne: Victorian Council of Social Services.

Wagamese, R. 1996. *The Terrible Summer.* Toronto: Warwick Publishing.

Ward, D. and Mullender, A. 1991. Empowerment and oppression: An indissoluble pairing for contemporary social work. *Critical Social Policy,* 32: 21-30.

Ward, J. 1989. *Organizing for the homeless.* Ottawa: Canadian Council for Social Development.

Warren R.L. 1983. Observations on the state of community theory. In R. Warren and L. Lyon (eds.), *New Perspectives on the American Community.* Homewood, Ill.: Dorey Press. - 1977. Organizing a community survey. In F. M. Cox et al. (eds.), *Tactics and Techniques of Community Practice.* Pp.23-35. Illinois: F.E. Peacock Publishers.

Weeks, W. 1994. *Women Working Together: Lessons from Feminist Women's Services.* Cheshire: Longman.

Weick, A., & Saleebey, D. 1998. Post modern perspectives for social work. *Social Thought* 18(3): 21-39.

Wharf, B. ed - 1992. *Community and Social Policy in Canada.* Toronto: McClelland & Stewart - 1990 *Social Work and Social Change in Canada.* Toronto: McClelland & Stewart.

Wharf, B. and M. Clague, eds. 1997. *Community Organizing: Canadian Experiences.* Toronto: Oxford University Press.

White, R.W. 1959. Motivation reconsidered: the concept of competence, *Psychological Review.* 65:5-197.

Whittingtton , L. 2007. Taxing trend, poor carry bigger burden than rich, *Toronto Star.* November 8, p. A7.

Whitmore, E. and Kerans, P. 1988. Participation, empowerment and welfare. *Canadian Review of Social Policy.* Issue #22.

Whitmore E. & Wilson, M. 1997. *Seeds of fire: social development in the era of globalism.* Fernwood Press and Canadian Consortium for International Social Development.

Wilkinson, R. and Pickett, K. 2010. *The Spirit Level, Why Equality is Better for Everyone.* London: Penguin Books.

Wolfson, M. (2002) Examining the territory of anti-oppressive social work. In (eds.) Lee, B. & Wolfson, M. Introductory readings in anti-oppressive social work. (Unpublished monograph) McMaster University School of Social Work. 5-16.

World Development Report. 1997. *The State in a Changing World.* Washington: World Bank.

Wycoff, H. 1980. *Solving Problems Together.* New York: Grove Press.

INDEX

Notes

Notes

Notes